Praise for _Classroom Discussions: Using Math Ta_

This book has had a direct, positive, and important influence on my math teaching. The ideas are clear and persuasive, and I gained new and important tools for engaging students and improving classroom math discussions. It's a terrific resource!

—Marilyn Burns, founder, Math Solutions

Using this book in book stuady groups and then coaching teachers to use the strategies presented has really changed teacher practice.

—Janie Merendino, math coach, Fairmont, West Virginia

This book gives teachers concrete tools—"talk moves"—that provide security and a framework to open up discussion in the math classroom. The talk moves will enhance daily conversations, professional development, and most of all the conversations heard in classrooms.

— Lori Murach, math program supervisor, Department for School Improvement, North East ISD, San Antonio, Texas

CLASSROOM DISCUSSIONS

Using math talk to help students learn

GRADES K-6

SECOND EDITION

Math Solutions
Sausalito, California, USA

Suzanne H. Chapin | Catherine O'Connor | Nancy Canavan Anderson

Math Solutions
150 Gate 5 Road
Sausalito, CA 94965
www.mathsolutions.com

Library of Congress Cataloging-in-Publication Data

Chapin, Suzanne H.
  Classroom discussions : using math talk to help students learn, grades K–6 /
Suzanne H. Chapin, Catherine O'Connor, Nancy Canavan Anderson. — 2nd ed.
      p. cm.
  Includes bibliographical references and index.
  ISBN 978-1-935099-01-7 (alk. paper)
  1. Mathematics—Study and teaching (Elementary) 2. Discussion. I. O'Connor,
Catherine, Ph.D. II. Anderson, Nancy Canavan. III. Title.

  QA135.6.C47 2009
  372.7--dc22

                                                        2009022068

Editor: Jamie Ann Cross
Production: Melissa L. Inglis-Elliott
Cover design: Jan Streitburger
Cover image: © iStockphoto.com/Bonnie Jacobs
Interior design: Joni Doherty
Composition: ICC Macmillan

Printed in the United States of America on acid-free paper
13   12   11   ML   6   7   8   9   10

A Message from Math Solutions

We at Math Solutions believe that teaching math well calls for increasing our understanding of the math we teach, seeking deeper insights into how students learn mathematics, and refining our lessons to best promote students' learning.

Math Solutions shares classroom-tested lessons and teaching expertise from our faculty of professional development consultants as well as from other respected math educators. Our publications are part of the nation-wide effort we've made since 1984 that now includes

- more than five hundred face-to-face professional development programs each year for teachers and administrators in districts across the country;
- professional development books that span all math topics taught in kindergarten through high school;
- videos for teachers and for parents that show math lessons taught in actual classrooms;
- on-site visits to schools to help refine teaching strategies and assess student learning; and
- free online support, including grade-level lessons, book reviews, inservice information, and district feedback, all in our Math Solutions Online Newsletter.

For information about all of the products and services we have available, please visit our website at *www.mathsolutions.com.* You can also contact us to discuss math professional development needs by calling (800) 868-9092 or by sending an email to *info@mathsolutions.com.*

We're always eager for your feedback and interested in learning about your particular needs. We look forward to hearing from you.

To the students and teachers of Project Challenge

Brief Contents

Contents

9. Planning Talk-Based Lessons

10. Troubleshooting

Preface
Talk in Action—Project Challenge Research

What is the basis for the descriptions and recommendations you will find in this book? One source is the research and teaching literature that deals with classroom talk and student learning. In the back of the book we include a number of references for readers who want to learn more. But in addition, we have experience in the planned use of classroom discourse to support students' thinking and reasoning in mathematics. We have seen tremendous changes take place in classrooms and in students, over a period of four years in one low-income urban school district.

From 1998 through 2002, we implemented Project Challenge, an intervention project funded by the Jacob K. Javits program of the United States Department of Education. The Javits Program was specifically looking for projects that would increase the number of ethnic and linguistic minority students in programs for gifted and talented students. For many years it has been the case that programs for gifted and talented students served primarily white, affluent students. In many poor urban districts, where students are primarily nonwhite and where many are English language learners, there have been few programs for gifted and talented students. When we started out, the goals of Project Challenge were to identify English language learners, minority students, and economically disadvantaged elementary and middle school students who had potential talent in mathematics, and to provide them with a reform-based mathematics curriculum that focused on mathematical reasoning and communication. We hoped that by combining a solid curriculum, instruction based on mathematical understanding, and a heavy emphasis on talk and communication about mathematics, we would be able to help these students become robust learners of mathematics: learners able to think deeply and insightfully, learners who would not give up when a problem was difficult, and learners who would legitimately come to think of themselves as mathematically able.

From the beginning, obstacles to these goals appeared with regularity. First, the students in the schools we worked with were not high-performing students. The district had no programs at all for gifted or talented students.

Some teachers and administrators suggested that there were very few gifted students in the system. About 85 percent of the district's students qualify for free or reduced-price lunch, and over 75 percent speak a language other than English at home. We began by evaluating the six hundred or so students in the fourth grade in September of 1998 to see if we could identify about one hundred to participate in the project starting later in the fall. On alternative assessments (created to reflect the local curriculum) and on standardized assessments of aptitude, very few of the students performed at a level that would indicate any special talent in mathematics. Of the approximately six hundred students we evaluated each year over the four years of the project, less than a dozen stood out each year as obviously talented in mathematics.

But our assumption in designing this intervention was that many students probably had abilities and interests in mathematics that could be nurtured and developed, even if these did not show up at the time on standardized tests. We were looking for potential in mathematics, not demonstrations of accomplishment. Each year, using teacher recommendations, student work, some standardized measures of aptitude, and records of prior achievement in mathematics, we selected about one hundred students to begin participating in a daily mathematics curriculum, organized into four classes each containing about twenty-five students. These students closely mirrored the demographic profile of all students in the district in terms of ethnicity and home language.

We worked with many teachers to combine solid curriculum materials (*Investigations in Number, Data, and Space* in fourth grade and *Connected Mathematics* in grades 5–7) with the strategic use of various forms of classroom talk. We instituted weekly quizzes as a way to reinforce the importance of studying and remembering the content introduced during each week. We gave each teacher daily "warm-up" problems in logic and spatial reasoning to work through with students every morning before classes began. In addition, we introduced major projects that students worked on at the end of the year, culminating in a mathematics fair. Other students and parents were invited to this fair.

From the beginning, we attempted to incorporate various forms of classroom talk into the mathematics work. During the first year, the one hundred students in our first cohort were in fourth grade. Many of them were reluctant to talk in class, or to speak loudly enough so that others could hear. Others were confused by the new forms of activity and participation, and still others resisted the whole process. But we persisted, working alongside committed teachers who worked hard to put these new forms of instruction into place.

Gradually, we began to see real changes in the ways our students were thinking and talking. After about seven or eight months of our first year's efforts, we noticed that students' reasoning had become more complex, more sophisticated, and more recognizably mathematical. Students were better able to give clear explanations for their problem solutions, their use of language became more precise, and their communication skills improved noticeably.

As our first cohort of students moved through fifth grade, we started to see results that were more striking. Even students who had been nearly silent the entire first year of the program began to speak up, explain their thinking, respond to other students' contributions, and ask and answer questions that reflected a growing interest in mathematics as well as a growing ability to think mathematically. Other teachers who taught these students in their language arts and social studies classes began to comment on their striking ability to verbalize their thoughts and explanations. Parents who had previously seemed disconnected from the program began to communicate that they were very happy with their children's growing interest in mathematics.

In addition, we got very strong support for our efforts in the form of results on standardized tests. At the beginning of the program, we administered the Test of Mathematical Abilities, Second Edition (TOMA 2) to our first cohort of students. Only 4 percent were rated as "Superior" or "Very Superior" (which indicates a "high probability of giftedness in mathematics") and 23 percent were rated as "Above Average." The remaining 73 percent were rated as "Average" or "Below Average" in their mathematical abilities. After two years in the program, however, we again tested those students who had remained in the program (approximately eighty). After two years, 41 percent were now "Superior" or "Very Superior," and 36 percent more were "Above Average." Only 23 percent of our first cohort were classified as having "Average" ability in mathematics after two years in the program, and none were "Below Average."

In order to examine student achievement growth over time, we also used data from the California Achievement Test (CAT). After three months in the project, our first one hundred students scored better on the CAT than 70 percent of a national sample. This score undoubtedly indicated that we had identified students who did have potential ability in mathematics. Two years later these same students took the CAT mathematics subtest again. This time, they scored better, on average, than 91 percent of a national sample. Furthermore, after three years in the program, 90 percent of the one hundred sixth graders in our first cohort placed in the top two categories on the Massachusetts state assessment (MCAS) in mathematics, a rate greater than that of nearby affluent suburbs.

The growth in achievement has continued for students who entered the program after the first year. We have compared the growth of the second cohort—roughly one hundred students who entered the program as fourth graders in the second year of Project Challenge. Like the first cohort of one hundred, their achievement growth was significant; in two years that cohort went from having a mean total mathematics score at the 74th percentile to a ranking at the 91st percentile. We found similar results for the third and fourth cohorts.

To what can we attribute these results? First, we attribute them to the very hard work of the teachers and students involved in the program. Second, we believe that a well-planned mathematics curriculum that emphasizes student understanding is a critical centerpiece to our story. The supporting activities—the projects, the weekly quizzes, the daily logic problem warm-ups, and an emphasis on high levels of achievement all played an important part in the high levels of performance we saw our students achieve. In addition, we believe that these results are due in part to the very productive use of classroom discourse in these classes, something we have carefully scaffolded since the beginning of the project. We think there are a variety of reasons why the classroom talk that occurred between students and teachers in these classrooms was supportive of mathematical thinking and learning:

- Talk about mathematical concepts and procedures caused misconceptions to surface and helped the teachers recognize and address what students did and did not understand.
- Discourse formats, such as extended group discussion and partner talk, played a part in helping students improve their ability to reason logically: When one student made a claim, the teacher would ask for evidence to support the claim. Examples or counterexamples to the claim provided fodder for reasoning. Over four years, this had a noticeable impact.
- Allowing students to talk about their thinking and problem solving gave them more to observe and listen to, and more chances to participate in mathematical thinking. This pushed them beyond their incomplete, shallow, or passive knowledge by making them aware of discrepancies between their own thinking and that of others.
- Classroom discussion provided motivation: Students became more motivated through taking an interest in their peers' claims and positions within a discussion.

In short, we believe that the ways we used talk in the classroom helped these students make their thinking public; it helped students to explicate and elaborate their reasoning; it allowed them to model, build on, and add to the development of complex ideas; and in at least some cases, it provided a socially grounded motivation to learn.

None of the participants would say that the work of Project Challenge has been easy. In some ways, our experiments with using classroom discourse to promote student learning have been the most challenging aspect of the program. But we believe that our results—the whole range of our results, from test scores to student testimonials—indicate that productive talk was a crucial part of the program. It enabled these low-income students, three-quarters of whom spoke a language other than English at home, to become mathematically articulate. They learned to express their mathematical thoughts to their peers and to their teachers. This was a formative experience for them, and it was a formative experience for us as well. Our experiences with Project Challenge are a large part of the reason that we decided to write this book, so that teachers who wish to support the learning of their students could build on what we have learned.

In the years since the first edition of *Classroom Discussions* was published, we have continued to work with teachers and students to support their use of academically productive talk. We have gathered more examples of classroom talk in mathematics learning at early grade levels, including kindergarten, and at higher elementary grade levels, as students prepare for algebra. We have expanded our range of vignettes to include these. We have added discussion questions to the end of each chapter, based in part on feedback we have gotten from teachers and teacher educators who have used our book in the past. Finally, we have added an index for every mathematical example we use, classified by grade level and mathematical emphasis.

Acknowledgments

In 1998, the authors began to work together on Project Challenge, a program to enhance learning opportunities for urban students with potential talent in mathematics. Suzanne Chapin brought her experience in professional development and mathematics education, Cathy O'Connor brought her background in linguistics and the study of classroom discourse, and Nancy Anderson brought her training in math education and her willingness to try new approaches to mathematical communication in the classroom. This book grew out of our collaboration. Its contents are based on our years of work in our respective fields, on what we learned during Project Challenge, and on subsequent research and professional development we have done together.

We would like to express our appreciation to the students of Project Challenge and to their families. They inspired us to write down our ideas so others might use them. We are also grateful to all the Project Challenge teachers who so willingly tried new methods and materials, even in the face of pressures from high-stakes testing. They were willing to think deeply about what it means to be talented in mathematics, and to spend many hours in demanding professional development activities. Our profound thanks go to Beth Brogna, Ali Brown, Patty Burge, Lauren Carilli, Roseanne Cataldo, Maureen DeFreitas, Janice Fields, Kathy Foulser, Laura Glavin, Monty Grob, Gina Lally, Mesook Lee, Claire Moran, Magaly Rodriguez, Alice Rourke, Rene Sacco, Sally Siriani, Alissa Stangle, Andrea Taddeo, Henry Utter, Tanya Walsh, and Carol Wolf, as well as other teachers, support staff, project staff, and district administrators who offered time and support of many kinds. Furthermore, we appreciate the advice we received from teachers, professors, professional development experts, and students on what to include in the second edition of *Classroom Discussions*. A special thanks to Jennifer McPherson, Lainie Schuster, Carolyn Felux, Marji Freeman, Linda Honeyman, Chris Brunette, and Rusty Bresser, and to the many educators who have been using this book to support talk in the classroom.

Marilyn Burns has had a tremendously positive impact on the form and contents of the volume; it has been a pleasure to work with her.

Many of the ideas and practices described in this book came from the work of individuals that Cathy O'Connor has had the opportunity to collaborate with over the past decade. She is very grateful for help and discussion over the years from Lynne Godfrey, Maggie Lampert, Sarah Michaels, Robert Moses, Pam Paternoster, Lauren Resnick, Vicki Bill, Matthew Robert, Marty Rutherford, and many others.

We are greatly indebted to our funders. The Spencer Foundation has supported Cathy O'Connor's work on language in mathematics classrooms in several ways over the past decade. Project Challenge itself was funded by the Jacob K. Javits Gifted and Talented Students Education Program (Grant No. R206A980001). The opinions expressed in this book do not necessarily reflect the position, policy, or endorsement of the U.S. Department of Education or of the Spencer Foundation. And although we are grateful to all of the individuals and institutions cited, none of these individuals or institutions should be assumed to endorse the contents of this volume.

Finally, we would like to express our appreciation to all the students in classrooms across the United States who are trying to make sense of mathematics by talking about key ideas. We are deeply encouraged and inspired by your hard work and consistent efforts to talk productively and animatedly about mathematics!

Connections to NCTM's
Principles and Standards for School Mathematics

Communication is featured as one of the standards in NCTM's *Principles and Standards for School Mathematics* (2000) at all grade levels. Every example in this book demonstrates how teachers can foster good mathematical communication. In addition, each example illustrates how communication is incorporated into instruction focused on mathematical content and procedures. The table below highlights one standard for each example; however, other standards are also addressed in individual examples.

NCTM Standard	Grade Level	Chapter	Mathematics Content
Algebra	3	2	Solving equations using guess-and-check
Algebra	5	Case Study 2	Algebraic expressions and equations (case study)
Algebra	6	6	Equality using balance scales
Connections	1	4	Addition strategies
Connections	1	7	Addition symbols
Connections	2	5	Subtraction
Connections	6	Case Study 3	fair games (case study)
Data Analysis and Probability	3	Case Study 1	Data analysis (case study)
Data Analysis and Probability	6	Case Study 3	Experimental and theoretical probability (case study)
Geometry	K	7	Sorting objects by attributes

NCTM Standard	Grade Level	Chapter	Mathematics Content
Geometry	1	2	Characteristics of triangles
Geometry	3	7	Classification of 3-D figures (no dialogue)
Geometry	6	7	Concept of similarity (no dialogue)
Geometry	6	7	Meaning of *congruent* (no dialogue)
Geometry	6	9	Area of circles
Measurement	2	7	Meaning of *quarter* (no dialogue)
Measurement	2	9	Units (no dialogue)
Measurement	3	Case Study 1	linear measurement (case study)
Measurement	4	3	Area of parallelograms
Number and Operations	3	1	Commutative property of multiplication
Number and Operations	3	4	Subtraction with regrouping, estimation
Number and Operations	4	2	Even and odd numbers
Number and Operations	5	2	Fraction concepts; division of fractions
Number and Operations	5	3	Subtraction of decimals
Number and Operations	5	4	Decimal operations
Number and Operations	5	4	Distributive property of multiplication over addition, double-digit multiplication
Number and Operations	5	8	Fractions comparison
Number and Operations	6	2	Division of fractions
Problem Solving	3	5	Money

NCTM Standard	Grade Level	Chapter	Mathematics Content
Problem Solving	4	5	Multiplication and division
Problem Solving	6	5	Ratios (no dialogue)
Reasoning and Proof	K	6	Inductive reasoning
Reasoning and Proof	4	6	Deductive reasoning
Reasoning and Proof	5	Case Study 2	Equivalent representations of numbers
Representation	2	5	Addition basic facts
Representation	2	3	Equivalent representations of numbers
Representation	2	5	Column addition (no dialogue)

PART

I

Getting Started:
Mathematics Learning
with Classroom Discussions

1

Academically Productive Talk: An Overview

The students in Mrs. Schuster's third-grade class are discussing a question she has set out for them to consider: "Does the order of the numbers in a multiplication sentence affect the answer? Explain why or why not." In order to explore this question, they are generating examples of multiplication sentences and testing what happens when they change the order of the factors. Students know many of the basic multiplication facts but have not yet learned an algorithm for multidigit multiplication.

> **NCTM Standard:**
> Number and Operations
>
> **Grade 3**

One student has made a conjecture that the order of the factors does not make a difference—"the answer is the same no matter which number goes first." Students are agreeing with this conjecture by bringing up other examples that work, such as $3 \times 4 = 12$ and $4 \times 3 = 12$. Mrs. Schuster then asks if this conjecture works with larger numbers and suggests they use calculators to check. Students are able to generate many examples to verify the conjecture, but explaining *why* the products are the same is not as straightforward as carrying out the multiplication.

1. Eddie: Well, I don't think it matters what order the numbers are in. You still get the same answer. But the multiplication sentences are different because they mean different things.

2. Mrs. S: OK, Rebecca, do you agree or disagree with what Eddie is saying?

3. Rebecca: Well, I agree that it doesn't matter which number is first, because two times five equals ten and that's the same answer as five times two. But I don't get what Eddie means about the multiplication meaning different things.

4. Mrs. S: Eddie, would you explain what you mean?

5. Eddie: Well, I just think that the two times five that Rebecca used can mean two groups of five things like two bags of five apples. And five times two means five bags of two apples. Those aren't the same at all.

6. Tiffany: [Hand up, waving] But you still have the same number of apples! So they do mean the same!

7. Mrs. S: OK, so we have two different ideas here to talk about. Eddie says that order does matter, because five times two and two times five can each be used to describe a different situation, like two bags of five apples or five bags of two apples. So the two number sentences mean different things. And Tiffany, are you saying that those two number sentences *can't* be used to describe two different situations?

8. Tiffany: No, I mean that even though the two situations are different, the answer is the same.

9. Mrs. S: OK, so you're saying that order doesn't matter because the answer is the same?

10. Tiffany: Right.

11. Mrs. S: OK. We need to think about this. In Eddie's statement, order makes a difference in the situation you're describing. In Tiffany's statement, order doesn't make a difference in the answer we get. So when does order make a difference in multiplying two numbers together?

Mrs. Schuster is using classroom talk to deepen students' understanding of the commutative property of multiplication. She knows that this mathematical idea may be clear enough for the operation of addition, but that it gets complicated when we introduce multiplication. She knows that in the case of addition, students can easily see that the number sentence $2 + 3$ and the number sentence $3 + 2$ can be used to describe the same situation. It doesn't really matter whether we mention the three pears or the two apples first. In the case of multiplication, however, if we focus on the particulars of the problem situation, the order of elements in the number sentences suddenly matters. As Eddie points out, two bags of five apples and five bags of two apples are very different.

Mrs. Schuster knows that this is one of many points in the early grades where students' mathematical reasoning and their appreciation of real-world problem situations can come into apparent conflict. Yet in the long run, students' abilities to use mathematical expressions to model real-world situations will be central to their progress in mathematics and science. She knows that it is therefore worth time and effort to clarify things here in her third grade, and she has chosen to use classroom talk as a tool to support that aim.

For almost two decades, the National Council of Teachers of Mathematics has been urging teachers to emphasize communication—talk and writing—as part of mathematics teaching and learning. Their arguments make sense: The mathematical thinking of many students is aided by hearing what their peers are thinking. Putting thoughts into words pushes students to clarify their thinking. Teachers can spot student misunderstandings much more easily when they are revealed by a discussion instead of remaining unspoken. And the previous classroom interchange exemplifies what we are aiming for: a respectful but engaged conversation in which students can clarify their own thinking and learn from others through talk.

But for many teachers, it has not been easy to implement new ways of using talk in mathematics class. Researchers have found that few American classrooms display consistent or even occasional use of student talk. Instead, most classroom talk consists of the teacher lecturing, asking students to recite, or posing simple questions with known answers. Of course, lecturing, recitation, and quizzing are useful instructional tools. They form the bedrock of most teachers' instructional practice and we would not want them to disappear. However, they have limitations, as do all forms of talk!

As teachers, we have many different academic goals, and many things we want to achieve in our classrooms. We need as large, diverse, and powerful a set of instructional tools as we can find. The purpose of this book is to enable you to enhance and expand the array of instructional tools you know how to use. We will introduce you to a variety of discourse-based tools—ways of using language in teaching mathematics that will allow students to engage more fully in mathematical thinking and reasoning. These include conversational moves and ways of structuring interaction in your classes that will help you achieve the goals you have for your students.

Some of your goals may be social: You want your students to be able to listen to one another respectfully, to cooperate, and to build on one another's ideas. Some of your goals will be both social and cognitive: You want your students to be able to make mathematical conjectures, present evidence, voice agreement and disagreement with the claims of others, and support their own positions. And, finally, some of your goals will center on your students' learning of core mathematical concepts and procedures. In this book, we aim to help you integrate all of these goals and support them through the skillful use of classroom talk.

When should students talk, and about what? If we simply ask students to talk, without thinking carefully about our purposes, we may end up with irrelevant, hard-to-manage talk that serves no clear academic purpose. Sometimes this aimless talk may be pleasant; sometimes it may be unpleasant. But in either case it probably will not significantly advance student thinking and learning. Instead, for talk to be productive, we believe that it must be carefully integrated with the content of the mathematics lesson. Our goal is not to increase the *amount* of talk in our classrooms, but to increase the *amount of high-quality* talk in our classrooms—the mathematically productive talk.

How can we tell when the talk in our classrooms has been productive, and not a waste of time? It seems clear that we can't simply rely on our feelings. Think back to the last time you had a conversation that you enjoyed. It may or may not have been intellectually significant. Obviously, the best conversations—in or out of school—are the ones that are fun and exciting, and also intellectually or personally important. But we cannot use fun and excitement as our only criteria for whether classroom talk has been productive. We have to find ways to recognize and appreciate which forms of talk are most mathematically productive for our students, and for a particular lesson or topic. In this book, we provide ways for you to develop a sense for when talk is mathematically productive for your students.

How Classroom Talk Promotes Student Learning

Classroom talk may support and promote student learning in mathematics both directly and indirectly. Classroom dialogue may provide *direct* access to ideas, relationships among those ideas, strategies, procedures, facts, mathematical history, and more. Through classroom discourse, all of these aspects of mathematical thinking can be discussed, dissected, and understood. Classroom dialogue also supports student learning *indirectly*, through the building of a social environment—a community—that encourages learning. Through classroom discourse of certain types, students are encouraged to treat one another as equal partners in thinking, conjecturing, exploring, and sharing ideas. Mutual respect is fostered when norms exist that set expectations for respectful and civil discourse.

These two results of talk, direct and indirect, are of equal importance. If we use talk to establish a supportive learning environment, but we do not succeed in creating productive talk about the actual content of mathematics, our students are not likely to succeed in learning the mathematics we want them to know. On the other hand, if we fail to build a supportive learning environment—one in which students can talk about their mathematical thinking without fear of ridicule—then many students will not participate at all. Throughout this book we address both the social aspects and the content-focused aspects of productive classroom talk.

Cognitive Aspects of Student Talk in Mathematics Learning

We've all experienced learning about a concept by listening to a teacher talk about it. After we listen to the teacher we may feel that we understand the concept. However, when asked to put the concept into words, we may discover that our understanding is not as deep as we thought. We may become inarticulate, even speechless. We don't yet have the understanding necessary to put the idea into words clearly. Yet unless we are put in a situation where we *must* talk or write about the concept, we may never come to realize that our knowledge is incomplete, shallow, or passive.

How can we push learners beyond incomplete, shallow, or passive understanding? One way is to incorporate student talk into lessons about the ideas they are trying to understand. Asking students to talk about mathematical concepts, procedures, and problem solving helps them understand more deeply and with greater clarity. It can make clear to them what they do and do not understand, and what other students think about these same issues. Often the first step in setting out to learn something involves realizing that you don't understand it. And sometimes it is this first step that is most difficult to elicit from our students. Getting students to talk about mathematical ideas or procedures can bring to the surface their gaps in understanding. It's important to note that the students are not the only beneficiaries of hearing their own thinking made public. Such talk also allows teachers to hear students' misconceptions and thus identify what students do and don't understand.

There are other benefits as well. Certain forms of talk may promote specific kinds of reasoning. For example, discussion, either in small groups or with the whole class, can play a critical part in helping students improve their ability to reason logically. Many people think that logical abilities are something we are born with (or born without), and that teachers cannot do much to change them. In fact, many researchers claim that logical reasoning can be strongly affected by teaching. The basic components of logical reasoning can be very effectively taught in the context of a discussion. For example, within a discussion, when one student makes a claim, the teacher can ask for evidence to support the claim. The examples or counterexamples to the claim can then be discussed and taken apart by the group. Each student hears the reasoning of others and can make a contribution when ready to do so. In this way students gradually learn how to make and support arguments.

When we give students a text to read, we allow them time to read it more than once, to consider the details. Yet we often forget that when we are talking to the class, presenting new material or explaining, our words and ideas swiftly pass by. Students can't call them back and reflect on them to reconsider ideas, pose questions, or work out details. By carefully using certain talk moves in the mathematics classroom, however, we give students time and space to consider more deeply the content we expect them to learn by allowing them to revisit what has just been said. We all know that humans learn through observing, listening, and doing. Skillful use of classroom talk gives students more to observe, more to listen to, and more chances to participate in mathematical thinking.

Finally, talk gives students practice in reflecting on their own thinking processes. Expert thinkers are able to coordinate the ideas and understandings inside their heads with ideas and information outside, in the world. When engaged in thinking or solving problems, expert thinkers keep track of their moment-to-moment understanding or lack of understanding. When they realize they don't understand something, they immediately address their confusion by asking a question, or stopping the process completely until they find a way to address what they don't understand. But this ability to expertly adapt and respond to one's own internal processing does not develop overnight. Students need a great deal of practice to become expert thinkers in this respect. And in the context of a lecture or recitation, they do not get any practice in this particular *self-regulative* aspect of thinking. Based on our experience, we have concluded that certain kinds of discourse practices support the development of expert thinkers. In this book, we will provide details on how to bring these practices into your classroom.

Social Aspects of Student Talk in Mathematics Learning

In the world of adults, mathematical and scientific work are often carried out by groups of people working together. The ability to communicate clearly and precisely is essential. But this ability—like all the capacities mentioned previously—does not develop overnight. It takes many years of striving to make oneself clear to others. Finally, it takes motivation. We all know adults who do not seem interested in communicating clearly with others!

As teachers, how can we encourage our students to do the hard work necessary to become clear communicators? In order to make the effort to communicate clearly, people need the motivation of knowing that others *want* to hear what they have to say. A number of researchers have observed that certain forms of classroom discourse seem to motivate students to make their thoughts clear. If students know that the teacher and their classmates will hold them accountable for making themselves clear, many of them will make great efforts to do the best they can to be clear and comprehensible.

Another benefit of classroom talk is to build students' confidence about their own ability to engage in intellectual discussion. Some students have not engaged in group intellectual discussion before and may find it stressful to talk in front of their classmates. Students bring with them to school a great variety of experiences in using talk to explore intellectual topics. In some communities, for example, it is considered normal and desirable for children to engage in argument and discussion with adults. Such children may have more confidence in the value of their own ways of expressing their thoughts. In fact, it may be hard to stop them from taking the floor! In other communities, children are not supposed to assert themselves in this way—it might be considered rude, pushy, or obnoxious. In these communities, adults may be entitled to discuss their thoughts, while children are considered apprentices. There are many cultural variations: In some communities, such behavior may be considered acceptable for boys, but not for girls. In any case, children who have been taught that they should take an observer's role in intellectual discussions may find it very challenging or even upsetting to take an active role in a classroom discussion.

Nevertheless, to engage in serious mathematical and scientific work in high school, college, and beyond, people must be able to assert themselves in ways that are expected by members of those communities. In fact, some students leave the serious study of mathematics and science in high school or college because they find the intellectual discourse intimidating or uncomfortable. We have found that helping students learn to talk in the ways valued by scientists and mathematicians results in real changes in how students present their thoughts and ideas, and in how they feel about themselves as thinkers. We believe it will eventually help them do well in advanced high school and college courses, where the subject matter requires students to feel at home with scientific and logical argumentation.

When a teacher succeeds in setting up a classroom in which students feel obligated to listen to each other, to make their own contributions clear and comprehensible, and to provide evidence for their claims, that teacher has set in place a very powerful context for student learning. Over time, students come to value their classmates' contributions and strive to make their own contributions of value to others. The class as a whole develops an understanding about values held by mathematicians and scientists all over the world: precision, clarity, intellectual honesty, effort, and thoroughness. But to accomplish this takes effort, planning, and many months of work. We have included in the chapters that follow a number of strategies, techniques, and examples to help you get started in the challenging but ultimately very rewarding work of using classroom talk to help your students learn.

DISCUSSION AND REFLECTION

1. One of the key skills you will develop in using this book is the ability to work with students whose contributions are initially unclear, helping them move toward clarity. This kind of work is not easy at first. To prepare for this, try to recall a time when you could not explain your thinking to others because the ideas you were dealing with were new and complex. What would have helped you at that time?

2. This book will also help you develop the ability to tell when talk in your classroom is academically productive. Can you recall a time when you held a discussion in your class that *was not* academically productive? What happened? What was it like? Can you recall a time when you held a discussion that *was* academically productive? What were the qualities of that discussion? Do you remember anything you did to make it productive, or did it just seem to happen spontaneously?

3. Think back in your own education. Can you recall a teacher who made you feel that he or she really *wanted* to understand what you had to say? Try to picture a conversation with that teacher. What was it like?

CHAPTER 2

How Do We Begin? The Tools of Classroom Talk

As teachers, we elicit responses from our students in various ways—with questions, commands, hints, jokes, and so on. When students become familiar with our inventory of phrases and expressions, they usually know what we expect of them. Although we rarely stop to think about our most common conversational prompts, they are among our most important instructional tools. From our work in Project Challenge, we have found it useful to think carefully about these tools: It matters what you say and how you say it.

In this chapter we present a number of examples of talk in action in mathematics lessons and describe the tools that teachers use to implement classroom talk. The tools include "talk moves" that support mathematical thinking, "talk formats" that suggest different ways to organize students for conversation, and ideas for creating a classroom where respect and equal access to participation are valued norms. Narrative examples, or "cases," illustrate how the basic tools of talk look in action in four different classrooms.

Ground Rules for Respectful Talk and Equitable Participation

First and foremost, before any talk moves can be implemented, the teacher must establish ground rules for respectful and courteous talk. You will not be able to use the moves described here successfully unless you have established a classroom culture in which students listen to one another with respect. If students are afraid that their ideas will be ridiculed, they will not talk freely, no matter what inducements you offer. They must feel that their classroom is a safe place to express their thoughts. Therefore, your first step in creating the conditions for productive classroom talk must involve setting up some clear ground rules for interaction. It is very important to put this step first. Even one hostile or disrespectful interchange can put a serious damper on students' willingness to talk openly about their ideas and thoughts. It is imperative that you consistently maintain the ground rules for respectful and courteous talk, and that your students know there will be no exceptions.

The ground rules must center on each student's obligation to treat others with respect. No name calling or derogatory noises or remarks are ever allowed. "I was just joking" cannot be an acceptable defense for a disrespectful remark, and students must know that you will hold them to a high standard. There must be clear consequences for violation of these rules. You may need to remind students of these rules every day until the rules become a routine part of your classroom culture. We recommend creating a poster or wall chart and prominently displaying it so that you can make reference to it when necessary.

As you establish the conditions for respectful and courteous talk, you will also need to set the conditions for full participation: All students must have the opportunity to engage in productive talk about mathematics. This means that you must make sure of three things:

1. that every student is listening to what others say;
2. that every student can hear what others say; and
3. that every student may participate by speaking out at some point.

Your ground rules for respectful and courteous talk must include a rule that obligates students to listen attentively as others talk. This is respectful behavior, but just as important, it is pragmatic behavior. It enables students to participate in the ongoing talk. If they do not know what was just said, they cannot possibly build on it.

While establishing these ground rules may sound difficult, many teachers have had success within the first few weeks or months of teaching this way. In Chapter 8 we introduce specific suggestions to help you put these norms in place.

Productive Talk Moves: Steps Toward Real Discussion

In this section we introduce a number of *talk moves* that we return to repeatedly throughout the book. We have found each one to be helpful in achieving the goal of supporting mathematical thinking and learning through talk. For each one, we describe the move, illustrate it with a brief classroom example, and then explain the teacher action required.

First, however, we will give an overview of what these moves are designed to accomplish. If you don't know why you are using these moves, they may seem like arbitrary maneuvers instead of tools that will help you reach your instructional goals.

Four Steps Toward Productive Discussions

In order to reach the goal of holding academically productive discussions in your class, you need to accomplish each of the following four steps. Without these, you will not have the conditions you need to support real, substantive discussion that supports student learning. The talk moves described in this section will help you accomplish these four steps.

• **Step 1: Helping Individual Students Clarify and Share Their Own Thoughts**

If a student is going to participate in the discussion, he or she has to be able to share thoughts and responses out loud, in a way that is at least partially understandable to others. If only one or two students can do this, you don't have a discussion—you have a monologue or, at best, a dialogue between the teacher and a student.

• **Step 2: Helping Students Orient to the Thinking of Other Students**

If a student is simply waiting to speak, and is not *listening* to others and *trying to understand them*, he or she will not be able to contribute to a real discussion. Your ultimate goal involves sharing ideas and reasoning, so it is important to steer students away from a series of individual, disparate thoughts.

• **Step 3: Helping Students Deepen Their Reasoning**

Even if students express their thoughts and listen to others' ideas, the discussion can still fail to be academically productive if it does not include solid and sustained mathematical reasoning. Some classroom discussions are superficial—most students are not skilled at pushing to understand and to deepen their own reasoning. Therefore, the teacher's role includes continuous and skillful use of the talk move *press for reasoning*.

• **Step 4: Helping Students Engage with Others' Reasoning**

The final step involves students actually absorbing the ideas and reasoning of other students and responding to them. This is when real discussion can take off, discussion that will support robust learning.

Talk Moves That Help Students Clarify and Share Their Own Thoughts

Say More (asking an individual student to expand on what he or she said)

Sometimes a student response to a question is very telegraphic. Because the student doesn't say much, it's hard to understand. At this point you can ask the student to expand: "Can you say more about that?"; "Tell us more about your thinking. Can you expand on that?"; or Can you give us an example?"

This "family" of talk moves sends the message that the teacher wants to understand the student's thinking. It sends a signal that the teacher wants more than just a correct answer. It also gives the student time to regroup and clarify, as in the following example:

Ms. Davies has given her fourth graders a series of numbers, and in a whole-group discussion has asked them to say whether the numbers are even or odd. They had established the day before that if you can divide a number by two, with no remainders, then it is an even number. Paulo has tackled the number twenty-four. His contribution is telegraphic, and incorrect.

NCTM Standard:
Number and
Operations

Grade 4

1. Ms. D: So Paulo, what do you think? Is twenty-four an even number or an odd number?

2. Paulo: Umm . . . odd.

Ms. Davies could now choose to move on, or to tell Paulo that his answer is incorrect and remind him of the previous day's discussion. She chooses instead to use a "Say More" talk move.

3. Ms. D: Paulo, can you say more? Can you tell us more about your thinking?

Paulo thinks, and then says the following:

4. Paulo: Well, if we could use three, then it could go into that, but three is odd. So, then, if it was . . . but . . . three is even. I mean odd. So if it's odd, then it's not even.

Ms. Davies is confused by this somewhat garbled utterance, but she wants to understand Paulo's reasoning, so she tries again with a "Revoicing" move. . . .

Revoicing (asking a student to verify your interpretation and clarify his or her thought)
When students talk about mathematics, it's often difficult to understand what they say. And if you as the teacher have trouble understanding a student's reasoning, the student's classmates will likely not do any better. Yet given your goals to improve the mathematical thinking and reasoning of all students, you cannot give up on an especially unclear student. Deep thinking and powerful reasoning do not always correlate with clear verbal expression.

Therefore, teachers need talk moves that can help them deal with the inevitable lack of clarity of many student contributions. They need tools that will allow them to interact with the student (without putting the student on the spot) in a way that will encourage that student to clarify his or her own reasoning.

One such tool has been called "revoicing." Revoicing is *not* just repeating. In a revoicing move, the teacher essentially tries to repeat some or all of what the student has said, and then *asks the student to verify* whether or not the teacher's revoicing is correct, as in the next stage of our example. In doing this, she leaves room for the student to *clarify* the original intention.

After hearing Paulo's contribution in (4), all Ms. Davies could grasp was that Paulo *might* be saying that twenty-four is odd because he divided it by three and got no remainder. She vaguely recalls that this is a common misconception among students: If division by two with no remainder yields an even number, then division by three with no remainder must yield an odd number! By phrasing this guess as a question, she is asking Paulo if her understanding is correct. By *waiting for his answer*, she gives him a chance to clarify.

5. Ms. D: OK, let me see if I understand. So you're saying that twenty-four is . . . an odd number . . . because you divided it by three?

Seven or eight seconds go by. Ms. Davies waits. Finally Paulo answers.

6. Paulo: Yeah. Because three goes into it, because twenty-four divided by three is eight.

As it works out, Paulo verifies that he did intend to claim that twenty-four is an odd number, and he gives his reason. By creating a space in the conversation for Paulo to respond, Ms. Davies has learned that he probably does hold this basic misconception about even and odd numbers. She has gained a foothold in the discussion that she did not have after simply hearing his contributions in turns (2) and (4). Now Ms. Davies may include other students in this small and impromptu discussion, to make sure that she addresses all students' understanding.

Talk Moves That Help Students Orient to Others' Thinking

Who can repeat? (asking students to restate what has been said)
When a student says something potentially important, you may want to incorporate that into the ongoing discussion. But if other students did not hear it, or were not paying attention, they will not be able to take the next step and think about it. Other ways to express this are "Who can put this into their own words?" or "Who can restate what Paulo said?" Following Paulo's turn in (6), the teacher asks "Who can repeat?"

7. Ms. D: Can anyone repeat what Paulo just said in his or her own words? Miranda?

8. Miranda: Um, I think I can. I think he said that twenty-four is odd, because it can be divided by three.

9. Ms. D: Is that right, Paulo? Is that what you said?

10. Paulo: Yes.

It's important to note that this is *not* being used as a management move. Some teachers use this move to "catch" students who are not listening, but if you use it only in this way students may not be inclined to participate. They will be more enthusiastic if you generally use it in a positive way. At the beginning of your efforts to use productive classroom talk moves, some students may resist repeating. It's important to get across that they are allowed to say "I didn't hear" or "I didn't understand," but they must then ask the other student to repeat his or her point, and then you must follow up by asking them to repeat it.

Talk Moves That Help Students Deepen Their Reasoning

Press for reasoning (asking students to explain their reasoning)
To deepen the focus on shared reasoning, all students must get used to explaining *why* they say what they say. There are many ways to ask this question, depending on the age of the student and the topic under discussion. Here are some examples. Can you think of other ways to press for reasoning?

Why do you think that?	What is your evidence?
What convinced you that was the answer?	What makes you think that?
Why did you think that strategy would work?	How did you get that answer?
Where in the text is there support for that claim?	Can you prove that to us?

Some students are not used to explaining their thinking in this way, and may at first be puzzled. "I chose that because . . . like . . . it was the right answer?" How did you know? "I just . . . I followed the directions." In these cases, you will need to be persistent.

At this point, Ms. Davies could work to deepen Paulo's reasoning and at the same time make sure that everyone else understands what he is saying. She guesses that others will hold the same misconception, and to address it, everyone must be clear about what he is saying.

11. Ms. D: So Paulo, can you tell us why that makes twenty-four an odd
               number? Can you explain your reasoning?

12. Paulo: Well, you divide by three. And eight is the answer. And
               there's no remainder. So like . . . even—even is when you
               divide by two and there's no remainder. So since three is
               odd, this one is odd.

As you work on deepening and clarifying one student's reasoning, other
students need to be following along. Even if the speaker is mathematically correct and concise, that does not mean that everyone will follow it. Many students will tune out as they hear a classmate produce a long and complex piece
of reasoning. This is an ideal time to use the "Who can repeat?" move, and ask
for volunteers to put the student's reasoning into their own words. This helps
everyone deepen their own understanding, and thus, the entire class moves
forward toward a more academically productive discussion.

Even in cases where the student is not correct, all students can benefit
from understanding the reasoning behind it, particularly when a common
misconception is at stake. Therefore, Ms. Davies decides to make sure that
everyone is following.

13. Ms. D: Wow, Paulo, you said a lot. Can anyone put that into his or
               her own words? Eva?

14. Eva: Well, I would say that if a number is even then you can
               divide it by two and there's no remainder, so if you divide it
               by three, well, three is an odd number. So if you don't get a
               remainder when you divide it by three, maybe it's odd.

From her reaction, Ms. Davies guesses that maybe Eva is also a student
who would benefit from thinking about this more, despite the previous
day's lesson!

Talk Moves That Help Students Engage with Others' Thinking

After everyone hears and understands the claim, and the reasoning behind it,
they are ready to take the step of really engaging with that claim.

*Do you agree or disagree . . . and why? (asking students to apply their
own reasoning to an idea)*

This talk move really brings students into direct contact with the reasoning of
their peers. Often teachers simply ask for "thumbs up if you agree, thumbs
down if you disagree." While this can provide some useful information, it is

usually not helpful in getting students to deeply engage with others' reasoning. It is crucial that you follow up with the question "*Why* do you agree?" or "*Why* do you disagree?" Otherwise, students may provide generic answers without really thinking through their position. Other versions of this question include "Who has a similar idea or a different idea about how this works?" and "Does that make sense to you? Why does that make sense?"

Ms. Davies decides that students are now ready to engage with what she knows is a misconception that Paulo and others probably hold. So she asks for students to take a position on the idea.

15. Ms. D:	So, let me ask you: Who agrees with what Paulo said, and who disagrees?	
16. Jamie:	Well, sort of, like, I disagree?	
17. Ms. D:	OK, so why do you disagree with what he said? Can you explain it to us?	
18. Jamie:	Because I thought that we said yesterday that even numbers could be divided by two. And I know Paulo said that. But, like, I think you can divide twenty-four by two. And it's twelve with no remainder. So isn't that even?	

By using the agree/disagree move, Ms. Davies has now set up a way for all students to engage with this central issue.

Who can add on? (asking students to add their own ideas)
Sometimes a student may explain her own reasoning or make a claim in a way that is clear enough and significant enough to allow others to easily respond, as the case with Jamie's claim. This presents an opportunity to really help students engage with their classmate's reasoning and perhaps sustain a productive discussion. Asking "Who can add on?" or "Who wants to respond to that?" invites anyone to join in and respond. You can also personalize this move by calling on a particular student.

19. Ms. D:	So who wants to add on to that? Can someone add more to this? Tell us why you agree or disagree with Jamie or with Paulo.	

Thirty seconds go by as Ms. Davies waits for hands to go up. These students know that in their classroom, it is not always the same swift two or three students who answer all the questions. They know that Ms. Davies will wait until a number of students think through her question. Finally, Eduardo raises his hand. He is an English learner, and rarely talks. Slowly, he reveals his understanding and deepens the reasoning the class can share.

20. Eduardo: Yes, I am agreeing with Jamie's idea, because if something is even it can be divide by two. And if we divide twenty-four by three, we can also divide it by four. And we can divide it by six, also. So I think we should stay with two only for finding even numbers.

Wait time (giving students time to think, and time to answer)
Last but not least, by any means, is the well-known talk tool that involves . . . not talking! Wait time, as first described by Mary Budd Rowe (1974), involves waiting *at least* four to five seconds after you ask a question, and then waiting again for the same interval *after* the student responds to the question.

By waiting patiently, Ms. Davies has made it possible for Eduardo, a second-language learner, to make an important contribution that she and other students can build upon in the ensuing discussion. But this move is not easy for her. Although the research is clear on the value of wait time, this tool is actually quite difficult to adopt consistently. We all tend to feel uncomfortable with silence, as though we are putting a student on the spot. Yet few students can speedily put together an answer to a complicated question about their own reasoning. So if we do not use wait time consistently and patiently, students give up and fail to participate, knowing that they cannot beat the clock, so to speak. So it is easy to see that wait time is a talk move that can help you accomplish all four of the steps described. In later chapters, we again address this and related moves designed to give students the time they need to think and reason mathematically.

Three Productive Talk Formats

Talk Format 1: Whole-Class Discussion

Talk Format 2: Small-Group Discussion

Talk Format 3: Partner Talk

Along with thinking about talk moves that guide students' learning, it's also useful to consider the talk formats available to teachers. Talk formats are different ways that teachers configure classroom interactions for instruction. For example, Ms. Davies took advantage of all five talk moves and used the talk format of whole-class discussion, having her entire class participate together in mathematical thinking and reasoning. Every classroom teacher makes use of a variety of talk formats, and these formats are among the major tools that teachers use to accomplish their goals for student learning. Each format carries with it certain opportunities and certain limitations.

Each format has its own "rules for talk." Some of these rules are rarely discussed, but students know them, nevertheless. For example, in the traditional and familiar talk format that we might label *direct instruction* or, in the higher grades, *lecturing,* the rules go something like this: The teacher has the right to talk, and students must not talk unless the teacher calls out their names. *Quizzing* is another commonly used talk format in which the teacher asks questions for which he or she knows the answers and expects the students to know the answers as well. The rules are as follows: The teacher calls on a student and evaluates the answer given as to its correctness. "Jamie, how much is three times eight?" "Twenty-four?" "Good." In research on classroom talk this is called the IRE format, for *initiation* (by the teacher), *response* (by the student), and *evaluation* (by the teacher). Other talk formats include *sharing time, group recitation,* and *student presentations.*

While there are many academic purposes that may be served by using these formats for mathematics instruction, in this book we focus on three talk formats—whole-class discussion, small-group discussion, and partner talk. We have found these talk formats to be particularly supportive of maximizing opportunities for mathematical learning by all students.

Talk Format 1: Whole-Class Discussion

The talk format that appears most prominently in this book is whole-class discussion. In this talk format, the teacher is in charge of the class, just as in direct instruction. However, in whole-class discussion, the teacher is not primarily engaged in delivering information or quizzing. Rather, he or she is attempting to get students to share their thinking, explain the steps in their reasoning, and build on one another's contributions. These whole-class discussions give students the chance to engage in sustained reasoning. The teacher facilitates and guides quite actively, but does not focus on providing answers directly. Instead, the focus is on the students' thinking.

It takes students a great deal of practice to become solid and confident mathematical thinkers, and this talk format provides a space for that practice. In whole-class discussion, the teacher often refrains from providing the correct answer. He or she does not reject incorrect reasoning, but instead attempts to get students to explore the steps in their reasoning, with the aim that they will gain practice in discovering where their thinking falls short. Invariably, these discussions reveal many examples of faulty reasoning, mistakes in computation, and misunderstandings. These flaws, however, are the raw material with which teachers can work to guide students' mathematical learning. And, in the process, students become more confident in their ability to stick with making sense of concepts, skills, and problems. They gradually lose some of the anxiety and avoidance that many students display when confronted with complex mathematical ideas.

The purpose of whole-class discussion is to provide students with practice in mathematical reasoning that will further their mathematical learning. To accomplish this, the focus is on the students' ideas, not on the correctness of their answers. This does not mean that we are advising teachers to deemphasize correct answers and mathematical truth. In our view, the ultimate goal is for students to achieve mathematical power through precision, accuracy, insight, and reliable reasoning. However, we have found that it's important for students to have opportunities to practice their reasoning in discussions without an immediate focus on correct answers.

How is students' learning of mathematics supported when teachers don't let them know when their thinking is misguided or an answer is incorrect? Aren't there times when it's better to tell students that their answer or idea is wrong? To answer these questions, it's important to think about what learning of mathematics involves. More specifically, when confronted with any new mathematical concept or skill, it's important to consider where the source of the knowledge is for the student.

Sometimes the source of mathematical knowledge lies outside a student and the only way that a student can have access to the knowledge is from an external source, such as a book, a television program, the teacher, or another student. For example, the mathematical symbols we use to represent ideas are socially agreed-upon conventions, and the source of learning these symbols lies outside the student. There is no way for a student to "discover" the meaning of a plus sign—we show it to students and tell them what it means. The same is true for the operation signs for subtraction, multiplication, and division; for the relational symbols for equal, greater than, less than; even for the way we write the numerals. These symbols have no meanings that are inherent to them but rather are mathematical conventions that we all agree to use for ease of representing and communicating mathematical ideas. The same is true for the terminology we apply to mathematical ideas—*triangle, prime number, even, fraction,* and so on.

When mathematical knowledge is linked to social conventions, direct instruction is appropriate for furthering students' learning.

When mathematical concepts and skills are not linked to social conventions but, rather, have their own internal logic, the source of knowledge is not external to the student. Instead, students learn by processing information, applying reasoning, hearing ideas from others, and connecting new thinking to what they already know, all for the goal of making sense for themselves of new concepts and skills. The source of the knowledge, of creating new understanding, lies within the student, and making sense is the key. We can tell a student, for example, that the order of the numbers in a multiplication problem doesn't alter the answer, that 2×5, for example, produces the same product as does 5×2. But this is an idea that students can figure out for themselves, from experimenting with problems, thinking about what happens to the products when factors are reversed, and then talking about their ideas as the students in Mrs. Schuster's class did in the example presented in Chapter 1.

Simply "telling" students through direct instruction is not sufficient for teaching ideas in which the source of the knowledge is inside the student. In order for children to learn, understand, and remember, they need experiences to interact with the idea, think about it in relation to what they already know, uncover its logic, and then apply their thinking to this new idea. Using talk in a whole-class discussion provides students with opportunities to make sense of new ideas. Such discussions may reveal students' confusion, partial understandings, and misconceptions, but these are also part of learning and are important information for teachers to have when planning instruction. Explaining their reasoning is important for all students as it helps them to cement and even extend their thinking. Over the long run, we have seen that asking "Why do you think that?" has profound effects on students' mathematical thinking and on their "habits of mind" in general.

Talk Format 2: Small-Group Discussion

In this book we make a distinction between whole-class discussion and small-group discussion. In small-group discussion format, the teacher typically gives students a question to discuss among themselves, in groups of three to six. While the rules for whole-class talk formats are generally familiar to students, students need help becoming familiar and comfortable with the rules for small-group discussion. In this format, the teacher circulates as groups discuss and doesn't control the discussions, but observes and sometimes interjects when appropriate. The teacher necessarily plays a diminished role and therefore cannot ensure that the talk will be productive. Students can spend time on off-task talk, and there is no guarantee that students will treat one another in an equitable manner. This format has many important functions in mathematics class. However, it figures less prominently in this book. Rather, our focus here is on how teachers can actively create conditions for talk that will be reliably productive in terms of mathematical thinking and reasoning.

Talk Format 3: Turn and Talk, or Partner Talk

Small-group discussion is distinct from what we will call *partner talk* or *turn and talk* (also sometimes called "think-pair-share"). In this talk format, the teacher asks a question, gives students thirty seconds to a minute to think to themselves (no hands!) and then gives students a short time, perhaps a two minutes at the most, to put their thoughts into words with their nearest neighbor. While this is happening, the teacher circulates and listens to discover what students are thinking. He or she can then go back into the large-group discussion with a better sense of how to proceed, while students have had a chance to clarify their thinking in a low-stress format. When the teacher then asks students to report what they said in their partner talk, many more will feel confident in doing so.

This format has numerous benefits, and works directly to help you accomplish the four steps introduced in the previous section. For example, it supports Step 1: Helping Individual Students Clarify and Share Their Own Thoughts. Students who are keeping up with the lesson but are hesitant about voicing their thoughts will have a chance to practice their contribution with just one conversational partner. Students who have not understood completely can bring up their questions with their partner, and perhaps formulate a way to ask their questions to the whole class. For many students, particularly those who are English learners, this two-minute aside is invaluable. They can emerge from the partner talk ready to participate in the whole-group discussion.

This talk format can also help with Step 1: Helping Students Orient to the Thinking of Others. When you ask a student to report after a turn-and-talk, you can say "Tell us what *your partner* said." For students who would prefer to use the airtime for themselves, this helps get across the message that all students are responsible for listening to others and for being able to repeat back or restate what has been said. Similarly, even after two or three students have repeated the reasoning expressed by their classmate, not all students will have it. This is the perfect time to call for a turn-and-talk to allow everyone to see if they can put it into their own words. After the turn-and-talk, you can call on students who might not have been able to repeat or reformulate at the beginning of the sequence of explanation. By this time, many more students will be able to understand, to the point of being able to restate. This move is particularly useful in classrooms with numerous English learners or wide ranges of preparation or ability.

This talk format also helps support Steps 3 and 4, which allow you to help students deepen their reasoning and engage directly with their classmates' thinking. When a student has talked through a complex piece of reasoning, the teacher can say "Does everyone follow that? Let's do a quick turn and talk about her reasoning to make sure we all follow it." Similarly, after you pose a question about who agrees or disagrees, you can call for a brief turn and talk to support all students' participation in working with their classmates' reasoning.

Four Cases: What Does Productive Talk Look Like?

The following narrative examples, or cases, show you how talk moves look in action in the classroom. These cases, or examples, are composites based on actual classes we have taught or observed. The examples in this chapter are from grades 1, 3, 5, and 6. Each case begins with a brief description of the mathematical ideas or problems that are central to the lesson, along with a description of what the class has done so far. We then present the interaction in the form of a script, tracking the teacher's and students' contributions to the conversation.

Case 1: "I disagree with Juana's solution because four won't work."

In Ms. Day's third-grade class, the students had been finding solutions for pairs of equations that are number sentences in which unknowns are indicated by

NCTM Standard:
Algebra

Grade 3

squares and triangles. For each pair of equations, students must figure out one value for the square and one value for the triangle that makes both sentences true. Students were instructed that all squares have the same value and all triangles have the same value. For example, in this case, students had been considering the following two number sentences and have been asked to figure out what values of the square and triangle make both equations true.

$$10 - \square = \triangle$$
$$\square + \square + \triangle = 13$$

(In order for both sentences to be true, the square must have a value of 3 and the triangle must have a value of 7.)

A problem like this is useful for a number of reasons. First, it gives children practice with arithmetic as they try out different numbers to make both sentences true. Second, it provides children early exposure to two ideas that are central to algebraic thinking—finding a value for an unknown, and finding a solution that simultaneously solves two different equations. Third, the problem is accessible to almost all students because it can be solved using a guess-and-check strategy. Third graders have no way to manipulate these equations algebraically, so they have to start with the strategy of guessing two numbers that might work, and plugging them in to check whether they do work. Finally, because there are two number sentences for which the numbers must work, students must perform the logical operation of checking whether the numbers they choose work for both sentences.

Ms. Day knows that some of the students understand that they are finding a solution that works for both equations, while others do not. Although she has explained to them that the value they choose for the square and triangle must remain the same for both sentences, many of them do not seem to comprehend her explanation fully. She decides to use a session of classroom talk to help them.

First, Ms. Day gives the students five minutes to work on the problem individually. As they work, she circulates through the room looking over their shoulders. She notices that Juana has not grasped the connection between the two number sentences, while Jaleesa has already solved the problem. David seems to be wavering between treating each number sentence as an isolated problem and connecting the two as one system to be solved. Ms. Day refrains from giving students any assistance during this time. After the five minutes are up, she starts the whole-class discussion with a statement:

1. Ms. D: I'd like someone to explain the solution you got, and I'll write it on the board. Then we can see who agrees, who disagrees, who has the same answer, or who has a different answer. Juana, what was your solution?

2. Juana: Umm, I think the square can be six, and then the triangle is four.

3. Ms. D: [Writes on the board: $\square = 6$, $\triangle = 4$.] OK, so tell us what your reasoning is.

4. Juana: Well, if you put them in that sentence, then ten minus six is four.

5. Ms. D: OK, so let's hear what people think. Did other people get the same answer? A different answer? What do you think about what Juana said? Jaleesa, your hand is up. Did you agree or disagree with Juana's solution? And tell us why.

6. Jaleesa: Well, I sort of disagree, because four doesn't work.

7. Ms. D: Hmm, so you think four doesn't work. But look, in this sentence here, it does work. Juana says the square is equal to six. Ten minus the square, which is six, equals the triangle, which is four. That works, right? [Looks around . . .] I'm confused. Can someone else explain what Jaleesa is saying? How about you, David?

8. David: I think I know what Jaleesa is saying. She's saying that four doesn't work in the *second* sentence—square plus square plus triangle equals thirteen.

9. Ms. D: So, Jaleesa, is that what you were saying?

10. Jaleesa: Yes, because in the second sentence if you use four for the triangle then the two squares will have to equal up to nine and that can't work. Because in the first one they're six.

11. Ms. D: Wait, I'm not sure I'm following that. I'm a little confused here. You're going kind of fast. David, do you want to try to say what Jaleesa said in your own words?

12. David: OK, I think she means that the triangle number has to be the same number for the first sentence *and* the second sentence. And the square number has to be the same for both sentences too. So if you put four in for the triangle on the first sentence, then you have to put four in for the triangle on the second sentence. And that won't work.

13. Ms. D: That won't work? Is that what you meant, Jaleesa?

14. Jaleesa: Yes, because . . . can I show you on the board?

15. Ms. D: Sure. Come on up.

Notice that Ms. Day has used the *repeating* talk move in several ways here. In line 7, she asks David to repeat Jaleesa's position. Then, in line 9, she asks Jaleesa if David is correct in his summary of her position. In line 11, she models confusion, and asks David to once again put Jaleesa's contribution "into his own words." Then, in line 13, she gives Jaleesa another chance to clarify. By the time Jaleesa comes to the board, her own position has become clearer to her and she is eager to share it.

16. Jaleesa: OK. [She writes the first sentence, encircling the six with a square and the four with a triangle:]

$$10 - \boxed{6} = \triangle{4}$$

OK, *this* one *works.* But now we have to put the *same* numbers in the *second* sentence and *it* has to work *too* [She writes $6 + 6 + 4 = 13$, drawing squares around the 6s and a triangle around the 4:]

$$\boxed{6} + \boxed{6} + \triangle\!\!\!4\!\!\!\triangle = 13$$

But *this* one doesn't work. [She sits down.]

17. Ms. D: OK. Hmm. So Juana, what do you think about that? Do you agree or disagree with what Jaleesa said? And tell us why.

18. Juana: Well, I guess I didn't think that we had to put the *same* numbers in both sentences. I thought we could use different ones.

19. Ms. D: Yes, this kind of problem is harder than just filling in one sentence, isn't it? We have to fill in two at the same time! We have to make sure that *both* sentences are true. Let's do another one. This time you can spend three minutes working with the person next to you. [Ms. Day writes two different equations on the board:]

$$\square - \triangle = 15$$
$$\square + \triangle + \triangle = 21$$

Recognizing and Understanding the Teacher's Moves
A great deal is going on in this series of exchanges. Let's focus on the teacher's purposes and her use of talk. While many teachers already use the instructional strategy of asking students to share their solution to a problem, our focus in this case is on Ms. Day's use of talk to bring the students to a *common ground of understanding.* She knew that not all students had understood the constraints of the problem, even though she had done her best to explain it. Her immediate purpose was to clarify one aspect of the math problem: The problem solver has to consider *both* sentences simultaneously in order to find a valid solution. She had observed that some students, like Jaleesa, understood this. Some students, like David, were wavering. And still others, like Juana, did not understand this constraint.

This situation, where different levels of understanding can be found side by side in the same class, is extremely common and is always a challenge. It is one reason that teachers sometimes shy away from carrying out a whole-class discussion. How can we have a discussion involving all students if only some of them understand the problem? But Ms. Day used the students' contributions in a systematic fashion to clarify a misconception that she suspected many students held, not just Juana.

So why did Ms. Day say what she did? Why did she call on the students she called on? Ms. Day first brought the misconception to the forefront by asking Juana to present her solution. She did not correct Juana, but asked the students in an open, neutral way whether anyone agreed or disagreed with the solution. She knew that Jaleesa would disagree, and would present some form of argument against Juana's claim. So she called on Jaleesa. Jaleesa did disagree, but did not provide a full explanation of why she disagreed with Juana's solution. Right after Jaleesa gave this partial explanation, Ms. Day expressed confusion.

Why does Ms. Day say in Line 11 that she is confused? Was she really confused? No, but she knew that other students were. Jaleesa's explanation was quick and Ms. Day knew that it would be difficult for some of the other students to follow. An explanation that cannot be understood is not worth much to the other students. In instances like these, the teacher must try to expand the time and space available for the class to understand what one student already knows. So here Ms. Day makes a skillful move: She brings a third student into the conversation, David, who is not entirely clear about the constraints of the problem. By asking him to repeat Jaleesa's explanation, she is hoping to draw him (and others) into Jaleesa's thinking and lead him to a fuller acceptance of the two-sentence constraint on the problem. Finally, after David helps construct a fuller explanation, Ms. Day returns to Juana, and allows her to revisit her original analysis. By moving on to another, similar example, and allowing students to talk to each other as they solve it, Ms. Day is using talk in yet another way to solidify students' understanding.

It takes students a great deal of practice to become solid and confident mathematical thinkers, and the talk format of whole-class discussion provides a space for that practice. Accordingly, within a class discussion, the teacher often refrains from providing the correct answer. The teacher does not reject incorrect reasoning, but instead attempts to get students to explore the steps in that reasoning, with the aim that they will gain practice in discovering where their reasoning falls short. In this case, Ms. Day did not correct Juana's misconception directly, but instead asked other students to react to what Juana had said. As we said earlier, whole-class discussions will reveal many examples of faulty reasoning, mistakes in computation, and misunderstandings. Ms. Day decided to use these as her raw material to help her students develop their problem-solving abilities.

When Ms. Day refrains from correcting the students in this part of the discussion, she is not losing sight of her ultimate goal: that her students achieve mathematical power through precision, accuracy, insight, and reliable reasoning. She knows, however, that her students need to practice their reasoning in complex problem solving without an immediate focus on the answer. After this discussion, Ms. Day will summarize and review the correct solutions, along with the generalizations that the group has made based on their discussion.

Case 2: "This is a triangle because it just looks right."

Mrs. Sigler's first-grade students are learning about geometric figures. The students have been given a set of polygons to sort into two groups: triangles and other shapes. Within the set there are many different sizes and kinds of triangles, including scalene, equilateral, isosceles, and right triangles. The triangles are cut out of colored paper and are either red, green, or blue. Other shapes are also in the set—squares, rectangles, hexagons, and parallelograms. Students are working in groups of four. Mrs. Sigler notices that one group of students has separated the equilateral triangles from all of the other triangles and grouped them alone. They have placed most of the other triangles in the "other" category.

NCTM Standard:
Geometry

Grade 1

1. Mrs. S: I see that you have separated the shapes. What is this group of shapes called? [Points to the set of equilateral triangles.]

2. All: Triangles.

3. Mrs. S: I'd like each of you to explain your thinking to me. I'd like each of you to explain to me why all of the shapes in this group are triangles [points to the equilateral triangles] and all of these are not triangles [points to some triangles in the "other" group].

4. Ollie: This [points to one equilateral triangle] just looks like a triangle.

5. Mrs. S: In what way?

6. Ollie: It's short and fat and just looks right.

7. Yoon So: Yeah. This one [points to a scalene triangle] is too skinny and pointy. It isn't a triangle.

8. Mrs. S: What do you think, Paul?

9. Paul: Well, you know these are maybe triangles [indicates the group of equilateral triangles] because you know they just look like triangles.

10. Mrs. S: What does a triangle look like?

11. Paul: Hmmm. [Paul looks around the room and then points to a poster of geometric shapes. The shapes on the poster are all regular polygons and the triangle on it is equilateral.] Like that one. See, triangles just look like this [cups hands into the shape of an equilateral triangle]. They're flat on the bottom.

12. Mrs. S: Ollie, what did Paul just say?

13. Ollie: These are a triangle [cups his hand].

14. Mrs. S: What else did he say?

15. Ollie: They have to sit on their bottoms—there aren't pointy parts on the bottom.

16. Mrs. S: OK. Look at this. [She takes one of the large equilateral triangles from the triangle pile and turns it so a vertex is pointing downward.] Is this a triangle?

17. Paul: [Turns the triangle so it is sitting on a side.] Now it is.

18. Mrs. S: Sim, you have been very quiet. What do you think? Is this a triangle? [Turns the equilateral triangle around so the point is again facing down.]

19. Sim: I don't think so. I don't know.

20. Mrs. S: Why don't you think it's a triangle?

21. Sim: I don't know. [Long pause.] Maybe it is. Because I can turn it and it looks like a triangle.

Mrs. Sigler has been asking each student in turn to justify their categorization of the equilateral triangles as the only "real" triangles. Mrs. Sigler has seen that the children in this small group have a very restricted idea of what a triangle is. This is quite typical for young children: Their definitions for geometric shapes are based on their visual memory of their previous experiences with that shape. Equilateral triangles are typically used to illustrate the concept of "triangle." One teacher we know calls this the *Sesame Street* level of understanding geometric shapes.

Some readers might find this small-group interchange to be somewhat slow and laborious. Is the teacher really moving the children toward changing their understanding? Yes, but first she must assess what they believe, find out how they think about the question. And to do this, she is getting them to *externalize* their ideas by asking them each to speak in turn. Notice that with each new contribution, their low level of understanding gets a little bit more obvious. Even though the teacher pushes them to justify their categorization of the triangles, they only offer reasons like it "looks right." It doesn't seem that the talk is moving the group very far into new understandings, but at this point, Mrs. Sigler does have a pretty clear picture of the level of this group's understanding. She sees that this classification task has not been an effective instructional activity at this point. She decides to bring out another set of materials the next day.

The next day, Mrs. Sigler brings out a large box of strips made of cardboard of different lengths, with holes at the ends. They can be fastened together by the use of brads.

From the previous day's discussion she knows that the students are simply identifying the names of geometric shapes with a typical image. They are not considering the defining properties of a triangle, such as the fact that a triangle is any closed figure with three straight sides. So she gives each child three strips from the box, choosing three strips that she knows will make a triangle. She asks them to use the strips and the fasteners to create a triangle. By choosing the 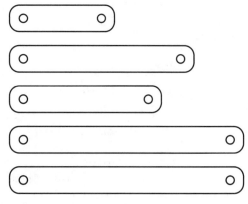 strips, she has made sure that all varieties of triangles—equilateral, isoceles, and scalene—will be produced by at least one or two students in the class.

After each child has made a triangle, Mrs. Sigler tapes them all to the front board. She then holds a large-group discussion about the triangles.

1. Mrs. S: Let's look at these. Does anybody notice anything about the shapes? Cecile?

2.	Cecile:	All of them are made from three strips.

3.	Mrs. S:	Does anybody see a triangle that was made from more than three strips?

4.	Students:	No, no. They all have three.

5.	Mrs. S:	I notice that all of these triangles are not identical; they don't all look the same. How are they different? Pooja?

6.	Pooja:	Some of them are big and some are small.

7.	Mrs. S:	What makes a triangle big or small? See these two triangles? [Mrs. Sigler takes one large triangle and one small triangle and places them next to each other on the board.] What did someone do to make them different?

8.	Pooja:	You use long strips to make the big one and short strips to make the small one.

9.	Paul:	Mine is the big one and I used the really long strips.

10.	Mrs. S:	How many long strips did you use, Paul?

11.	Paul:	Three.

12.	Mrs. S:	Who else made a big triangle? [Points to a couple of triangles on the board that are large.] How many strips did you use?

13.	Cristobal:	I made that one over there. [Points to an isosceles triangle.] I used three strips.

14.	Mrs. S:	Who made a small triangle?

15.	Ben:	I did! I used three strips, too!

16.	Ali:	Me, too. My triangle took three strips.

17.	Mrs. S:	OK, so now let's use a word that people use to talk about some geometric shapes. We can use the word *side*. This triangle has three sides—one, two, three. [Mrs. S points to each side as she counts.] How many sides does Ali's triangle have? [Here Mrs. S points to Ali's triangle, a long and thin scalene triangle made with two longer strips and one short one.]

18.	Ali:	My triangle has three sides.

19.	Marsha:	But Mrs. Sigler, I don't know if that's a triangle. It doesn't look like the triangles from yesterday.

20.	Mrs. S:	That's an important question. Can somebody repeat for us what Marsha just said? Ali, can you repeat what Marsha just said?

21. Ali: She said that my triangle isn't really a triangle because it doesn't look like the ones we put in the triangle group yesterday.

22. Mrs. S: Marsha, is that what you said?

23. Marsha: Yes, but I didn't mean that Ali's triangle wasn't a triangle. I just meant that it didn't match the ones from yesterday in our group.

24. Mrs. S: OK, so Marsha has asked a really important question. Is this shape a triangle? And what about those triangles from yesterday? Remember yesterday, when we were sorting triangles? [General acknowledgment comes from the students.] Some of you thought that a shape like this [points to Ali's triangle] didn't belong in the same group with triangles that looked like this [points to an equilateral triangle on the board]. So we have a really important question here. [She pauses . . . all eyes are on Mrs. Sigler.] Just what *is* a triangle?

Recognizing and Understanding the Teacher's Moves

Mrs. Sigler has brought the discussion to a very important point: All of the children's attention is now focused on whether or not all of the shapes they have just constructed are triangles. She now has several choices. She could tell them that Ali's shape is a triangle and ask them to figure out why. She could ask them what they think, and see where the discussion leads. She could provide some direct instruction about the properties of triangles, starting with the fact that they have three sides and are closed figures and then asking the students to check whether all the figures on the board meet those two conditions.

Mrs. Sigler has succeeded in using classroom talk to bring these first graders to a point where they are ready to engage with the idea that triangles that are not equilateral triangles are also properly called triangles. What talk moves did Mrs. Sigler use with these first graders? Notice that she asked many students to reiterate the idea that three strips are needed to make a triangle, even though everyone had agreed that all the shapes on the board had used three strips. Students need time to generalize important ideas; in this case these first graders had to consider the fact that all of the different-looking shapes have three sides. Although this idea is less complex than those we describe in some other examples in this book, it's an important idea for these first graders. They deserve the time it will take to make sure that everyone has seen the same generalization.

The slow and gentle nature of the talk in this first-grade classroom is also reflected in other ways. Mrs. Sigler lets these students spend time in their small groups working with an activity while she talks to the small groups. Then she moves the activity to a whole-class format, making sure that all students have had a chance to think about and talk about the material that will be discussed in the large group.

Notice that although Mrs. Sigler makes sure to give students time to consider the problem and to listen to one another, she does not shrink from difficult material. For example, Mrs. Sigler does not hesitate to introduce correct mathematical terminology. She uses the term *geometric shapes* and she directs the students to use the word *side* when talking about their triangles. She could have spent even more time with this, particularly if she had had many English-language learners in the class.

Finally, it is very important to note that even with these young children, Mrs. Sigler allowed the students to consider her questions for quite some time without providing them with answers. She could have started the first day by simply telling the students that they were wrong in their categorizations, that all three-sided closed figures are triangles. In some situations one might want to proceed in this way, and we would not rule it out as an option. But Mrs. Sigler chose the more indirect route, in the belief that letting students follow the ideas at their own pace and in their own way would more likely result in their being ready to face the question that Marsha brought up. Her ultimate aim is to use classroom talk to bring students to understand the criteria for what makes a shape a triangle, thereby moving them beyond their *Sesame Street* understanding of this geometric shape.

Case 3, Episode 1: "So you drew a picture of the tarts?"

Ms. Stangle's fifth-grade class is focusing on a problem that is designed to give them experience with fractions:

Ms. Stangle wants to make peach tarts for her friends. She needs two-thirds of a peach for each tart and she has 10 peaches. What is the greatest number of tarts that she can make with 10 peaches?

NCTM Standard:
Number and Operations

Grade 5

Ms. Stangle has the students work on the problem on their own for ten minutes. At the end of the ten minutes she doesn't know what types of solutions students have come up with because she had an unexpected visitor to the classroom and did not get a chance to circulate and look at their work. So she is wading into murky waters. However, she does know that some students will have difficulty setting up the problem, others will have difficulty representing the facts accurately, and still others will have difficulty with computation.

1. Ms. S: Who wants to present their solution? How about some hands here? OK, Marco.

2. Marco: Well, first I looked at them all and then I made lines on each one and then I counted.

3. Ms. S: Marco, I'm not really sure I follow you. It sounds like you drew a picture of the tarts and the peaches, is that right?

4. Marco: Well, yeah.

5. Ms. S: We can't really follow what you say about your solution unless we can see the picture in our minds. We have to be able to listen to you and really understand what you're describing. Would you like to tell us again about the details of what you drew?

6. Marco: Um, OK. I drew the ten peaches and then I cut each one into three parts. Then I counted all the parts. So it was thirty parts. And the problem says that each tart needs two parts of a peach.

7. Ms. S: Hold on, I'm getting lost again. I thought the problem said . . . well, wait. So you're saying that I can take any two parts of a peach and that will be enough for a tart? Is that what you're saying?

8. Marco: Two of the three parts.

9. Ms. S: OK, so let me see if I can draw what you're describing. Here are my ten peaches [draws ten circles] and here I'm dividing each one into three parts [draws unequal partitions of each peach; see Figure 2–1].

              Did anyone else have a picture like this?

10. Students: [Several shifting restlessly] Nooo! Not like that!

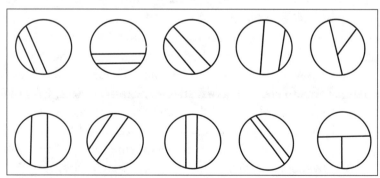

FIGURE 2–1 Ms. Stangle's representation of Marco's solution.

11. Ms. S: No? How come [innocently looking surprised]? What's wrong with this? I've cut each peach into three parts.

12. Ginny: No, it has to be equal or it won't be thirds.

13. Ms. S: Oh, so the problem says it has to be thirds? Is that right?

14. Ginny: Yes.

15. Ms. S: OK, so Marco do you want to add to your statement of your solution?

16. Marco: OK. I drew ten peaches and I drew lines that cut them into *equal thirds!* And then I drew ten tarts and I matched them up.

Recognizing and Understanding the Teacher's Moves

You might wonder why Ms. Stangle didn't just ask Marco to draw a picture on the board. After all, it's good mathematical practice to have students present their graphic representations to the class. What is Ms. Stangle trying to do here? Why is she subjecting the students to this ordeal of clarification? Why is she being so cautious in making sure that their meaning is absolutely clear? She could not be as obtuse as all that—surely she knew that Marco knew he was counting thirds, not just random parts of a peach.

In our work we have found that one of the most effective ways to increase students' attention to precise language is to engage in just such episodes as the fragment presented here. When the teacher sets a very high criterion for clarity, when she herself "fails" to understand what the students are saying until they are utterly clear, she is modeling for them an attention to detail in language that will serve them in a variety of ways. Experiences like these will eventually lead students to use language more precisely, because it raises their level of awareness of the audience. They will also begin to scrutinize the language of others more carefully. We have seen this kind of awareness lead to clear gains in reading comprehension, both in mathematics and in English language arts.

In this excerpt Ms Stangle skillfully uses the technique of revoicing. She repeats what the student has said, clarifying, adding, or making more obvious some problematic feature of it. She then asks the student whether that is the correct interpretation. In the first few lines, she uses this conversational move in order to get Marco to clarify his first statement from Line 2. Like many students, Marco is not particularly skilled at anticipating what his audience will need. An outsider to the classroom would not understand him when he says, "Well, first I looked at them all and then I made lines on each one and then I counted." And although the other students have been working on the same problem, there is no guarantee that their solutions look the same. Therefore, Marco's description has to be clear enough for others to envision exactly what he has done, and to connect it to what they have done.

Ms. Stangle could have asked Marco to draw his picture on the board, and in fact she often does just that. But in this excerpt, she skillfully uses classroom discourse to get Marco to reach a higher level of verbal precision. In Line 9, she takes his words literally and draws a picture that matches what he has said (although it does not match his intentions). As other students see the discrepancy, they grow slightly anxious and want to correct it.

Case 3, Episode 2: "Thirds of tarts or thirds of peaches?"

17. Ms. S: Can somebody repeat what Marco did for his solution so far? Cheryl?

18. Cheryl: I think he said he drew a picture of the ten tarts, and then he, like, drew a picture of the ten peaches. Then he cut the tarts into three pieces each. And he drew, like, lines to the peaches.

19. Ms. S: OK, so does everyone agree with Cheryl's rendition of what Marco said? Was that what Marco said? Does anyone want to weigh in here? Ginny?

20. Ginny: Well, it was almost the same, but Cheryl said that Marco drew ten tarts and cut them into three pieces each. And I think he said that he drew ten *peaches* and cut them into three pieces, three *thirds*, each.

21. Ms. S: So Marco, would you clarify? Which one did you do? Did you cut the tarts into thirds in your picture or did you cut the peaches into thirds?

22. Marco: [Looks suspiciously at Ms. Stangle.] Umm, I'm not sure now.

23. Ms. S: OK, who can help out? Did anyone else have a picture where they divided either the tarts or the peaches into thirds? Tyavanna?

24. Tyavanna: I drew ten peaches? And . . . um . . . like . . . um, I think that's what you have to do because you have to show the thirds of the peaches? 'Cause that's what you have to figure out to make the tarts. Not the other way around.

25. Ms. S: OK, can somebody repeat what Tyavanna just said? Kenny, can you repeat it in your own words?

26. Kenny: Well, I think she's saying that we have to draw pictures of the ten peaches so we can draw the thirds of each peach. She's saying we don't have to draw thirds of each tart. But I didn't draw the peaches at all.

27. Ms. S: OK, so you did it a different way? Will you tell us how you started out?

28. Kenny: I wrote the fraction *three-thirds* and I wrote it once for each peach. Then I added up all the three-thirds and I got thirty thirds. So then I knew how many thirds I had to work with. Then I knew that each tart had to have two thirds, so I just divided two into thirty and I got fifteen. So I knew there could be fifteen tarts.

Recognizing and Understanding the Teacher's Moves

Notice how at the beginning of Episode 2, in Line 17, Ms. Stangle asks Cheryl to repeat what Marco said. This move quickly puts students on notice that they must listen to their classmates' contributions and cannot simply sit and wait for their turn. They must actively engage in trying to understand what others are saying. In fact, Cheryl incorrectly repeats what Marco said, perhaps because she does not understand or perhaps because she has made a simple speech error. We do not know which is the reason for her error, and neither does Ms. Stangle. Nevertheless, Ms. Stangle brings other students into the process of clarifying and correcting. As part of this process, she asks Tyavanna to explain her understanding, and Tyavanna is able to shed some light on the situation.

Why does Ms. Stangle choose to ask Kenny to repeat what Tyavanna has said (Line 25)? Is it because she thinks he isn't listening and she wants to call him back? Or is it because she wants to make sure that all students have heard and understood what Tyavanna has just said? Ms. Stangle could have both intentions: Her skillful use of this request for students to repeat could serve both functions simultaneously. But some readers may ask whether this set of moves—the questioning about details and the requests for repetition—isn't awfully time-consuming, and perhaps even annoying. How could one run every class this way? Who has the time? Doesn't this focus on precision drive people crazy?

Ms. Stangle does use these techniques with regularity, but there are many times during lessons when she does not require students to achieve the same degree of precision as in Episode 1. For example, when students encounter a new idea, and are trying to come to grips with it, their language typically becomes imprecise and even incoherent. A moment's reflection reveals that this is true of adults as well—when we are dealing with new concepts and unfamiliar ideas, any of us may sound quite inarticulate! As the cognitive demands on us increase, our ability to talk precisely may deteriorate precipitously. Knowing this, teachers like Ms. Stangle strike a delicate balance. She does not require absolute precision of students as they are working through new ideas. When they are engaged in the most demanding kinds of thinking, she is less stringent in her attention to clarity and precision. On the other hand, when students are more comfortable with the mathematical ideas, she can afford to emphasize the precision of their language. Her students encounter these demands for precision often, and thereby come to understand and accept the need for precision. They develop an appreciation for the effort we all must make to communicate clearly, in mathematics and elsewhere. And although at first students do not like to have to repeat what other students have just said, over time they become remarkably attentive and skilled at keeping track of where the conversation is going. It is in just such settings that teachers are able to eventually achieve real advances in mathematical understanding through talk.

Case 4: "Discuss this with the person next to you."

When we divide a whole number by a fraction, such as two divided by one- fourth, the quotient, eight, is larger than the dividend! For most students, this is a confusing new result that does not connect well with their previous experience of division. In lower grades, division problems typically yield answers that are *less* than the dividend. Also, this problem does not lend itself to being interpreted in the way students usually interpret division situations, as "sharing." How can you share two pies among one-fourth of a person? And what does the answer of 8 mean in terms of the most common situations associated with division, like sharing? In the face of this departure from the students' favorite meaning of division, many teachers resort to simple computational rules: to divide some number by a fraction, you simply "invert and multiply" or "multiply by the reciprocal of the fraction." But very few students understand why this works.

NCTM Standard:
Number and Operations

Grade 6

To help his sixth-grade students develop understanding of division by fractions, Mr. Harris plans several days of instruction. First he discusses with the students the fact that in this set of lessons they will encounter some new ideas about division. He writes on the board a simple division problem with whole numbers:

$$12 \div 4 = \underline{\quad}.$$

He asks the students to give an example of what the problem might mean. Students respond with "sharing" interpretations. For example, one student says, "If you share twelve pies among four people, how many pies will each get?" Mr. Harris reminds the students of another way to interpret a division problem, as making equal groups rather than sharing. He counts out twelve sheets of paper and tells the students that they will use them to make booklets. "We need four sheets for each booklet," he says. "How many booklets can we make with these twelve sheets of paper?" The answer is obvious to the students, and Mr. Harris models it by putting the paper into piles, or groups, with four in each, having the students do the subtraction to figure out how many sheets of paper are left each time he makes a group of four. In this way, he reviews interpreting division as repeated subtraction.

Next Mr. Harris writes on the board:

$$2 \div \tfrac{1}{4}$$

He presents the puzzle of dividing two pies among one-fourth of a person. The students all agree that this does not make much sense to them. Then he gives another interpretation of the problem, as dividing the two pies into equally sized groups with one-fourth of a pie in each group. By drawing pictures, he illustrates the process of successively subtracting one-fourth of a pie from two pies to arrive at eight groups, thus showing how the answer of 8 is derived. (See Figure 2–2.)

Finally, Mr. Harris writes on the blackboard the following table of number sentences, in which 2 is divided by some unit fraction.

$$2 \div \tfrac{1}{2} = \text{?} \qquad 2 \div \tfrac{1}{9} = \text{?}$$

$$2 \div \tfrac{1}{3} = \text{?} \qquad 2 \div \tfrac{1}{20} = \text{?}$$

$$2 \div \tfrac{1}{5} = \text{?} \qquad 2 \div \tfrac{1}{50} = \text{?}$$

$$2 \div \tfrac{1}{6} = \text{?}$$

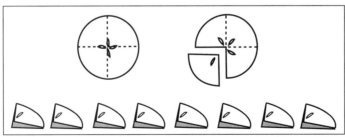

FIGURE 2–2 Mr. Harris's diagram showing $2 \div \tfrac{1}{4} = 8$.

Mr. Harris calls on different students to read each number sentence aloud using this sentence structure: "How many times can we subtract one-fifth from two?" "How many times can we subtract one-fiftieth from two?" And so on. He then asks students to talk together in groups of four to solve the entire set of number sentences. He gives them twenty minutes to do this as he circulates around the room checking in with different groups.

Mr. Harris's Use of Small-Group Discussion

Mr. Harris thinks that the students need time to think about the answers to the problems. He knows that if he asks them to do so individually, then students who are having difficulty could be stranded without help. Therefore, Mr. Harris uses the small-group format and asks students to work together on the problems. This provides support for the students, giving them a chance to talk with one another about their thinking. It keeps all of them engaged with the problems. And it allows Mr. Harris to circulate and check on the students' understanding. When he notices that most groups have written answers for all of the problems, Mr. Harris asks the students for their attention. Then, calling on students to report their answers, he fills in the chart. As students report, he revoices their answers and then reinforces the repeated subtraction interpretation: "So you found that two divided by one-sixth is twelve, because you can subtract one-sixth from two . . . *twelve* times. Is that right?" Finally the table looks like this:

$$2 \div \tfrac{1}{2} = 4 \qquad\qquad 2 \div \tfrac{1}{9} = 18$$

$$2 \div \tfrac{1}{3} = 6 \qquad\qquad 2 \div \tfrac{1}{20} = 40$$

$$2 \div \tfrac{1}{5} = 10 \qquad\qquad 2 \div \tfrac{1}{50} = 100$$

$$2 \div \tfrac{1}{6} = 12$$

1. Mr. H: OK, so now we've filled in the chart. Does anyone see a pattern?

Mr. Harris waits for ten seconds. He asks again: "What pattern do you see?" The students are staring at the board, perusing the table. No hands are raised. Mr. Harris again uses "wait time" with determination, but then begins to think that perhaps this situation calls for more support. He decides that the students need to voice their questions and externalize their thinking with one another first, before they tackle talking about this complex problem in the context of the whole class.

2. Mr. H: Turn and talk to your partner about the table. Do you see a pattern that relates the quotient to the first two numbers? See if you can come up with an answer that you and your partner agree on.

The room explodes in talk. Students had ideas about the pattern, but they lacked an easy way to express their ideas. Many students are reluctant to speak up when they are not absolutely sure of themselves. However, if they have time to talk to one other person, a peer, in an environment where only that one other person will be paying attention to their initial attempts to give voice to their ideas, they can lose some of their reluctance to think out loud.

Mr. Harris's Use of Partner Talk

At this point, let's consider one of the benefits from Mr. Harris's use of talk. Although many of the students may have noticed a pattern, they are unable or unwilling to describe it aloud at the start. Partner talk or "turn and talk" is especially effective when students reach an impasse—the teacher gives students a short time, perhaps a minute or two at the most, to put their thoughts into words with their nearest neighbor. Some students have partially formed mathematical ideas but are hesitant to try them out in front of a whole-class group. Mr. Harris also has students who are learning English as a second language who may be hesitant for both linguistic and mathematical reasons. All students can benefit from the two minutes of partner talk, particularly when faced with a knotty new problem. This talk practice is simple, but it can have a profound impact on ensuring equitable participation in the classroom. While a few students may always be ready at a moment's notice to give an answer to anything, the whole class suffers if the teacher is unable to create the conditions for equal access for all students.

After the two minutes, Mr. Harris continues:

3. Mr. H: So let's hear what you have decided about the pattern in the chart. Verette?

4. Verette: Me and my partner think the pattern is that the answer is twice as much as the bottom number.

5. Mr. H: Let's hear from others. George.

6. George: We think you take the denominator and multiply it by the first number, and then you get the quotient.

7. Mr. H: Is the pattern that Verette found the same as the pattern that George found? Paula?

8. Paula: I think they are the same, because Verette said the bottom number and George said the denominator, and those are the

same thing, and you multiply them by the first number, which is two.

9. Mr. H: Does the pattern work for every single case? Let's check each example. If we take the first number, two, and multiply it by the denominator in the first example, two, what do we get? Four. It works. Let's try the next one. Marcia, can you talk us through that one? [Mr. Harris continues through the entire chart, having individual students talk through the calculation for each one.]

Recognizing and Understanding the Teacher's Moves

Notice how Mr. Harris uses the contribution of different students in a sequential fashion to build understanding for the entire group. He does not simply announce the pattern at the start. Nor does he correct or clarify the contribution of the first student, Verette. Instead of evaluating Verette's formulation, he asks for another formulation from a different student. The next student, George, presents the same generalization but in different terms. Still Mr. Harris does not evaluate, but instead moves on to ask whether these two are the same. The third student, Paula, gives yet a third formulation of the same generalization in slightly different words, combining George's and Verette's contributions.

Mr. Harris's moves here are not necessarily the best or only way to handle this conversation. He could certainly have homed in on Verette's contribution and elicited more detail, as he has done many other times. But we offer this example as a way of showing how a skillful teacher can use the contributions of students to accomplish several goals at once. First, Mr. Harris is giving the students practice in putting their mathematical reasoning into words. Second, he is letting students who need more processing time hear several different versions of the target generalization. And third, he is modeling for students the practice of listening to one another, and conveying their obligation to try to make sense of one another's words.

As the lesson goes on, Mr. Harris gives the students another set of examples, in which the dividend for each problem is 3, not 2, and the divisor is still a unit fraction with a numerator of 1. He again asks them to look at the examples and find a pattern. And he again uses partner talk to give students time to see that once more the quotient equals the dividend times the denominator (e.g., $3 \div \frac{1}{5} = 15$).

All in all, Mr. Harris invokes partner talk nine times during the entire lesson. And the rewards are great. With a step-by-step, careful, and systematic approach, Mr. Harris gives plenty of time for students to process the current question with their partner, and he uses students' subsequent contributions to solidify everyone's understanding. This leaves the students ready to work the next day on generalizing still further, beyond division by unit fractions (e.g., $2 \div \frac{2}{5}$ or $3 \div \frac{2}{5}$). The computations in problems like these are more difficult: Repeated subtraction of $\frac{2}{5}$ from 2 is not as straightforward as repeated subtraction of $\frac{1}{5}$ from 2. And while the answer to $2 \div \frac{2}{5}$ is a whole number, 5, as were all the answers in the earlier tables, the answer to $3 \div \frac{2}{5}$ isn't a whole number. If you subtract $\frac{2}{5}$ from 3 seven times, you are left with $\frac{1}{5}$, which isn't enough to subtract another $\frac{2}{5}$. It's only half of what's needed. The answer to $3 \div \frac{2}{5}$ is $7\frac{1}{2}$, which means that you can subtract $\frac{2}{5}$ from 3 seven and a half times. This is complex for students to grasp. Nevertheless, by continuing slowly and carefully, alternating among partner talk, small-group discussion, and whole-class discussion, and building on students' contributions, Mr. Harris was eventually able to lead students to adopt the strategy of "multiply the dividend by the reciprocal of the divisor." But in their case it would not simply be a computational trick; it would be undergirded by a real understanding of the mathematical relationships. In Mr. Harris's view, what the students accomplished would not have been possible without the extensive use of the talk moves and strategies we have been describing.

Integrating Talk and Content

Each of these teachers had taken the time to set up classroom norms for respectful and courteous discourse. They had also made it possible for all students to have equal access to participation. Their students are obligated to listen quietly and to speak up when they make a contribution. They are not allowed to express disrespect, and they follow standard turn-taking procedures.

These teachers rely on three talk formats: whole-class discussion, small-group discussion, and partner talk, using whole-class discussion and partner talk most often to get students to focus on mathematical reasoning, both their own and that of their classmates. Each of these teachers uses other talk formats as well, but in these lessons we paid special attention to these two because they facilitate the kind of mathematical thinking we are interested in supporting. Within the context of these talk formats, each teacher made skillful use of the talk moves introduced in this section.

But the talk formats and talk moves together still do not add up to a full and coherent lesson. As the teacher, you must integrate the tools of talk with the mathematical content, adjusting and refining both to the particulars of your own unique teaching situation. To help you, we suggest a three-part cycle that you will engage in again and again as you incorporate productive talk into your mathematics class. (See below.)

PRODUCTIVE TALK: THREE-PART CYCLE

1. Planning and Projecting: Creating a Road Map

Your first step is to plan carefully for a specific lesson. You need to spend time identifying the important mathematical ideas, concepts, and procedures you'll be talking about, as well as potential misconceptions or difficulties that students might have. You also need to plan which talk formats you will use, and how you will incorporate the specific talk moves we've introduced.

2. Improvising and Responding: In the Midst of the Lesson

As we all know, if you are actively engaging with students, even the most carefully planned lesson involves improvisation. You cannot be sure that things will go as you planned. And when you make extensive use of student talk, you introduce an element of uncertainty. Therefore, part of the cycle of introducing productive talk into your mathematics class necessarily involves improvisation and responding in the moment. And although you may not remember everything that happens in the lesson, you will aim to keep track of how your plans actually did or did not unfold as you expected.

3. Summarizing and Solidifying: So Where Are We Now?

During a talk-intensive lesson there will be moments when you and your students will feel overwhelmed: too much will have been said, and you will feel that you are losing focus. At these times, it's important to step back and review what has been said so far, and what the most significant points have been. Furthermore, after every such lesson, you will want to spend some time reflecting on what important mathematical ideas, conjectures, claims, and arguments have emerged during the class. When you return the next day, it will be important for you to present to the students a review of the most important aspects of the previous day's discourse. Talk-intensive lessons can be difficult to summarize, but as the teacher you will want to make sure that you take a few moments to review, clarify, and solidify the important points that have been made. This will also help you as you return to the "planning and projecting" part of the cycle.

DISCUSSION AND REFLECTION

1. For many teachers, the thought of using partner talk as many times as Mr. Harris does in Case 4 may seem disruptive. Go back over the case and consider other ways the discussion might have been conducted. In your own use of partner talk, have you found positive results? Have there been drawbacks? If so, how could you address the drawbacks?

2. One of the main goals of using classroom talk moves like those described here is to manage the unavoidable complexity and lack of clarity that occurs when students are learning something new and complicated. Consider each of the five talk moves. Could each be useful when you are faced with a student contribution that is completely unclear? Or are some better than others? Construct a situation in your classroom in which you are faced with an uninterpretable response and describe what you will do.

3. In the cases in this chapter, and throughout the book, you will see instances of students making assertions or observations that are mathematically incorrect. In many cases, because the emphasis is on sustaining student discussion and developing deeper understanding, the teacher chooses not to correct or call attention to these mistakes. What are some of the consequences of such choices? Have you had this experience? How did you deal with it? How might you deal with it in the future?

PART

II

The Mathematics:
What Do We Talk About?

3

Mathematical Concepts

Mathematical knowledge is sometimes classified into two categories: conceptual knowledge and procedural knowledge. Conceptual knowledge consists of well-defined concepts, more informal mathematical ideas, and relationships among ideas, concepts, and skills. For example, conceptual knowledge of division includes knowledge of the relationships between division and multiplication, and division and subtraction. It involves information about the different representations for division, the uses of remainders, and how remainders are affected by the size of the divisor. It includes an understanding of mathematical properties such as associativity and commutativity, and knowledge of which properties hold true for division. When students have conceptual knowledge of division, they can talk or write about these relationships and can give examples of problems and tasks that could be solved using division. Carefully guided classroom talk is an especially effective method for developing concepts and building connections among mathematical ideas.

Procedural knowledge, on the other hand, involves knowledge of facts, symbols, rules, and procedures. In the case of division, students with procedural knowledge know or can retrieve basic division facts, can use symbols to represent division, and can perform short and long division computations accurately and efficiently. It's possible to have procedural knowledge of a topic and to have little or no conceptual knowledge. However, without knowledge of the important concepts and ideas, it's impossible to truly understand that topic. For example, when students lack conceptual knowledge of division, they may have difficulty deciding if a problem-solving situation can be solved using this operation, they may not recognize when a quotient is unreasonable, or they may not understand that they can use multiplication to "undo" division.

They exhibit fragile understanding of division—understanding that is neither deep nor comprehensive.

Conceptual understanding is sometimes described in terms of how information is represented and structured in the mind of the student. When teachers indicate that students have conceptual understanding, they usually are referring to the fact that the students have an "integrated and functional grasp of a number of mathematical ideas" (National Research Council 2000). Their knowledge is "organized into a coherent whole which enables the students to learn new ideas by connecting them to what they already know." Other researchers argue that understanding occurs through the activity of participating in communities of learners who together become more and more competent in doing and making sense of mathematics. We believe that productive talk promotes both interpretations of conceptual understanding: It can be useful in helping students build individual mental connections, and it is the core activity of a community of learners who together are trying to make sense of mathematical truths.

The role of connections in understanding is considered central by the vast majority of psychologists and educators. When students are able to connect ideas and concepts to procedures and representations, learning is especially robust. Thus, one of the things we want to talk about in mathematics class is how concepts and relationships among concepts connect to what students already know. We believe that talk can be used to assist students in organizing what they already know into larger and more powerful conceptual structures—the "big ideas" of mathematics—and in developing a community of budding mathematicians.

NCTM Standard:
Representation

Grade 2

Exploring a Mathematical Concept

In a second-grade classroom, the teacher, Mrs. Hollinger, asked students to work individually and use base ten blocks to show the number 37 in different ways. About half of the students represented 37 with three "ten" blocks and seven "one" blocks, whereas the other half used thirty-seven "one" blocks. One of the students used one "ten" block and twenty-seven "one" blocks. Another student used two "ten" blocks and seventeen "one" blocks. Mrs. Hollinger wanted her students to understand that all of these groupings showed the quantity 37. Whereas she could *tell* her students that the four combinations of blocks were equivalent, she thought that if she asked students to talk about the different combinations possible they would gain insight into grouping by tens and ones. She hoped that they would conclude that three tens and seven ones uses the fewest blocks, is the most efficient grouping, and connects directly to the numeral that represents the quantity.

First, Mrs. Hollinger initiated small-group discussions, organizing students into groups of three to share what they had done individually and then to work together to generate other combinations. She asked groups to try to show the quantity 37 in four different ways. After groups had time to work, she called the class to attention. She asked a student to bring one combination of blocks to the front of the room and place them so everyone in the class could see them. Then she asked other students to display different combinations, continuing until all four grouping combinations were displayed—three tens and seven ones, two tens and seventeen ones, one ten and twenty-seven ones, and thirty-seven ones. Mrs. Hollinger then asked the class, "How can we be sure that each of these four different combinations of base ten blocks equals thirty-seven?" Mrs. Hollinger was not sure that all students agreed that the different groupings were equivalent, so she asked students to count the value of each pile of blocks displayed. Two students counted by tens and ones, and the other two counted just by ones, but all four verified that each combination of blocks equaled 37. (See Figure 3–1.)

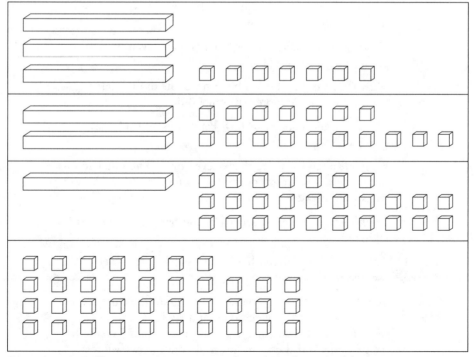

FIGURE 3–1 Different representations of 37 using base ten blocks.

After students had counted all of the piles, one student stated, "The piles look different but they are the same amount." Another student added, "The three tens and seven ones pile uses the smallest number of blocks." Mrs. Hollinger then chose students to explain to the class how they decided on their combination of blocks.

1. Mrs. H: Liana, can you explain one way you used blocks to show thirty-seven?

2. Liana: I used three tens and seven ones since you can count like ten, twenty, thirty. Then I had to use ones to get to thirty-seven.

3. Mrs. H: How is your combination the same or different from one of the others?

4. Liana: I used tens and took a tens block for each ten. The thirty-seven ones doesn't use any tens blocks.

5. Mrs. H: So you used all the tens you could, right? [Liana nods.] Peter, can you explain another way, a different way?

6. Peter: I counted out thirty-seven ones. Then I took one ten and put away ten ones. So I counted the rest. I have one ten [points to one ten] and twenty-seven ones.

7. Mrs. H: Could you have divided the other twenty-seven ones into groups of ten the way Liana did?

8. Peter: Mine is sort of like Liana's but I have lots of ones left. I could have made more tens but I didn't.

9. Mrs. H: Deacon, could you tell us how Peter showed thirty-seven using tens and ones?

10. Deacon: He made a ten from the thirty-seven ones. Then he had lots of ones left. [He starts counting the ones and Mrs. Hollinger waits.] Twenty-seven ones.

11. Dave: I think you could make what Deacon has into two tens by taking some from the ones.

12. Mrs. H: Are you saying that another way to show thirty-seven is to use two tens?

13. Dave: Yup. Here, I'll show everyone. [Dave takes the thirty-seven one blocks, counts out ten ones and trades them for one ten. He does this twice, and holds up two tens.] Here are two tens and there are still more ones left, seventeen ones left.

Each time that a student contributes or weighs in with his or her thoughts, it provides the class with more to work with as they consider the different ways 37 can be represented. Notice how Mrs. Hollinger revoiced Dave's comment to focus on the key point of using two tens.

14. Mrs. H: OK, so Liana used three tens, and Peter used one ten, and Dave used two tens. What else can we say about the different number of tens and the number of ones we can use to show thirty-seven? Crystal?

15. Crystal: You can have one, two, or three tens.

16. Luis: Can't you also have zero tens?

17. Mrs. H: Do you agree or disagree with the idea that we can show thirty-seven using zero, one, two, or three tens? Talk to your partner.

Mrs. Hollinger now has the class at a point where all options for the number of tens have been stated. You might think she would want to move to a new topic. However, this idea that a number can be represented using different numbers of tens and ones is quite complex. Students need more time than the short exchange here to grapple with the concept. So Mrs. Hollinger poses the question again and asks everyone to talk about it. She walks around listening to the students discuss the question and then states, "I would like Crystal, then Leonard, Simi, and finally Brian to share."

18. Crystal: Yes, you can have zero tens. Like the one that uses thirty-seven ones blocks.

19. Leonard: You can show thirty-seven in all of these ways. See, you just keep trading ones for tens. Zero tens, then one ten, then two tens, and three tens. [Leonard moves blocks around to show trading ten ones for one ten.]

20. Simi: We [Simi and her partner] didn't know this but I see now how you can trade. Ten ones is the same as one ten.

21. Brian: I think there is a problem. If you have one ten and twenty-seven ones, is that the number one-two-seven? Thirty-seven and one-two-seven aren't the same.

22. Mrs. H: Brian, are you saying that you can make thirty-seven using one ten block and twenty-seven ones blocks but wonder about writing that as one-two-seven?

23. Brian: Yeah. What do we call one ten and twenty-seven ones?

24. Students: One ten twenty-seven ones.
               Another name for thirty-seven.
               One-two-seven.
               I'm not sure.

25. Mrs. H: So let me ask you this. If we can use zero, one, two, or three
               tens to show thirty-seven with base ten blocks, why do most
               of the time we think of thirty-seven being made with three
               tens and seven ones? Think about how we write it as
               thirty-seven, not one ten and twenty-seven ones. Talk to
               your partner for a minute and then be ready to share your
               ideas with the class.

Mrs. Hollinger had not expected the question from Brian about how to record these representations. One of the benefits of talking about concepts is that students' questions, misunderstandings, and confusions are revealed. After two minutes of partner talk, the discussion in Mrs. Hollinger's class continued as students shared their ideas about how grouping by tens is related to the symbols we use to represent the quantities.

The concept of grouping by tens is important to place value, as is the concept that we use the most efficient grouping by ten to represent quantities numerically. In addition, the fact that we can represent the same quantity using a different number of tens is a key concept in making sense of the standard subtraction algorithm. Mrs. Hollinger realized that talking about these concepts furthered students' conceptual understanding. Also, listening to students gave her a better grasp of what individual students did and did not know.

What talk formats are featured in this lesson? Mrs. Hollinger primarily uses whole-class discussion but uses small-group discussion one time and periodically moves the class to partner talk. Mrs. Hollinger finds partner talk an effective method for getting every student involved in the talk, and her second graders are at the beginning stages of being proficient at talking productively in pairs. What talk moves does Mrs. Hollinger use? First, she asks many students to explain the grouping methods they used. Occasionally she revoices their explanations, to make sure that everyone heard or to emphasize a point such as the number of tens. It's important as well to ask students to describe how their methods differ from those already described. Finally, Mrs. Hollinger uses a variation of the "do you agree or disagree and why" talk move in order to get students to apply their own reasoning to others' contributions by reflecting on a grouping method different from their own.

Building Relationships

As teachers, we sometimes take it for granted that students will understand various forms of representation in the same ways that we do and readily build relationships among them. But a set of base ten blocks looks to many students just like any set of different-sized blocks; the materials do not automatically convey the structure of the base ten system. Even when students understand what the blocks are meant to indicate, classroom talk can help them interpret and link symbols, objects, and the linguistic expressions that describe them. As seen in the previous vignette, talk can be used productively to get students to ask questions about what these forms of representation mean, and how the meanings are connected.

Ms. Sanchez regularly uses discussion in her fourth-grade classroom to help students build relationships. One of the concepts she is responsible for teaching is area. She wants her students to understand that area is a measure of how much surface is covered; it is not a length. Within this big topic, there are many relationships. For example, when measuring area, the size of a unit and the number of units needed to cover a surface are inversely proportional. If you measure the area of a rug with square meters you will need fewer units than if you measured the same rug using square centimeters.

NCTM Standard:
Measurement

Grade 4

Ms. Sanchez's students have already engaged in many activities and discussions about area concepts. They have decomposed a shape into two or more parts, found the areas of the parts by counting or multiplying, and then recombined the parts to determine the area of the original figure. They have generated a formula for finding the area of rectangles and now can apply the formula in many situations. Students also have learned to use the terms *base* and *height* to label the dimensions of rectangles and triangles.

In this next vignette, Ms. Sanchez asks her students to justify some of their observations about dimensions and areas of parallelograms that are formed back into rectangles. She asks them to follow the steps shown in a worksheet. (See Figure 3–2.)

□ You will need two copies of this worksheet.
□ For each of the parallelograms, cut out one copy. Draw in a height and cut along it.
□ Reshape the pieces into a rectangle.
□ Answer these questions:
　1. What are the base and height of the parallelogram?
　2. What is the area of the parallelogram?
　3. What are the base and height of the corresponding rectangle?
　4. Has the area changed? Why or why not?

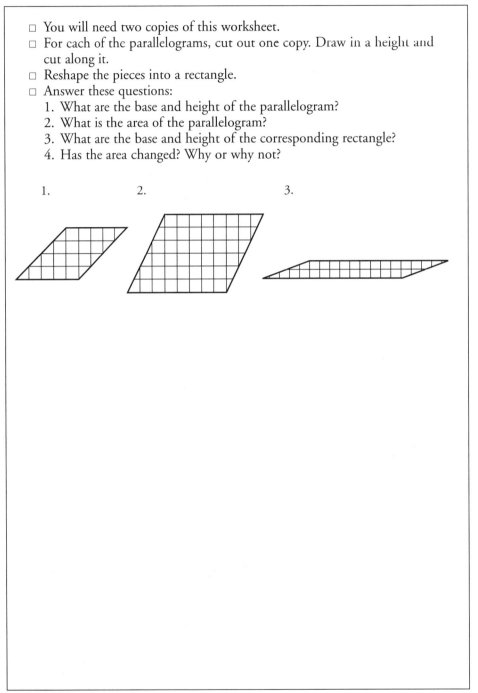

FIGURE 3–2 Student parallelogram worksheet.

Then the class discussed the questions.

1. Ms. S: Let's talk about the first parallelogram and the questions you answered about it. [Ms. Sanchez waits for students to look at their answers before calling on Ben.]

2. Ben: For the first parallelogram, the base is five and the height is four. I made the cut along this line [Ben points to the height.] And the area is twenty.

4.
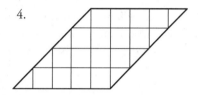

3. Ms. S: You gave us some numbers but I'm not sure what they stand for. Could you give us some more information?

4. Ben: Uhm. The five and four are just units. And the area is twenty.

5. Ms. S: Roberta, please repeat what Ben just said.

6. Roberta: The base is five centimeters and the height is four centimeters and the area is twenty.

7. Ms. S: I heard Ben describe the dimensions using units and Roberta used centimeters. How do we decide on the labels for the dimensions? Why can't we just say five and four? Talk to your partner.

Determining what units to use to measure an attribute is an essential component of the measurement process. Often diagrams do not include labels, so students must interpret the numbers and apply their own labels. Ms. Sanchez thought she would be able to immediately start talking about area, but she hears that students have many misconceptions about labels and interpreting dimensions, so she decides to slow down.

8. Eileen: I measured the picture. Those little squares are half a centimeter long, not a centimeter, so I don't think we should say five and four centimeters.

9. Janet: They aren't inches. I don't know what they are.

10. Ms. S: Would everyone measure and confirm that the little squares are not one centimeter on a side, but instead have a side length of zero-point-five centimeters.

11. Ryota: Ms. Sanchez, can we say the base is five half-centimeters?

12. Ms. S: Yes, we can. But it is more common that the label describe a whole unit such as centimeters, rather than a fraction of a unit such as half-centimeters. But sometimes the actual unit is not a common measure such as inches, yards, centimeters, millimeters, and meters. Ben?

13. Ben: That's why I just used the word *units*. There are five units along the base. The word *units* can stand for anything.

14. Ms. S: Yes, we need labels so we know what the numbers represent. When we aren't sure of the labels, such as in this case, we can use the general term *units*. Units here can stand for measures such as centimeters or feet.

This short interchange has been helpful in its focus on units, but Ms. Sanchez feels that she needs to make a decision. Where is this discussion going? Should she continue to discuss units? There are no predetermined guidelines as to how to facilitate a discussion or when to continue or when to redirect. In this case, Ms. Sanchez really wants her students to talk about area, so she makes an instructional choice, one that all teachers must make daily, and refocuses the class.

15. Ms. S: OK, so let's label these dimensions using the term *units*. But what does the twenty represent? Twenty units?

16. Andrei: Twenty squares, I mean twenty square units. It's like what we talked about a while ago. We have to cover the surface so you use something that covers it.

17. Sabra: I agree with Andrei. He said twenty square units and that's how many I got when I counted.

18. Ms. S: Alright. So the dimensions of this parallelogram are five units for the base and four units for the height. It has an area of twenty square units. Next, you cut this parallelogram and made it into a rectangle. Janet, what is the area of the rectangle? What are its dimensions?

19. Janet: They are all the same. Twenty and five and four.

20. Ms. S: Twenty what? Five what? Four what?

21. Janet: [Laughing] Twenty square units, five units, and four units.

22. Ms. S: Here's the important question. Why are they the same? Talk to your partner for a minute about this.

Ms. Sanchez walks around the room, listening in to the partner talk. She is listening with a purpose—who to select to talk about why the areas and dimensions are the same. She wants to give students who have not talked a chance to speak, and she wants to make sure she selects students who have a solid explanation and those who don't. Why choose students who are inarticulate or unclear on the reasoning? By forcing the whole class to try to make sense of an answer—or to clarify the reasoning—she is going to ensure that more students are engaged with the ideas. Learning can occur only if her students are truly pondering the relationships. To facilitate the discussion, Ms. Sanchez in advance cut out multiple copies of each parallelogram from a transparency. Now she asks students to cut one of the transparency copies in the same way as they cut the parallelogram from the worksheet, and show on the overhead projector how they adjusted their cut pieces.

23. Leland: I cut the parallelogram along the line and moved the piece like this. [Leland shows how he moved the piece to make a rectangle.]

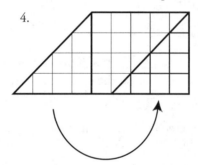

24. Ms. S: First, what's that line called that you cut along?

25. Leland: Hmm, a diagonal?

26. Ms. S: We call this the *height* because it is the distance straight up from the base. Please restate what you did using the word *height*.

In order to build vocabulary, students need to use mathematical words. Ms. Sanchez regularly corrects students as in this exchange. Furthermore, she always requires the student to then use the word or phrase in context. When teachers consistently require students to use mathematical vocabulary, the students start using these words more regularly on their own—in part because they know they will be corrected if they don't!

27. Leland: I cut the parallelogram here on the height, and then I took this piece and moved it here to form a rectangle. The base is the same.

28. Ms. S: And why is the base the same?

29. Leland: This part of the base was on this side, and I just moved it over. But I didn't make it longer or shorter, I just moved it.

30. Ms. S: How about the height? Did the height stay the same when the parallelogram was transformed?

31. Deval: The height also stays the same. See. This piece is slided over but the height hasn't been changed in any way.

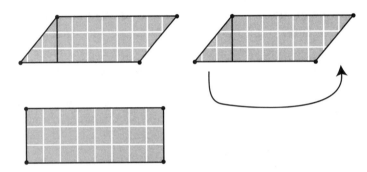

32. Lily: And the area is the same too. We didn't take away or add square units. We just moved them around a bit.

33. Ms. S: Lesley, will you repeat what Lily just said?

34. Lesley: The area is the same because you just move a piece but you don't take anything away.

35. Sabra: There are still twenty square units. The pieces have just been put together in a different order.

36. Ms. S: So let's summarize what we found with the first parallelogram. When we cut it along a height and rearranged the two pieces into a rectangle, the base lengths of the two shapes were the same, the heights of the two shapes were the same, and the areas were the same. Let's examine the next two parallelograms. What did you find?

Mrs. Sanchez has used this discussion to help students develop some understanding of the relationship between the areas of a parallelogram and a rectangle with the same base and height. She will continue to ask students to notice that when the dimensions are the same, the areas are equal. Talking about these ideas helps students generalize how to find the area of any parallelogram.

Uncovering Misconceptions and Errors

Classroom talk not only helps students develop conceptual understanding, but also is effective for revealing and clarifying students' partial understandings and misconceptions. In the process of making sense of experiences, students often generalize ideas in incomplete ways. For example, as seen in Chapter 2, if young students' experiences with triangles involve only viewing pictures of equilateral triangles oriented along a base, their generalization of the concept "triangle" may be very limited—they might conclude that scalene triangles are not triangles or that a triangle that is resting on a vertex is not a triangle. Talk is a powerful tool for revealing students' partial understandings of a concept or their misconceptions about that concept.

NCTM Standard:
Number and Operations

Grade 5

Mr. Lyman used talk to learn about his fifth-grade students' generalizations (and misconceptions). One topic that Mr. Lyman felt was not too difficult for his students was decimal addition and subtraction. Yet he noticed that when he didn't list the numbers vertically, one under the other with the decimal points lined up, many students made errors. Because of comments by a few students, he began to suspect that their understanding of decimals was procedural and not very complete. One day, when students were working in small groups on decimal word problems, he noticed that one group of four students incorrectly solved the computation 25 − 17.7 by setting up the exercise with the 2 and 5 underneath the two 7s:

$$
\begin{array}{r}
17.7 \\
-2\,5 \\
\hline
\end{array}
$$

Mr. Lyman decided to probe the understanding of the students in the small group.

1. Mr. L: I noticed that you have been adding and subtracting decimal numbers to solve these word problems. How are decimals the same or different from whole numbers? How is adding and subtracting decimals the same or different from adding and subtracting whole numbers? Take a minute to think about what you know about decimal numbers and how we add and subtract them. Then I'll talk with your group about this.

After giving them a couple of minute to talk among themselves, Mr. Lyman listened carefully to his students' ideas. At first he allowed them to make their points without much commentary from him, but then he began to ask clarifying questions as alternative understandings emerged.

2. Sarah: Decimals are like regular numbers; you just line them up and add them.

3. Corey: Yeah, it's easy because we all know how to add and subtract.

4. Kei: Decimals are numbers with a dot in them.

5. Mr. L: Sarah, what do you mean by "like regular numbers"?

6. Sarah: You know, like the numbers we use to count with—tens, hundreds, thousands.

7. Mr. L: So decimals are exactly the same as the counting numbers?

8. Sarah: Yes.

9. Mr. L: What do other people think? Are decimals the same or different from our regular counting numbers?

10. Kei: They are the same. You just line everything up on the right side and then add or subtract.

11. Mr. L: Could you give us an example, Kei?

12. Kei: Sure. Eight point two plus seven point nine. [Kei records and solves the addition problem correctly.] I lined up the two and the nine on the right and then just added. You bring the decimal point straight down.

$$\begin{array}{r} 8.2 \\ + 7.9 \\ \hline 16.1 \end{array}$$

13. Bob: I think you have to line up the decimal points.

14. Mr. L: What do you mean?

15. Bob: Well, if the problem was eight point twenty-five plus seven point nine, you don't line up the five and the nine. [Bob writes the following on his paper as he speaks to the group.]

$$\begin{array}{r} 8.25 \\ + 7.9 \\ \hline \end{array}$$

16. Mr. L: Bob, would you please say those numbers again but read them
             so we hear the place values?

17. Bob: Sure. Let's add eight and twenty-five hundredths and seven
             and nine tenths. I think we should line up the decimal points,
             not the last two numbers. It should look like this. [Bob records
             the addition on his paper.]

$$8.25$$
$$+\ 7.9$$

Teachers regularly must decide how to respond to an interaction similar to this one. One response is to tell students how to line up the numbers and to offer some explanation as to why this is the case. Another possible teacher response is to ask Bob to explain his reasoning in order to establish for the group the correct procedure. This has the benefit of another student providing the justification for the choice. We have found that a third alternative that uses talk productively is for the teacher to give no indication of the right or wrong answer—in this case how to line up the decimal numbers—and instead to send the question back to the students.

18. Mr. L: Would you all discuss what Bob just said? Do we line up
             decimal numbers using the last digit or the decimal point? Also
             be ready to explain why you think your choice is correct.

Why use talk in this way? What are the benefits? Both the teacher and Bob understand the mathematics in this situation. But it is unclear exactly what the other three students in the group do and don't understand. By forcing them to engage with the ideas—namely, to take a position on how to line up the numbers—the teacher has prompted them to think more deeply about the mathematics. They will be listening more closely to each other now to see if their ideas are the same. They will be working to come up with a way to explain why their response is correct. If the reasoning behind their ideas is faulty (line up the last number on the right), other students will usually offer explanations, evidence, or counterexamples in their own words, words that often resonate more effectively with the other students. Bob will be able to add his ideas to the group in response to the other students, which will help move them all forward to understanding they need to line up the decimal points. But the main advantage of talking in this way is that the three students who will benefit the most mathematically from the exchange are being forced to talk and reason about the ideas.

19. Sarah: I don't think it matters which way you do it.

20. Corey: Let's use one of the word problems to see if it makes a difference. [She reads] "Gus put four gallons of gasoline into the gas can. He kept filling and adding another seven-tenths of a gallon. How much gas is now in the can?"

21. Kei: I think maybe Bob is right. I thought you just lined up the numbers but if you add four and point seven like this [Kei writes the problem down], the answer is wrong; it's too small. Like four gallons of gas plus seven-tenths more is more than four.

$$\begin{array}{r} 4 \\ + \ 0.7 \\ \hline \end{array}$$

22. Bob: I think it is because we have to add the same things—like we add hundreds and hundreds with big numbers so now we have to add tenths and tenths or ones and ones.

23. Corey: But where are the tenths in four? It kinda makes sense but not completely.

Mr. Lyman has already learned a lot using the small-group format for this short discussion. First, three of the students in the group did not think there was a difference between whole numbers and decimal numbers. He will need to probe further to really understand what they think. However, he doubts that many students in his class think of a decimal number as the sum of a whole number and a part of a whole. He now suspects that many students' conceptions of decimals are unrelated to quantity and that they instead think that a decimal is a number with a "dot" in it. When adding decimals, they do not consider the size of the numbers or the place values of the digits. By listening to students as they discussed their ideas in a small-group format, Mr. Lyman was able to hear from each student and learn about their superficial understanding. Sometimes talking with a small group can clarify and extend concepts for students, but in this case, Mr. Lyman realized that small-group talk was not enough and additional instruction would be necessary. Mr. Lyman used productive talk to get mathematical ideas and concepts visibly out on the table. Both he and the students benefited from this interaction; Mr. Lyman gained valuable information on which to build future lessons, and these students had an opportunity to start making sense of the addition algorithm for decimals.

DISCUSSION AND REFLECTION

1. This chapter has examined the complexities of talking about mathematical concepts. What is a math concept? How are concepts different from skills? For each of the teacher/student vignettes, make a list of the concepts that were discussed.

2. One of the benefits of talking about concepts is that students' misconceptions or confusions often are revealed. Describe some examples from your own teaching experiences in which you learned about a student's misconceptions. For one example, give suggestions on how talk might be used to help students address the misconception.

3. Pictures and models can help students build relationships as long as the salient features of the picture or model are clearly understood by students. How did Ms. Sanchez use classroom discussions to help students understand the pictures of the parallelograms and the relationships between the dimensions and area?

Computational Procedures

A computational procedure is a series of steps or actions that we use when operating on numbers. For example, when we add, subtract, multiply, and divide we use some sort of procedure. Some procedures are algorithms. An algorithm, in terms of arithmetic procedures encountered in grades 1 through 8, is a generalized set of steps used to solve any problem of a particular class. Algorithms are efficient, produce accurate results, and can be used to solve many similar tasks using the same process. The regularity of the steps, known by memory by most people, allows the solver to focus his or her energies on more complex or important aspects of a mathematics problem.

It's useful for students to invent their own procedures when learning concepts and skills. Sometimes these "invented procedures" are identical to widely used algorithms. For example, the partial-sums method for solving multidigit addition problems is one that many students discover on their own: When adding $37 + 49$, they first add the tens ($30 + 40 = 70$), then add the ones ($7 + 9 = 16$), and then add the partial sums ($70 + 16 = 86$). However, other times students' invented procedures are not algorithms; they produce a correct answer for that one particular problem, but are not generalizable and do not work for similar problems.

Why Talk About Computational Procedures?

When we teach computational procedures, our goal should be student understanding as well as skill. Discussions about students' invented procedures can help teachers achieve this goal. Mrs. Parker's first-grade class has been exploring pairs of numbers that add to the sums of 5 and 10. She wanted her students to apply what they learned about these number pairs to solve a problem.

After reading aloud to her class *Rooster's Off to See the World*, by Eric Carle, Mrs. Parker asked her students to work in pairs to find out how many animals went along for the trip. (On the trip, Rooster is joined by two cats, three frogs, four turtles, and five fish.) After approximately ten minutes, Mrs. Parker asked the students to explain how many animals were on the trip and how they figured this out.

1. Caitlin: I drew a picture of all of the animals. Then I counted and got fifteen.

2. Mrs. P: So, Caitlin counted her pictures to solve the problem. Who solved it a different way?

3. Ross: I used the blocks. I took one block for the rooster, two more for the cats, three more for the frogs, four more for the turtles, and five more for the fish. When I had all of the blocks I counted them. There were fifteen.

4. Mrs. P: So Ross, it sounds like your strategy is similar to Caitlin's. You both counted animals. Is that right?

5. Ross: Yes, I counted the animals. But I used blocks. So it's different.

6. Mrs. P: So both Caitlin and Ross counted the animals, starting with one and going all the way to fifteen. One used a picture and one used blocks. They both got fifteen animals went on the trip. Is fifteen animals the answer [lots of nods]? Did anyone else solve the problem by counting?

Notice that Mrs. Parker links the two counting methods together, establishes that the answer is fifteen animals, and then surveys the class to determine how many students are counting rather than adding number pairs. Her goal in this discussion is to talk about strategies that are based on combining numbers rather than counting, but she first needs to make sure everyone understood the problem, regardless of their method. Mrs. Parker calls on a student she observed who used addition.

7. Mrs. P: Amelia, would you please share how you solved the problem?

8. Amelia: I wrote down that there were one, two, three, four, and five animals on the trip. I put the rooster and the two cats together to get three. Then plus the three frogs makes six. Then I remember that six plus four more is ten. I know ten plus five is fifteen.

9. Mrs. P: Amelia, can you tell us again what you added and I'll write the number sentences on the board?

10. Amelia: One plus two is three. [Mrs. Parker writes on the board: *1 + 2 = 3.*] Three plus three is six. [Mrs. Parker writes: *3 + 3 = 6.*] Six plus four is ten. [Mrs. Parker writes: *6 + 4 = 10.*] Ten plus five is fifteen. [Mrs. Parker writes: *10 + 5 = 15.*]

11. Mrs. P: So Amelia, can you explain to us why you were adding these numbers?

12. Amelia: Because we want to put them all together and see how many are on the trip.

13. Mrs. P: Tell me about this first number sentence. Why did you write "one plus two equals three"?

14. Amelia: There is one rooster and two cats were with him on the trip.

15. Mrs. P: Billy, can you repeat what Amelia just said about where in the story the one and the two come from in her number sentence?

16. Billy: From the rooster and two cats.

Mrs. Parker writes the following under the number sentence on the board to provide a visual scaffold for those students who used counting. This also provides students with a record of the discussed thinking.

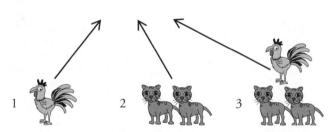

17. Mrs. P: Why did Amelia add three plus three? [She points to the number sentence *3 + 3 = 6* on the board.] Where did those numbers come from? Hoai?

18. Hoai: I don't know.

19. Mrs. P: Talk to the person next to you about the three plus three. What animals does each three stand for in the story?

Mrs. Parker now has the students thinking about addition, but she clearly lost some children when she jumped to the second number sentence. So she asks students to talk to the person next to them about what the numbers in this new number sentence represent. Partner talk is effective with young students when the question is very focused.

Mrs. Parker calls on three different pairs of students to share their understanding that one of the 3s represents three frogs and one of the 3s represents the rooster and cats together. She adds pictures of the animals underneath the number sentence. She does not worry about the order of the labels. The last pair of students she calls upon includes Hoai.

20. Mrs. P: So Hoai, you're saying that the rooster plus two cats makes three, then three more frogs make six animals in all? [She points to the numbers in the number sentence as she says this. Hoai nods.] That makes sense to me. Who can tell me where Amelia got the numbers for the next sentence?

21. Pete: There are six so far, then four more come, the turtles, so that's ten. Then five fish come, and that's fifteen.

22. Mrs. P: Talk to the person next to you about what Pete said. What animals does the six stand for? What animals does the four represent?

Following this, Mrs. Parker then establishes the meaning of Amelia's number sentence, $10 + 5$, by asking students to talk about each of the numbers. The final number sentence has pictures of the animals written under it.

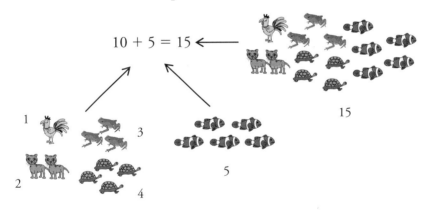

She then summarizes what they had talked about.

23. Mrs. P: So let's look at Amelia's method. Amelia solved the problem by adding two numbers at a time. She started by adding one plus two and then took that answer, which was the total

number of animals so far, and used it to keep adding. [Mrs. P writes on the board, *1 + 2 + 3 + 4 + 5*.] Could Amelia have started with a different pair of numbers? Vanessa?

24. Vanessa: Yes, we played that game and one of the pairs was four plus one is five. So that's five. Then there's another five and that's ten. And then there's three plus two, which is another five. That's fifteen.

25. Mrs. P: Vanessa, you said a lot. Let's back it up a little. What do you mean by "that game"?

26. Vanessa: The game where we looked for numbers that add to five. One of them was four plus one and another was two plus three.

27. Mrs. P: Are you thinking of the Sum Five game where we shake a cup and add beans to make five? Who else remembers that game? [Students nod.]

Mrs. Parker helps students connect to prior knowledge by jogging their memory about a previous experience in order to help them build upon existing knowledge. She also reintroduces the vocabulary word *sum*.

28. Mrs. P: What numbers did we discover have a sum of five?

29. Students: Four and one.
Two and three.
Zero and five.
Three and two.

30. Mrs. P: Who can explain how using numbers that add to five will help us solve the problem?

31. Kevin: The rooster and four turtles make five; the five fish is five. The two cats and the three frogs make five. There are lots of fives!

32. Leia: Like, we can make fives a lot. And it's easy to add fives since they make ten.

33. Mrs. P: Work with your partner and add these numbers from the problem. [Points to *1 + 2 + 3 + 4 + 5*.] Look for numbers that make five. What is the answer when you add these numbers? How many animals went on the trip?

By focusing the discussion on the meaning of the numbers in the number sentences in the context of the story problem, Mrs. Parker is helping her students understand addition. But she is also helping them learn number facts. She asks them questions that focus on facts to make five and then has them practice this way of solving the problem. Mrs. Parker is supporting her students' mathematical thinking skills, and she is helping them improve their own procedures. But because Mrs. Parker is interested in helping students use strategies other than counting, she focuses most of the discussion time on exploring the strategies that use addition (see Lines 8–21 and 27–33).

Notice how Mrs. Parker uses revoicing both to summarize students' contributions and to provide more time for everyone to think about the ideas. Mrs. Parker also knows that her first graders will benefit from hearing each explanation a number of times. This content is new for them, and they need many experiences where they link objects and symbols. Furthermore, when she asks them to repeat what another student said, she is giving them practice in paying attention to someone other than the teacher! While Mrs. Parker's students are not procedurally fluent, class talk is moving them toward reaching this goal.

Lessons that use talk can serve multiple purposes. Students can practice computational skills and also can deepen their understanding of the operation

NCTM Standard:
Number and Operations

Grade 5

by talking about what they are doing and why. Mrs. DeFreitas's fifth-grade students have been exploring different ways to solve multidigit multiplication problems. Some students use repeated addition, some use partial products, and some use the standard multiplication algorithm. As they apply strategies for multiplying, they also must justify their steps, thus reinforcing the idea that mathematics makes sense! In the following example, one student in Mrs. DeFreitas's class uses a particularly efficient mental procedure to solve the problem 19 × 12, based on the distributive property. Mrs. DeFreitas asks this student to explain his method to the class.

1. Kim Lee: I wanted to solve nineteen times twelve. This looked hard to me. So, instead I first did twenty times twelve because that's easier. It's two times twelve, which is twenty-four with a zero—two hundred forty. Then I did two hundred forty minus twelve, which is two hundred twenty-eight.

2. Mrs. D: Kim Lee, I want your classmates to really understand your procedure because I think they will want to use it themselves. Can you talk us through it again, this time a little more slowly?

3. Kim Lee: OK. Nineteen times twelve would be tough for me. Nineteen is close to twenty and twenty times twelve is easier because we know a shortcut for multiplying numbers that end in zero.

4. Mrs. D: Let me stop you for a minute. What's one way to interpret nineteen times twelve? Fran?

5. Fran: Nineteen groups of twelve.

6. Mrs. D: Then, twenty times twelve means twenty groups of twelve. Keep going, Kim Lee.

7. Kim Lee: Yeah, so once I figured out that twenty times twelve was two hundred forty, I subtracted twelve.

8. Mrs. D: Who thinks they can explain why Kim Lee subtracted twelve? Talk to the person next to you for a moment about this. [Partners talk for about one minute.] Go ahead, Felicita.

9. Felicita: The number *two hundred forty* is from twenty groups of twelve. We only want nineteen groups of twelve, so we have to get rid of one group of twelve.

10. Mrs. D: Is that why you subtracted, Kim Lee? [He nods.] Kim, as you talk us through your procedure, tell me what number sentences to write.

11. Kim Lee: OK, it's nineteen groups of twelve, which is close to twenty groups of twelve, so write *twenty times twelve*. [Mrs. D writes 20×12.] But now I take away one group of twelve, since I only want nineteen groups, so write *minus twelve*. [She writes $20 \times 12 - 12$.] The answer is two hundred twenty-eight.

12. Mrs. D: We can use parentheses to show what operation we do first. [She writes on the board $(20 \times 12) - 12 = 228$ and $19 \times 12 = (20 \times 12) - 12$.] Talk to your partner about these equations. Are these equations equivalent? Why or why not?

Mrs. DeFreitas doesn't spend a lot of time having students discuss the equations, but she wants to make sure that students understand that the equations are equivalent. She rewrites the second equation so that it starts with the expression, $(20 \times 12) - 12$.

$$(20 \times 12) - 12 = 228$$
$$(20 \times 12) - 12 = 19 \times 12$$

After a number of students have explained why they are equivalent, Mrs. DeFreitas writes one more equation and asks students to think about what it is saying mathematically, $(20 - 1) \times 12 = (20 \times 12) - (1 \times 12)$.

Next Mrs. DeFreitas asks everyone to solve another problem.

13. Mrs. D: Let's try Kim Lee's procedure for eighteen times thirteen. Work with the person next to you. [Partners work on solving this problem.]

One reason that Mrs. DeFreitas asks everyone to try Kim Lee's procedure is because she suspects that students are confused about which number to round, what to round it to, and how much to subtract. While students work she circulates among them, noting who is applying Kim Lee's method correctly and who is not. She notices that Jonathan's answer is correct while Sierra and Beatriz and Felicita have made different types of errors. She plans on using their errors in the discussion to help students better understand Kim Lee's method. Prior to the whole-class discussion, she mentions to each of these students that she will be calling on them to explain their thinking. This enables the students to prepare their thoughts.

14. Mrs. D: OK, now that you've had a chance to try Kim Lee's procedure, who would like to explain to us what you did? Beatriz?

15. Beatriz: Me and Felicita did twenty times thirteen to get two hundred sixty, because thirteen times two is twenty-six and then add a zero.

16. Mrs. D: What do you mean "add a zero"?

17. Beatriz: It's not thirteen times two, it's thirteen times twenty, so you need to put a zero down.

18. Mrs. D: Why?

19. Felicita: It's like the two is really a twenty but you pretend it's a two since that's easier and then put the zero back when you're done.

20. Mrs. D: Who can explain why they rounded eighteen to twenty?

21. Richard: Kim Lee's method works with friendly numbers, like ones that end in zero. So you look for a close number that ends in zero. Eighteen is close to twenty.

22. Mrs. D: Is that why you did it? [The girls nod.] Who thinks they can predict what we have to do next?

23. Jonathan: I think we do two hundred sixty minus twenty-six. The twenty times thirteen means twenty groups of thirteen but we only really want eighteen groups, so we need to take away two groups of thirteen, which is twenty-six.

24. Mrs. D: Does anyone else have a different prediction?

25. Sierra: I think it is two hundred sixty minus eighteen because you have to take away eighteen.

26. Mrs. D: Does anyone else have a prediction? OK, Felicita and Beatriz, tell us what you did.

27. Beatriz: We subtracted thirteen because that's what Kim Lee did in his problem. The answer is two hundred forty-seven.

Mrs. DeFreitas realizes that this discussion may be confusing to many in her class. She decides that she needs to slow everything down even further and summarize the main points students have made. Since there are a number of suggestions for what to subtract from 260, she decides to recap them and then recommence the discussion.

28. Mrs. D: OK. So we have several different predictions here, and several different answers have been mentioned. So let's take stock here. What do we agree on? So far, to solve eighteen times thirteen we all agree that you can multiply twenty times thirteen, which equals two hundred sixty. This is part of Kim Lee's method to work first with friendly numbers. But it is not clear what number should be subtracted from two hundred sixty. We have three predictions. The first prediction, I'll call it A, suggests that we should subtract twenty-six. The second prediction, called B, is that we should subtract eighteen. And prediction C is that we should subtract thirteen. I am going to write the number sentences on the board while everyone talks to their partner about the three predictions. Which of the predictions do you agree with and why? [Mrs. DeFreitas writes the following predictions on the board and gives students about two and a half minutes to discuss them.]

$$18 \times 13 = ? \quad \textit{Step 1: Multiply } 20 \times 13 \quad 20 \times 13 = 260$$

Step 2: Predictions
A: $(20 \times 13) - 26$

B: $(20 \times 13) - 18$

C: $(20 \times 13) - 13$

29. Mrs. D: OK, which prediction did you and your partner decide upon? Lindsey?

30. Lindsey: We got rid of prediction B because it's eighteen groups of thirteen changed to twenty groups of thirteen.

31. Mrs. D: Would you elaborate a bit more for us? I agree it is twenty groups of thirteen, but why is that important?

32. Lindsey: Since it's groups of thirteen, we think you subtract groups of thirteen, not a group of eighteen.

33. Kim Lee: I agree with Lindsey. I would subtract twenty-six since twenty times thirteen is over by two groups. You need to take away those two groups of thirteen, which is twenty-six. The answer should be two hundred thirty-four. I checked with the calculator and that's right.

34. Mrs. D: Peter, would you please explain in your own words what Lindsey and Kim Lee said?

35. Peter: They said that prediction B is wrong because twenty is too many groups of thirteen, so you have to subtract groups of thirteen, not eighteen.

36. Mrs. D: OK, let's look at the third prediction. Can someone explain why you think prediction C is either right or wrong?

37. Jonathan: It only takes away one group of thirteen, not two, like Kim Lee said.

38. Mrs. D: Beatriz, what do you think of what Jonathan and Kim Lee both said?

39. Beatriz: I think I get it. You don't always take away the number. You have to think about how much you rounded up and then take that many groups. We rounded up two so we have to subtract two groups.

Mrs. DeFreitas's class then used Kim Lee's procedure to multiply other numbers. They discussed the reasoning behind each step, especially how much to subtract and why. As they became more comfortable with the method, they discussed different number sentences they could write. Mrs. DeFreitas chose not to formally introduce the distributive property at this time because the class was still grappling with making sense of the idea of rounding up and subtracting. However, she would return to the topic and focus exclusively on the distributive property in a future lesson.

Did you notice how Mrs. DeFreitas asked more than one student to suggest what number should be subtracted from 20×13? Jonathan gave a correct answer, but Mrs. DeFreitas knew that not everyone in her class could immediately make sense of his reasoning. Thus, she called on two students she suspected might have incorrect predictions. This allowed the students time to really think about which number to subtract and to discuss their reasoning.

One effective talk strategy that assists students in reasoning about a particular answer is to set up a discussion around different positions. Instead of telling students that Jonathan's method to subtract 26 from 260 was correct, Mrs. DeFreitas summarized the three possible answers students had suggested. Discussing a variety of possible answers to a calculation can help students make sense of the numbers used. Teachers sometimes wonder if discussing wrong answers is in students' best interest. We have found that students learn more when they consider incorrect options and then reject them based on reasoning rather than on the basis of an authority's decision. When students make sense of a situation, they deepen their understanding of procedures and calculations. Also, as they align themselves with one position or another, their stake in the outcome increases their interest and attention.

Recall that Mrs. DeFreitas did not identify any prediction with a particular student's name but instead labeled the predictions in an impersonal way with letters. Sometimes teachers want to focus the discussion on the mathematics, rather than on the person who gave the response, so that incorrect responses are not associated with individuals. Other times teachers want to identify a procedure or conjecture with a particular student's name as a way to recognize that student's contributions.

It's important that students understand the algorithms they use, rather than just applying them in a rote fashion. When students are learning a computational procedure, understanding why it works will help them commit it to memory. One of the best ways to assist students in understanding and remembering procedures is to talk with them about the procedures. Talking about the math we are doing slows down and clarifies processes so that more students can understand them. Additionally, many students are motivated to compare their own ways of solving a problem with those of other students, which teaches them new computational procedures and strengthens their understanding of the workings of procedures they are more familiar with. Furthermore, by listening to students talk, teachers can gain insights into their understanding of procedures as well as into their misconceptions and mistaken ideas about computation. Fluency, however, requires practice, so teachers should be sure that students have ample opportunities to practice a procedure or skill once they have talked it through.

Procedural Fluency

In the following example, we illustrate one of the many ways that teachers can use talk to gain insight into their students' current level of procedural fluency—knowledge of procedures, knowledge of when and how to use them appropriately, and skill in performing them flexibly, accurately, and efficiently (Kilpatrick, Swafford, and Findell 2001). In the same example, we will see the teacher simultaneously supporting students' abilities to monitor their own use of computational procedures. Self-monitoring is an important characteristic of good problem solvers. Ms. Webster wants to review with her third-grade students a procedure for regrouping tens when subtracting and has decided to use the format of whole-class discussion. On the board, she writes the problem: 81 – 43. Then she allows time for everyone to complete the calculation individually.

NCTM Standard:
Number and
Operations

Grade 3

1. Ms. W: What is this problem asking us to find [nods to Juan, whose hand is up]?

2. Juan: You need to find the answer between eighty-one and forty-three.

3. Ms. W: We can call the answer in a subtraction problem the *difference*. [Ms. Webster writes *difference* on the board.]

4. Jane: You could also say, "What's eighty-one take away forty-three?"

5. Ms. W: Yes, we can. Good point. Now we often estimate the answer before we solve a problem. What is the purpose of an estimate?

6. Lisa: Because it's part of the problem?

7. Kenny: Maybe so we have a number, an answer, that we check?

Ms. Webster is a bit confused by both Lisa's and Kenny's responses. Students often are inarticulate and less than completely clear. Rather than restate what she thinks Kenny means, Ms. Webster instead revoices Kenny's contribution in the hope that he will clarify his thoughts.

8. Ms. W: So we estimate so we have a number or an answer that we can check? Is that what you said, Kenny?

9. Kenny: Kind of. What I mean is you use your estimate to see if you made a mistake or not. Like, if the estimate is around forty, then if you get an answer of sixty, maybe you made a mistake.

10. Ms. W: Marge, can you repeat what Kenny said.?

11. Marge: An estimate is like a guess of the answer. Like eighty-one is close to eighty and forty-three is close to forty. Eighty minus forty is forty, so an estimate will be close to that.

12. Ms. W: OK, Marge suggests we work with friendly numbers that are close to eighty-one and forty-three and that an estimate of forty is reasonable. Talk to your partner. Instead of giving one number as an estimate, let's give a range of numbers, such as thirty-five to forty or forty to forty-five. Do you think the actual difference between eighty-one and forty-three is going to be more than forty, exactly forty, or less than forty? Explain your reasoning.

Ms. Webster lets students discuss their reasoning about the estimate with a partner for a minute or two. She wants students to consider giving a range of values when estimating and to understand how an estimate can be used to monitor their accuracy. She then conducts a brief discussion in which students share their estimates. Next, she focuses on the subtraction algorithm.

13. Ms. W: Now what about when I want to find the actual answer? What should I do first? [She points to $81 - 43$.]

14. Lou: You need to see what's one take away three but you can't do that. So you cross out the eight and write seven above it. Then you write a one next to the one since it's eleven now. [Mrs. Webster writes this equation on the board.]

$$^7\!8^1 1$$
$$-4\ 3$$

15. Ms. W: Lou, can you explain your procedure to us? Why should I cross out the eight and write seven?

16. Lou: Since the one wasn't big enough to take away three you had to get some more. The eight has some more.

17. Ms. W: OK, I want to make sure I'm following you. Remember we've been talking about what these two-digit numbers like eighty-one really stand for. Lou, can you tell or show me what eighty-one looks like? You can use the base ten blocks if you wish.

18. Lou: It's eight tens and one one.

19. Ms. W: So in this problem [points to the 81] you said I should cross out the eight in eighty-one and write seven above it and the

one in eighty-one becomes eleven. Can you either explain to me or show me why this makes sense?

20. Lou: Well, you need to take away three ones but you only have one in eighty-one. So you take this ten [picks up a ten from the base ten blocks on the table] and trade it for ten ones. Those go over to your other one and now you have enough to take away.

21. Ms. W: Who else can explain to me why I cross out the eight and write a seven?

22. Lara: Lou traded one ten for ten ones, so now you only have seven tens left.

23. Ms. W: Who can explain to me why the one one became eleven ones? Wally?

24. Wally: Your ten new ones got added to the other old one to get eleven.

25. Ms. W: So at the start of the problem we had eight tens and one one and now we have seven tens and eleven ones. Which is more—eight tens one one or seven tens eleven ones or are they equal? Talk to your partner about this.

Ms. Webster knows that many students can perform the regrouping step in the standard algorithm but do not realize that these two quantities have the same value. She doesn't ask if the representations are equivalent, as many students will assume she wants them to agree. Instead she poses the question in such a way that students must take a position: Eight tens and one one is greater than, is less than, or is equal to seven tens, eleven ones. Ms. Webster will now do what Mrs. DeFreitas did in the last vignette—gather responses from her students, reiterate their ideas, and pose them as three options (labeling them 1, 2, and 3). Then she will ask students to decide which one they think is true and why. If students do not mention all three positions (for example, if no one thinks eight tens, one one is less than seven tens, eleven ones, Ms. Webster will volunteer this possibility).

Position 1   8 tens, 1 one is greater than ($>$) 7 tens, 11 ones
Position 2   8 tens, 1 one is less than ($<$) 7 tens, 11 ones
Position 3   8 tens, 1 one is equal to ($=$) 7 tens, 11 ones

Ms. Webster can take different actions to help the class reason about this question. She may remind students that we often "revise" our thinking just like we revise our writing, so if they hear something from another student that makes sense, they can always state: "I revise my thinking. I now agree with what April said." This removes the stigma of having to admit that a position they chose was wrong, which is difficult for some children. She can also support students' reasoning by encouraging them to use materials such as base ten blocks or pictures (especially when explaining why the two representations are equal) to justify their position. And she can ask students to discuss the words used to describe actions in subtraction, such as *borrow*, *trade*, and *regroup*. Many students interpret the word *borrow* to mean that the quantities are not equivalent. Many classes decide to only use the term *regroup* in order to remind themselves that quantities such as eight tens, one one and seven tens, eleven ones represent the same quantity.

Following the discussion of equivalent representations, Ms. Webster continued to question her students about the steps in the computation. Other questions she asked included, "How do I know when I'm done?" "Why do I compare my answer to my estimate?" and "Is there a way to check my work?"

The dialogue shows that Ms. Webster asks questions that focus on the meaning of the actions in a computational procedure. When Lou offered an answer that did not indicate much understanding, she spoke with Lou for a while to see what he did and did not know. Ms. Webster involved other students in this dialogue as well. She did this because from past experience she knows that many students struggle in the same way Lou does. Since this lesson was mainly a review, Ms. Webster used this question-and-answer session to model for students the questions one can ask oneself when working through computations.

In addition to increasing students' ability to monitor their own understanding of any procedure, Ms. Webster's question-and-answer whole-class discussion accomplishes other goals. Some of the questions she asks serve to link the base ten blocks to the traditional regrouping algorithm. When students understand the standard algorithm they are more likely to apply it in an efficient and effective manner. Ms. Webster also gives attention to the meaning of vocabulary that the students use. She questions what students mean when they say *borrow* and, once they've clarified, asks them to repeat their statements using more accurate terms such as *regroup* or *trade*.

Deepening Students' Understanding of Number and Operations

Talking about computational procedures can do more than clarify students' understanding of the ins and outs of those procedures. It may actually promote a more profound understanding of the numbers and mathematical operations at the center of those procedures. In other words, at the same time that talk is building facility with procedures, it may deepen conceptual knowledge as well.

Recall Mr. Lyman's fifth-grade class as described in Chapter 3. In the small-group discussion about $25 - 17.7$, Mr. Lyman realized that some students did not have a strong conceptual grasp of decimals and were also making computational errors when subtracting. He concluded that the whole class needed to revisit subtraction of decimals to deepen their conceptual understanding and to reinforce correct procedures. He decided to have students make up a problem that fit the computation and to help them consider what might be a reasonable answer.

> **NCTM Standard:**
> Number and Operations
>
> **Grade 5**

1. Mr. L: We just reviewed that it's important to line up digits so that we are subtracting ones away from ones, tens away from tens, and so on. Now let's look at yesterday's problem. It was twenty-five minus seventeen and seven-tenths. Who can tell me a story for this problem? Alexa?

2. Alexa: I was in a race that was twenty-five miles. I ran seventeen-point-seven miles so far. How many miles do I have left to go?

3. Mr. L: Alexa, would you restate your problem again but remember to use place value to say the numbers so we can think about their size.

4. Alexa: OK. I ran a race that was twenty-five miles long. By noon I had run seventeen and seven-tenths miles. How many miles do I have left to run?

5. Mr. L: Work with your partner for a few moments to see if you can solve this problem. [After two to three minutes, Mr. Lyman asks Kyle and Ben to explain their solution strategy.]

6. Kyle: This is what we did. Three more tenths gives her eighteen miles. Then she has seven more to go. So she has seven-point-three miles left.

7. Mr. L: And what is another way to say seven-point-three miles?

8. Ben: Seven miles and three tenths of a mile.

9. Mr. L: Can you write a number sentence for your solution? [Ben writes the number sentence: *17.7 + 7.3 = 25.0.*]

10. Mr. L: So, to find the difference, it looks like you added three more tenths to get another whole, which gave eighteen whole miles in all with seven more miles to go to finish the race. Is that what you did? [Kyle and Ben nod.] That's one way to solve this problem. Let's think now about how to solve it with subtraction.

Mr. Lyman knows that learning occurs when students connect different procedures. He wants to build from students' understanding of the situation to further their ability to solve problems like these using subtraction. He continues.

11. Mr. L: Yesterday, most of you thought that to solve twenty-five minus seventeen and seven-tenths, we should write it like this. [He writes the problem vertically, purposely misaligning the numbers.]

$$\begin{array}{r} 17.7 \\ -25 \\ \hline \end{array}$$

Talk to your partner about this for a few moments.

Mr. Lyman spoke with the math curriculum specialist in his school to learn more about the kinds of difficulties students have when subtracting decimals. He learned that students often set up these problems incorrectly when one number has more digits after the decimal point than does the other, or when one of the numbers in the problem does not explicitly show the decimal point. Some students do not understand that a whole number such as 25 can be written with or without a decimal point. Mr. Lyman called on Bob after students had time to reflect on how the problem was set up.

12. Bob: The problem is written wrong. The seventeen-point-seven—oh, I mean the seventeen and seven-tenths—should be under the twenty-five. The problem is twenty-five minus seventeen and seven-tenths.

13. Mr. L: What do other people think about this? Do you agree or disagree with what Bob just said? [Mr. Lyman looks at Aipana to indicate he is calling on her.]

14. Aipana: I agree, like in the other problems, the number that's being taken away goes underneath.

15. Mr. L: So, how do you think it should be written? Who would like to write it on the board? [Two students come up and write the two problems shown here.]

$$25 \qquad 25$$
$$\underline{-17.7} \quad \underline{-17.7}$$

16. Mr. L: So we have two different versions of the problem written here. What is the difference between them? Ken?

17. Ken: Well, in one, the twenty-five is all the way to the right, and the seventeen and seven-tenths is lined up under it. In the second one, the twenty-five is above the seventeen, and the point-seven sticks out to the right. But I'm confused. Twenty-five doesn't have a decimal point. So she lined it up as though it did. Shouldn't the twenty-five be to the right?

18. Mr. L: That's a question for us to consider. The number twenty-five doesn't have a decimal point as it's written here, but could it? Talk at your table about this for a minute. [Mr. Lyman goes over to a small group of three students and overhears the following interaction.]

19. Corey: No, it can't. That's why the first problem is right.

20. Silvia: I disagree. I think the decimal point goes right after the five since the five is five ones.

21. Jennifer: If the decimal point went right after the five it would be there and it isn't, so there just shouldn't be one.

After a moment of partner talk, Mr. Lyman asks for student reactions. By listening to different groups, he has a better sense of whom to call on. Sometimes a teacher wants to introduce an incorrect response so students reflect upon it. Other times teachers need to get the correct answer on the table for discussion. Finally, sometimes a student is selected because the teacher knows his or her contribution will add insight to the situation. Mr. Lyman decides to call on Silvia first.

22. Silvia: I think there should be a decimal point right after the five. In twenty-five, the five stands for five ones.

23. Sarah: If there could be a decimal point there, then why don't books always put it in? Shouldn't they tell us where it goes?

24. Mr. L: Sometimes you have a choice whether or not to show the decimal point. If there are tenths or hundredths or

thousandths you have to show the decimal point so we know the value of the digits, but if there are no decimal parts in the number you can decide whether or not to record the decimal point. When might it be important to write the decimal point in the number *twenty-five* and where would it go? Kyle?

25. Kyle: You can write the twenty-five as twenty-five-point-zero— that shows there are no tenths.

26. Mr. L: Do you agree, Corey?

27. Corey: Oh, yeah. Then you can do the problem.

28. Mr. L: You said "then you can do the problem." What do you mean? Can you explain that a bit more?

29. Corey: Now that we have twenty-five-point-zero, we want to take away seven-tenths from nothing so we need to borrow a one.

30. Phuong: Let me show you. [Goes to the board and adds the decimal point and zero to the second example and shows the regrouping.]

$$
\begin{array}{r}
\overset{4\ 10}{2\cancel{5}.\cancel{0}} \\
-\ 17.7 \\
\hline
\end{array}
$$

This becomes ten-tenths. Ten-tenths minus seven-tenths is three-tenths. Like Kyle said earlier, it took three-tenths of a mile to complete one mile.

This discussion ended with students explaining how to complete the regrouping procedure. Then, Mr. Lyman made the following comment.

31. Mr. L: Let's review what we just talked about. When we look at numbers we need to think about the digits and their values, meaning what place they are in. This goes for whole numbers and decimal numbers. Decimal numbers are numbers that include parts of wholes. For example, seventeen and seven-tenths means seventeen whole miles with seven more tenths of a mile, and twenty-five means twenty-five whole miles and zero tenths. When we add and subtract, we need to add and subtract things that are alike. These are the kind of things you need to think about as you add and subtract decimal numbers.

Students often forget and mix up the many rules for adding, subtracting, multiplying, and dividing with decimals. When students make sense of these rules—that is, when the steps are meaningful—they can more easily remember them. Furthermore, they can "reinvent" what to do based upon their understanding, determine when an answer is reasonable, and apply computational procedures to new situations. Does this mean that it's best to try to develop students' conceptual understanding of number and mathematical operations before exploring the computational procedures related to them? Unfortunately, students' progression through conceptual and procedural understanding is not always linear. Furthermore, robust understanding comes when procedures and concepts are connected. The most effective way to build robust understanding and strong procedural abilities involves consistently moving from concepts to procedures and back to concepts. Carefully planned classroom talk can provide an excellent vehicle for this back-and-forth process. Discussing the concepts on which procedures are based as well as the reasons behind the steps in any procedure can serve to strengthen students' understanding of both.

DISCUSSION AND REFLECTION

1. Reread the section on Mrs. DeFreitas's fifth-grade class discussion about the three possible answers to the multiplication problem 18 × 13. She chooses to post the three possible answers using letters. It is also possible to set up a discussion using the student names associated with claims or predictions. Can you think of occasions on which one approach might have clear advantages? When might that approach have disadvantages? How do you decide which one to use?

2. After the vignette about Ms. Webster's third-grade discussion of regrouping in subtraction, we make the following claim: "Talking about computational procedures can do more than clarify students' understanding of the ins and outs of those procedures. It may actually promote a more profound understanding of the numbers and mathematical operations at the center of those procedures. In other words, at the same time that talk is building facility with procedures, it may deepen conceptual knowledge as well."

   Consider Ms. Webster's discussion, or others in this chapter. Do you see evidence for our claim?

3. Sometimes teachers do not want students to discuss errors or misconceptions. What types of errors or misconceptions would you want students to discuss? Why? What type of errors or misconceptions would you rather not discuss? Why?

5

Solution Methods and Problem-Solving Strategies

Problem-solving strategies are a good topic for discussions in mathematics classes. To most educators, a "problem" in mathematics is a puzzling yet intriguing situation for which there is no immediate, apparent solution. In other words, when faced with a problem, a student can't immediately call upon a procedure or an algorithm to find the answer. In solving a problem, the solver makes a plan for reaching the solution and then carries out the plan. The procedures by which the solver accomplishes this are referred to as solution methods. Talk about solution methods and problem-solving strategies can reveal shallow understanding or holes in previously learned concepts, as well as misconceptions and overgeneralizations that may impede current and future learning. Once these issues are revealed, teachers can make instructional decisions, both immediate and long term, based on students' needs.

George Polya, perhaps the most influential figure in the history of mathematical problem solving, outlined a four-step problem-solving method:

1. understand the problem;
2. make a plan for solving the problem;
3. carry out the plan; and
4. look back and reflect on the answer in terms of the initial question.

While Polya's method may at first appear to be a lockstep approach to solving problems, it really describes a process of mathematical thinking and acting wherein the solver moves back and forth among the four steps until a solution is reached.

Problem-Solving Strategies and Representations

While a plan can draw from many possible strategies, commonly used problem-solving strategies include guessing and checking, looking for a pattern, using an algorithm, making a list or table, modeling the situation, making a drawing, writing an equation, and solving a simpler problem. Notice that many of these strategies involve representing a mathematical idea or relationship in a different form. Representations are tools that help us record and work with our mathematical ideas, communicate our thoughts to others, and clarify our own understanding. Students in the elementary and middle grades use a variety of forms of representation to record and communicate their thinking: symbols, drawings and pictures, tables and charts, physical materials, graphs, models, and oral and written language. The NCTM *Principles and Standards for School Mathematics* states: "Representing ideas and connecting the representations to mathematics lies at the heart of understanding mathematics" (NCTM 2000, 136). Some representations are conventions that are well known and accepted throughout the mathematics community, such as the addition, subtraction, multiplication, and division symbols we use to represent arithmetic operations (e.g., $+$, $-$, $\times$, and $\div$); and line graphs that are used to represent linear equations. Students should be able to understand these and connect them to other conventional representations. For example, division can also be represented with fractional notation ($8 \div 2$ and $\frac{8}{2}$), pictures, and objects; the points on a straight line graph that satisfy the corresponding equation can be shown in a table of (x, y) values.

As students try to make sense of problems, concepts, and procedures, some may create other representations that are idiosyncratic and not standard. Often, it is not essential for everyone in the class to discuss or experience these representations. For example, Doug, a second grader, adds a column of two-digit numbers by first looking at the tens column and recording one X on his paper for each group of ten. He then counts the number of Xs and records that numeral in the tens column. He next makes check marks for the ones and counts them before recording the numeral. Sometimes he has to adjust the numeral he writes in the tens column if there are enough ones to make another ten. Doug's use of Xs and check marks is a nonstandard way to keep track of the number of tens and ones.

NCTM Standard:
Representation

Grade 2

$$
\begin{array}{r}
23 \\
14 \\
+\ 31 \\
\hline
68
\end{array}
\qquad
\begin{array}{l}
X\,X\,X\,X\,X \\
\surd\,\surd\,\surd\,\surd\,\surd\,\surd\,\surd
\end{array}
$$

While this notation is helpful to Doug, it creates an unnecessary extra step for other students. Also, students who have performed additions using base ten blocks or paper representations (a line for a ten and a dot for a one) might find Doug's representation confusing. Thus, teachers must consider which representations are worth sharing with the whole class during problem-solving situations. Not all representations are created equal!

Whatever type of representation is used in a problem-solving situation, it's important for teachers to maintain a consistent focus on the meaning of the representation. Our goal is for students to be able to understand and explain the mathematical meaning of each part of their symbolic, graphic, or language-based representation. Furthermore, we want them to be able to understand and explain the connections among different representations. In first grade, this might involve a student being able to explain that each dot in a diagram stands for one piece of candy that the children in a math problem got from their parents, or that the number 4 stands for four dots, which indicates four pieces of candy. In the sixth grade this might involve students being able to explain that a ratio of two portions of lemon juice to one portion of sugar in a lemonade concentrate can be symbolized as $2:1$, or $\frac{2}{1}$, and can be shown on a bar diagram where one bar is twice as long as the other.

If taught in isolation, strategies and representations may appear to be the goals of instruction rather than powerful tools for mathematical thinking. However, within the context of problem solving, strategies and representations naturally occur and can be explored in great depth during discussions. As teachers, we sometimes take it for granted that students will understand various forms of representation in the same ways that we do. However, a set of base ten blocks looks to many students just like any set of different-sized blocks; it does not automatically convey the structure of the base ten system. Classroom talk can help students transform their understanding of that representation and its potential. Furthermore, even when students understand what the blocks are meant to indicate, it takes a long time for them to learn to interpret symbols, graphic objects, and the linguistic expressions that describe them. Here, too, talk

NCTM Standard:
Representation

Grade 1

can be used productively to get students to ask questions about what these forms of representation mean, and how their meanings are connected.

Let's examine how a teacher can use a discussion about a problem on addends to highlight students' problem-solving strategies and help students link different representations. Mr. Evans's first-grade students are discussing a problem about ten students who are going to an amusement park with Mr. Evans and Ms. Zito (another teacher). The children have to be with one of the teachers at all times. How many children can be in each of the two groups?

1. Mr. E:		Who would like to tell us how they solved this problem? Robin? What did you and your partner, David, do?
2. Robin:		We drew a picture. [Robin holds up her picture, Figure 5–1, for others to see.] This one shows five and five [points to the two equal groups], and here is one student and the other nine [points to the second grouping]. This one has six friends together and one, two, three, four, four in this group. Here is three and seven, and over here is a group with eight kids and another one with two kids. There are a lot of ways to put the children.
3. David:		I think we forgot one. Everybody could be in Mr. Evans's group and no one could go with Ms. Zito.
4. Mr. E:		Drawing a picture is a good problem-solving strategy. Talk to your partner about what Robin and David's picture means. Then in a few minutes I'd like Pedro and Briana and Suman and Josh to come up together and tell us in their own words about Robin and David's drawing.
5. Pedro and Briana:		This circle is one kid—see how it looks like a person? And this circle is for nine kids. That doesn't seem very fair. The nine kids are really squashed. Our picture is different. We didn't put arms and legs on people, just heads.
6. Suman and Josh:		Each of these [points to one of the circles of students on Robin's paper] is the students that go with one teacher, and these are the circles that go with the other teacher. There are eight students here and two students here. That makes ten.
7. Mr. E:		How do you know which circles go together to make ten?

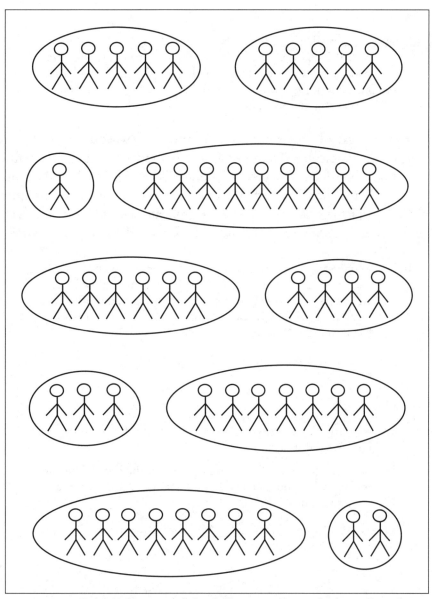

FIGURE 5–1 Robin's drawing of the different ways in which ten friends can be configured into two groups.

8. David: Ours are next to each other.

9. Josh: See we have lines connecting them [holds up his and Suman's picture].

10. Pedro: I can't tell. Let me count.

11. Briana: No, don't do that. Remember we put *E* for Mr. Evans and *Z* for Ms. Zito. See here. [Briana points to one circle with three marks and an *E* and another circle with five marks and a *Z*. She does not seem to recognize that these two circles don't account for all ten students.]

Mr. Evans next asks other students to comment on what the pictures show or to share their own pictures. He is using the talk move of "adding on" to further participation in the discussion, because young children need to share their unique experiences. But at the same time, Mr. Evans is also trying to help them generalize about how pictures can be used to solve problems. He holds off talking about the addends until he feels that everyone in his class understands the pictures.

12. Mr. E: So one way to decide how to put the students with the two teachers is to arrange the students in a drawing. Now let's use the pictures to help us write down the number of students that will go with each teacher. [Mr. Evans draws and labels a T-chart on the board.]

Mr. Evans's group	Ms. Zito's group

13. Robin: We started by putting five in one group and five in another. Then we did it again.

14. Mr. E: I'm going to record five in each group on the board. But I'm not sure what you mean by "did it again." David, can you tell us more about that?

Mr. Evans's group	Ms. Zito's group
5	5

15. David: Like, we made a circle with one person and the other group with nine. We just kept thinking about how to put the students with the teachers. We got six and four, three and seven, and eight and two. [Mr. Evans records the numbers.]

Mr. Evans's group	Ms. Zito's group
5	5
1	9
6	4
3	7
8	2

16. Mr. E: How did you know when you had found all of the different ways to place the ten students into two groups?

17. Robin: We just thought we were done.

18. Mr. E: Everyone who drew a picture, please look at it. Are there other ways to arrange the ten students into the two teacher groups?

Mr. Evans continued to collect data from the students. Some students mentioned number pairs that were already recorded, but others noticed that some of the pairs could be turned around. For example, Mr. Evans could have two students and Ms. Zito could have eight students. When no one mentions zero, Mr. Evans asks, "What if no one was in my group? How many students would be in Ms. Zito's group?" He plays an informal game with the class, picking one number in a row (e.g., 3) and asking what number goes with it to make 10 (e.g., 7).

Earlier, Mr. Evans noticed that Anthony and Nina made an organized list of addends. So he asks them to explain their strategy to the class.

19. Mr. E: Anthony and Nina, would you tell us how you solved this problem?

20. Anthony: We just wrote numbers. I wrote one and nine, then two and eight, three and seven, and I saw a pattern. One line was going up and the other was going down. [Mr. Evans makes a new T-chart on the board next to the other one and fills it in systematically.]

Mr. Evans's group	Ms. Zito's group
1	9
2	8
3	7
4	6

(*continued*)

5	5
6	4
7	3
8	2
9	1
10	0

21. Mr. E: Am I filling in this chart so it looks like how you wrote the numbers? [Anthony and Nina nod.]

22. Mr. E: Let's look at this chart. Who thinks they can explain what Anthony means when he says that one line is going up and the other is going down? Lindsey?

23. Lindsey: He means, like, in the picture, every time another person gets taken out, the other group gets one more and the other group is one less.

24. Byran   One number is counting up, and the other number is counting backward—nine, eight, seven, six, five, four, three, two, one, zero blast off!

25. Mr. E: Anthony, is that what you mean? [Anthony nods.] So Nina, how does this pattern help you figure out how to arrange the ten students into the two teacher groups?

26. Nina: We just followed the pattern. After five and five then comes six and four and then seven and three.

27. Karla   It's neat. Like with my fingers. One goes with nine, two goes with eight, three goes with seven. [Karla holds her hands up and puts one finger down and wiggles nine, then puts two fingers down and wiggles eight.]

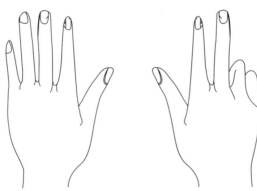

28. Mr. E: Let's all use our fingers to show numbers that together make ten in a pattern. Put ten fingers down, how many fingers are up? [He waits for everyone to try it.] So there could be ten kids in my group and zero in Ms. Zito's. Now put nine fingers down; how many are up? So in my group we could put nine students and in Ms. Zito's group we would put how many students? [Mr. Evans continues the pattern with fingers, linking the numbers to the two groups, for all pairs of addends.]

Later Mr. Evans reflects on the lesson. One purpose of this discussion was to introduce all students to the problem-solving strategy of drawing a picture. He wants to start building common knowledge of this strategy so that in the future, when a student says, "I drew a picture," the class already has common ground on which to build the discussion of their classmate's explanation. Another goal for the lesson was to assist students in understanding how relationships can be represented in drawings and tables. Mr. Evans knows that he will repeatedly need to ask students to talk about how they interpret different representations. He was especially pleased with the discussion about the organized list of addends to ten.

You might wonder why Mr. Evans did not pursue Robin's statement that "we just thought we were done" in response to his question about knowing when she had all of the pairs. Or why he didn't pursue the fact that Anthony and Nita missed forming a pair with zero and ten. There is a lot going on in every discussion. It is not easy in the middle of a discussion to respond to all comments. But because the discussion occurred, Mr. Evans knows that students need more experiences with zero and organizing data. He will be able to return to these ideas in future lessons.

Talking Through the Givens of a Mathematics Problem

Research on problem solving has revealed that good problem solvers spend a lot of time on Step 1 of Polya's method (understanding the problem and all the relevant relationships), while novices rush to try a plan without really thinking through the plan's effectiveness. Good problem solvers ask themselves key questions about the given and unknown information in the problem. They constantly monitor their own progress in solving the problem, reevaluating choices and sequences, as well as finding and correcting errors and oversights along the way. Talk can be used to help all students spend more time on Step 1.

NCTM Standard:
Problem Solving

Grade 4

Ms. Dunbar, a fourth-grade teacher, projects the following mathematics problem onto the board:

Mrs. Smith has to order pencils for all of the fourth-grade classrooms in the Miller School. Pencils come in packages of 48 pencils each. Mrs. Smith ordered 25 packages. Each of the 6 fourth-grade classes will get the same number of pencils. How many pencils will each class receive?

She tells the class that before they can begin to solve the problem, they first have to make sure that everyone understands the information in the problem and what the question is asking. She then initiates a discussion.

1. Ms. D: OK. First, read the problem to yourself twice. [Ms. Dunbar waits.] Who can tell us some information about this problem? Missy?

2. Missy: This problem is about pencils.

3. Kenley: And figuring out how many pencils to give each class.

4. Mrs. D: What else? Mohammed?

5. Mohammed: We have to figure out how many pencils there are altogether. You add or maybe multiply all the numbers.

6. Ms. D: I'm not ready yet to figure out what to do to solve the problem. I want to understand all the facts and ideas in the problem first. Can you give me a fact, Mohammed?

7. Mohammed: Mrs. Smith has to order pencils for all of the fourth grades in the school.

8. Ms. D: Yes, that is a fact. Who can give me another fact? Ellen?

9. Ellen: There are forty-eight pencils in one package of pencils.

10. Ms. D: Where did you get that information, Ellen? Would you please show us? [Ellen goes to the board and underlines the sentence *Pencils come in packages of 48 pencils each.*] Now everyone turn to your partner and share another fact from the problem.

Ms. Dunbar goes on to elicit information from the students, and she records the relevant facts on the board. Once the facts are established— 25 packages of pencils ordered, 48 pencils per package, six fourth-grade classrooms—Ms. Dunbar asks five different students to state in their own words what question they are trying to answer. Why do this? If she takes the time to make sure everyone understands the relationships and the question, she knows the ensuing discussions will be more valuable since everyone will be on the same page. Ms. Dunbar first calls on a student she thinks will be able to restate the question correctly, but then she calls on students who she knows are likely to still be confused.

11. Lily: We have to figure out how many pencils to give each of the fourth-grade classes.

12. Ms. D: Josh, what's this problem asking us to find?

13. Josh: I'm not sure.

14. Ms. D: OK. What can you do when you're not sure?

15. Josh: Ask someone? [Ms. Dunbar nods.] Lily, would you repeat what you just said?

16. Lily: We have to figure out how many pencils Mrs. Smith is buying, and then we have to give those pencils out to the fourth-grade classes. So we need to find out how many pencils to give to each class. Does that make sense? [Josh nods.]

17. Ms. D: Can you put that in your own words, Josh?

18. Josh: Mrs. Smith is buying a lot of pencils and we have to find the number. But then the pencils are going to be shared by the fourth-grade classes, so we have to figure out how many each class gets.

19. Ms. D: I agree. Andy, can you state the problem we are going to solve in your own words?

This type of interaction is common in many classrooms that use talk extensively. Sometimes students are not able to answer a question. What do we do? Ms. Dunbar has established the routine that when a student is confused or unable to answer a question for any reason, he or she simply asks for someone to repeat the question, repeat an answer, or repeat some information. This is not looked upon in a negative way; it is simply one of the classroom routines that allows everyone to get some form of support when needed. The important mathematical information is out in the public arena where students can hear it again. Notice that Ms. Dunbar does not chastise Josh for not knowing. Most students are legitimately confused when they say they don't know. They welcome a safe environment where there are ways to get information without feeling stupid. But in order to use this interchange to help Josh learn, it is important that Ms. Dunbar immediately return to him after he has listened to Lily and ask him to repeat what Lily said. When students know that their teacher will always return to them after a similar exchange, they really concentrate and work hard to understand the material.

Talking Through a Method for Solution

Having now engaged the class in a common and accurate interpretation of the problem, Ms. Dunbar asks students to work in pairs to solve the problem. Ms. Dunbar notes that Sam and Amanda are able to solve the problem while Missy and Mel are stuck. She notices that most students use multiplication and division, but one pair uses repeated addition. Some students make computational errors when dividing. Ms. Dunbar decides to use a whole-class discussion of the problem to address these issues.

20. Ms. D: Sam and Amanda, could you please explain the method you used to solve the problem?

21. Amanda: Sure. First we wanted to find out how many pencils Mrs. Smith ordered. We did twenty-five times forty-eight and got one thousand two hundred.

22. Ms. D: What made you decide to multiply twenty-five times forty-eight?

23. Sam: Because there are forty-eight pencils in each package and twenty-five packages in all.

24. Ms. D: Missy and Mel, can you explain why your classmates multiplied twenty-five times forty-eight?

25. Missy: It's a faster way to add forty-eight plus forty-eight plus forty-eight twenty-five times.

26. Mel: Yeah, they wanted to know how many pencils in all, so if there's forty-eight in one package and you have twenty-five packages, you need to multiply.

27. Ms. D: So now that they know there are one thousand two hundred pencils, who can predict what Sam and Amanda did next? Raphael?

28. Raphael: I bet they divided one thousand two hundred by six to get two hundred because we're splitting the pencils equally among six classes.

29. Ms. D: Is that what you did? [Sam and Amanda nod.] Alex, why do you think Sam and Amanda decided to use division?

30. Alex: *Divides* means *sharing*, and that's what we want to do with the pencils: take all those pencils and split or share them between the classes.

31. Ms. D: Is that how you knew? [Sam and Amanda nod.] Missy, can you repeat what Alex said in your own words?

32. Missy: He said that they divided since we're sharing the pencils equally.

33. Ms. D: Sam and Amanda, how did you two figure out the answer to one thousand two hundred divided by six?

34. Sam: It's two hundred. We just divided.

35. Ms. D: OK, but how else can we be sure that two hundred is the correct answer? Why doesn't everyone talk to their partners about this. [Partners talk for about two minutes.] Carla, I heard you and your partner describing your method. Would you share it with us?

36. Carla: If I were Mrs. Smith, I'd put all one thousand two hundred pencils into groups of one hundred 'cause that's easy to count. There would be twelve groups. Then, each class would get two of those groups and that's two hundred pencils.

Ms. Dunbar asked students who were confused to revoice and explain other students' explanations of their effective methods. She also asked students to predict what came next in solving the problem. When she did this, she checked back with the original speakers to see whether the prediction was accurate. As a result, many students who had not solved the problem or who had made mistakes were able to make progress in their understanding of the problem and one solution method.

Talking about methods of solution and problem-solving strategies can also enable students to gain insights into mathematical relationships. For example, as the discussion continued, one pair of students in Ms. Dunbar's class solved the pencil problem by dividing 48 by 6 (to find the number of pencils each class gets from one package) and then multiplying the answer, 8, by 25, for a total of 200 pencils. Students were surprised that the problem could be solved by dividing first and then multiplying; Sam and Amanda's method involved multiplying first, then dividing. The class discussed both methods, and then wrote number sentences to represent both of them—for example, $(48 \times 25) \div 6$ and $(48 \div 6) \times 25$.

Discussing methods of solution and problem-solving strategies also helps students learn more sophisticated problem-solving methods. Mrs. Steinfeld, a sixth-grade teacher, presented her students with a drawing of a large jar filled with

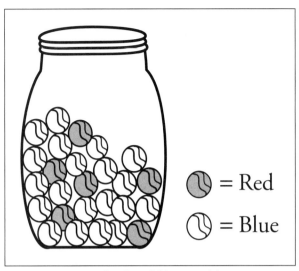

FIGURE 5–2 Jar of red and blue marbles.

six red and twenty blue marbles. (See Figure 5–2.) She asked the students to figure out how many more marbles she should put in the jar, and what color they should be, so that there will be three times as many blue marbles as red ones. In the class discussion, many students revealed that they had used a drawing to find the answer, circling groups of three blue and one red to decide how many to add. Mrs. Steinfeld then called on Bora, who remarked, "I noticed that there were twenty-six marbles altogether. You said there had to be three times as many blue marbles as red ones so that means three blue for every one red or four marbles together. So I have to have a total number of marbles that is divisible by four. But there are twenty-six marbles in the jar you drew. So that's not a multiple of four. But twenty-eight is divisible by four, so I need to add two marbles. Add one more blue and one more red marble, because if I have twenty-one blue and seven red, it works."

Mrs. Steinfeld then called on several of Bora's classmates to explain Bora's method as a way to assess their understanding of her explanation. Bora had to talk about her reasoning a few times before Mrs. Steinfeld felt that most students understood it. She also asked others to explain why Bora's method was both reasonable and efficient. In addition, Mrs. Steinfeld was able to use Bora's reasoning that the number of marbles in the jar must be a multiple of 4 to help explain why there is more than one answer to the problem—the jar could be filled with a different number of marbles that is a multiple of 4, such as 32 or 36.

The number of red and blue marbles to be added would be different depending on the total number of marbles in the jar. Finally, Mrs. Steinfeld presented the class with two similar problems and encouraged them to use Bora's method. These "marble" problems were also then discussed. Notice that Mrs. Steinfeld didn't assume that simply hearing a more sophisticated method would lead to its implementation by others. She required students to explain Bora's solution method and then to apply the method to new problems.

Increasing Students' Self-Monitoring of Their Thinking

As students talk about solving problems, they become more aware of their own understanding and can better monitor their own strategies and solutions. Monitoring your understanding of a topic calls for reflecting on what you do and do not understand. This kind of self-monitoring is sometimes referred to as a "metacognitive" activity. We have found that the process of explaining one's thinking aloud assists students in clarifying their own ideas and can help them correct their own mistakes, especially when teachers and classmates ask probing questions. The goal is for students eventually to monitor their own comprehension and ask themselves questions that will help them modify and refine their thinking.

NCTM Standard:
Problem Solving

Grade 3

Mr. Cooper, a third-grade teacher, wrote the following problem on the board:

> *The juice machine only takes quarters, dimes, and nickels.*
> *List all possible coin combinations you can use to buy a box of*
> *juice that costs 35¢.*

He gave the students time to work on the problem individually, and then he initiated a discussion.

1. Mr. C: Jaire, could you tell us how you solved this problem?

2. Jaire: I have a list here on my paper. I know that a quarter and a dime is thirty-five cents, then three dimes and a nickel is thirty-five cents, then you can also get it with seven nickels.

3. Mr. C: We've talked a lot about how important it is to look back at your work when you think you have found a solution. How did you check your work?

4. Jaire: I checked my addition and each one added to thirty-five cents. So I knew I got it right.

5. Mr. C: Jaire has a list of some different coin combinations. He has checked to make sure that each one adds to thirty-five cents. Who would like to respond to Jaire's work? Rebecca?

6. Rebecca: Well, I think you might want to check if you had all of the combinations. I have three that aren't on your list.

7. Mr. C: Rebecca, can you give some advice to Jaire on what he can do to find these other combinations?

8. Rebecca: Well, I set my list up so that I wrote all of the ones that used a quarter first, then I wrote all of the ones that used dimes next. That way I wouldn't skip any.

9. Mr. C: Does anyone else have advice for Jaire? Louie?

10. Louie: Well, it's still a list and it kind of goes in order like Rebecca's, but I started with the way to use the least amount of coins, which was one quarter and one dime. Then I kept the quarter and changed the dime to two nickels. I kept doing that, changing from only a few coins to more.

11. Mr. C: How many people think they have every single possible combination? OK, I can see that most people think they might have missed a few. Let's see if we can make our lists more complete. Jaire, would you see if you can find some more coin combinations using one of the suggestions your classmates have offered?

12. Jaire: OK, I'll try the one that starts with a quarter.

Instead of using the discussion to reveal to Jaire the missing coin combinations, Mr. Cooper used it to support thoughtful reflection about the overall process. He knew that many students, like Jaire, probably had missed some combinations through lack of a systematic strategy. Therefore, he took the time to have two students talk through their systematic approach for finding all the combinations. As a result, Jaire and others will likely complete the list of possible combinations while learning how to reflect on the implementation of a strategy to maximize its effectiveness.

We believe that students improve their ability to choose and reflect on an appropriate strategy when they discuss the methods and strategies of a problem. Mrs. Lombardo consistently asks her fourth-grade students these questions:

- Why did you choose this strategy or representation?
- Did you consider any others? Which ones?
- Why did you consider those?

- How can you show the relationships in the problem?
- When have we used this strategy before?
- Why does it make sense to use the same strategy on these problems?
- Can you think of other problems where using this strategy would be appropriate?
- Can you represent the problem in a different way?

On their own, students do not always see the mathematical connections among problems. When asked to consider such connections, however, students can do this well. The implications for learning can be profound. Generalizing about a specific problem-solving method enables students to figure out whether this method is appropriate when presented with a new problem. Having the chance to generalize problem-solving methods, strategies, and representations, and to discuss connections among problems, helps students avoid using a method or strategy when it is not appropriate. When students are taught to use a strategy without discussing why and when to use it, they may be less successful in applying that strategy in sensible ways when confronted with new problems.

Assessing Student Learning

Analyzing students' work samples is one way to uncover patterns of errors and misconceptions. Data gathered during classroom discussions also help teachers grasp what students know and don't know. Let's examine what one teacher, Mrs. Rice, learned about her students' understanding following a brief discussion and how she used this knowledge to plan her instruction for the next day. Mrs. Rice had the following word problem on the board when her second-grade class returned from recess.

NCTM Standard:
Connections

Grade 2

> *There are 12 girls and 9 boys present today in the class next to ours. How many more girls are there than boys?*

After giving students time to solve the problem individually, she asked them to share their method with their partner. Then Mrs. Rice began a whole-class discussion.

1. Mrs. R: Who can tell us how they solved this problem?

2. Janice: We used these little teddy bears. [See Figure 5–3.] We put twelve red ones in a line for the girls. Then we put nine blue ones in another line for the boys. We saw that the line for the girls had three more. So there are three more girls than boys.

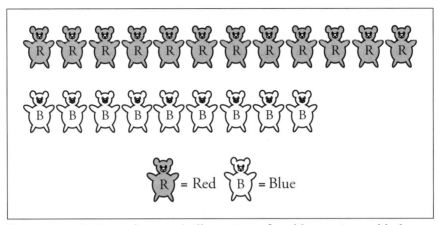

FIGURE 5–3 Janice and partner's illustration of problem, using teddy-bear counters.

3. Mrs. R: Who solved the problem a different way? Darryl?

4. Darryl: We made a picture of twelve girls and nine boys. We crossed them out one boy, one girl until there were three girls and no more boys to cross out.

5. Mrs. R: Did anyone use subtraction to solve the problem? [No hands.] Did anyone try to use twelve minus nine to solve the problem?

Mrs. Rice chose this simple problem from her textbook. It is a comparison subtraction problem where two quantities are compared. Mrs. Rice has mainly used a take-away model for subtraction; she is using this problem to gather formative assessment data to help her plan future lessons. A few students have generalized that they can use subtraction but they do not volunteer right away; other students are clearly confused by the idea that subtraction might be used. She decides to probe for more information.

6. Kirsten: That wouldn't work.

7. Mrs. R: Why not?

8. Kirsten: 'Cause twelve minus nine means twelve take away nine. We're not taking anything away.

9. Mrs. R: OK, so you're saying that this problem doesn't tell you to take the boys away from the girls? [Kirsten nods.] What do some other people think? Could you use subtraction here? Matthew?

10. Matthew: I don't think so. There's nothing being taken away here. It's not like the boys are leaving or something.

11. Salem: Well maybe. It works. Twelve take away nine is three and that's the answer.

12. Mrs. R: Salem, tell us more about what you are thinking.

13. Salem: If one thing is more, you can take the other away to see how much.

14. Mrs. R: Can you give us a different example?

15. Salem: Ten cookies and three cookies. How much more do I have than you?

16. Mrs. R: Are you saying if Salem has ten cookies and Mrs. Rice has three cookies, how many more cookies do you have than me? [Salem nods.]

17. Mrs. R: OK, talk to your partner about this problem. Can we use subtraction to find out how many *more* cookies Salem has?

When students talk about how they solve word problems, teachers have an opportunity to assess students' understanding of content applied to situations. For example, Mrs. Rice realized that her students could solve this problem by modeling, but many of them had not generalized that comparisons can be solved using subtraction. Based on this discussion, Mrs. Rice decided to include more problems involving comparisons in her lessons. She made a note that she would focus on the vocabulary of comparison situations, *more than* and *less than*, and that she needed to keep the numbers small until students had grasped that subtraction could be applied. She also noted that by discussing problems, it was likely that students would learn from each other more efficient solution strategies such as Salem's.

DISCUSSION AND REFLECTION

1. Make a list of the problem-solving strategies you think are most important for students at your grade level to be able to use. Write or find a mathematics problem that uses the math you are currently teaching and can be solved using two of these strategies. Design a talk lesson around this problem. See Chapter 9 for planning suggestions.

2. We stated in this chapter that representations can be powerful tools for mathematical thinking. Give an example from your own teaching or this chapter in which a representation (e.g., a picture, manipulative material, graph, equation, or word problem) clearly helped a learner understand a relationship or mathematical idea. How can talk be used to extend an individual student's insights to other members of the class?

3. Sometimes a student whose confidence is quite fragile will present a solution method that is deeply flawed. What might teachers do to help the class see that discussing different solution methods, right or wrong, helps move everyone toward understanding the mathematical truth of the situation? How do we do this and be sensitive to the individual needs of students?

6

Mathematical Reasoning

Reasoning stands at the center of mathematics learning. Many mathematics educators consider the NCTM standard concerning reasoning and proof to be its most important. Susan Jo Russell, coauthor of the *Investigations in Number, Data, and Space* curriculum, makes a number of points explaining why instruction must focus on reasoning.

> Mathematics is a discipline that deals with abstract entities, and reasoning is the tool for understanding abstractions. . . . First, mathematical reasoning is essentially about the development, justification, and use of mathematical generalizations. In the classroom where mathematical reasoning is at the center of activity, the solution of an individual problem is closely linked to the generalizations behind that solution. Second, mathematical reasoning leads to an interconnected web of mathematical knowledge within a mathematical domain. Third, the development of such a web of mathematical understanding is the foundation of what I call "mathematical memory," what we often refer to as mathematical "sense," which provides the basis for insight into mathematical problems. Fourth, an emphasis on mathematical reasoning in the classroom, as in the discipline of mathematics, necessarily incorporates the study of flawed or incorrect reasoning as an avenue toward deeper development of mathematical knowledge. (Russell 1999, 1–2)

Why Talk About Reasoning?

Reasoning is an integral part of doing mathematics. We reason when we examine patterns and detect regularities, generalize relationships, make conjectures, and evaluate or construct an argument. These activities are fundamental to making sense of content. Therefore, it seems natural to talk about mathematical reasoning in mathematics class.

Beyond these basic reasoning activities, however, there are more specialized types of reasoning that we want students to encounter, and teachers can use classroom talk to present these to students as well. For example, spatial reasoning and algebraic reasoning both have an important place in mathematics and are used to solve many types of problems. Spatial reasoning forms the cornerstone of all work with visual images such as geometric shapes, graphs, and tables. Students need to be able to perform a variety of operations on images, such as rotating shapes, translating between two-dimensional shapes and three-dimensional solids, and visualizing graphical data. Reasoning that involves topics such as variables, equations, and functions is often referred to as algebraic reasoning. Algebra is essential for success in mathematics and, therefore, all students should be provided with opportunities to reason algebraically. Each type of reasoning has characteristics or components that are specific to its type, and productive classroom talk is an especially effective way for teachers to help students master the complexities of logical thinking in all areas.

In addition, there are many general reasoning tools and skills that well-educated students should have available for use in mathematics, the sciences, social studies, and the humanities. For example, it's important for students to gain experience using the processes of deduction and induction. These forms of reasoning play a role in many content areas. Deduction involves reasoning logically from general statements or premises to conclusions about particular cases. Induction involves examining specific cases, identifying relationships among the cases, and generalizing the relationship. Productive classroom talk can enhance or improve a person's ability to reason both deductively and inductively.

Reasoning Deductively

How do we help students learn to reason deductively? One way is to regularly ask students to provide evidence for their claims regardless of the mathematical topic. This can be accomplished in almost all discussions, using one of the talk moves described in Chapter 2—asking students *why* they agree or disagree with someone else's reasoning—and pushing them to give examples that support their position. Another way is to provide instruction and practice focused specifically on the processes of deduction. Deductive statements can be especially confusing to children because of the use of negations and logical connectives (e.g., *and, or, if–then,* and *if and only if*). Discussing the interpretation of a negation or the inferences that can and cannot be made from particular statements helps students become skillful in drawing defensible conclusions.

Mrs. Wolfe started using logic problems a few years ago as a way to teach about deduction and has been pleased with the results. Every Tuesday at the start of their math period, she asks her fourth-grade students to talk about their reasoning when solving one matrix logic problem. Her students like these problems and look forward to Tuesdays! She has found that students at first do not know what type of conclusions can reasonably be made from given statements. However, by the end of the year, her students have improved in their ability to make inferences and reason deductively. Mrs. Wolfe thinks that talking about these types of problems in a very purposeful way has been a key ingredient in their success.

In the following vignette Mrs. Wolfe uses discussion to introduce the process of elimination—drawing a conclusion based on the fact that all other options have been eliminated. In addition, she shows students how they can use an array or matrix, a table of rows and columns, to organize the information and draw conclusions. Mrs. Wolfe writes the following problem on the board. It is typical of the problems she uses every Tuesday to help students learn to reason deductively:

NCTM Standard:
Reasoning and Proof

Grade 4

> Art, Bill, and Debby play first base, second base, and third base on their school's baseball team, but not necessarily in that order. Art and the third baseman went with Debby to the movies yesterday. Art does not play first base. Who's on first?

She does not give the students time to work on the problem on their own, but instead asks them to read the problem three times before initiating a class discussion.

1. Mrs. W: This logic problem requires us to reason from the statements that are given in the problem. Who can read us one of the statements and then tell us what conclusion you made from that statement? Jason?

2. Jason: I know that Art is not the first baseman because it says that Art does not play first base.

3. Mrs. W: I noticed that the statement you used to draw that conclusion is not the first statement in the problem. Is this OK to do?

4. Jason: I think so. I looked for a fact.

5. Mrs. W: In most logic problems it's OK to take statements out of order. What else can we conclude? Zach?

6. Zach: I think Art plays second base. It says that Art and the third baseman went with Debby to the movies, so Art is a different person from the third baseman.

7. Mrs. W: OK, so Zach thinks that Art plays second base. Do people agree, disagree, have questions? Yuree.

8. Yuree: I don't understand why you think that Art plays second base.

9. Zach: We know that Art doesn't play first from what Jason said. Then this other sentence says that Art went with the third baseman to the movies, so that just leaves second base, because Art and the third baseman are two different people. So Art can't play third base. Do you see what I'm saying?

10. Mrs. W: Caroline? Do you want to add on to this?

11. Caroline: I made a list, like first base, second base, and third base, and put the name next to the right place.

12. Yuree: But how did you know Art goes next to second base?

Mrs. Wolfe recognizes that Caroline's explanation is not helping Yuree and others follow the logic of the situation. While she could use the revoicing or repeating talk moves, she decides that this is the time to introduce a matrix as a way of organizing what is known. She had previously prepared a worksheet with a labeled three-by-three matrix on it and hopes to talk with her students about how one can deduce something using the process of elimination.

13. Mrs. W: This is a bit confusing, isn't it? Let me show you a method that might help you keep track of the facts. [As she is talking, Mrs. Wolfe draws a matrix on the blackboard.] First, I make a rectangular array showing rows and columns. We've used arrays when talking about multiplication and division but we're going to use one here in a different way and call it a *matrix*. I label each column with the names of the people because I am trying to match them up with the bases. [Mrs. Wolfe writes the names of the students above each column.] Where do you think I put the bases? Louise?

Art	Bill	Debby

14. Louise: Maybe on the other side? On the rows?

15. Mrs. W: Right! [She writes a base next to each row.] Now each of these small inside squares matches a name with a base. This square [points] is where second base and Debby meet, so I could put a YES or a NO in it to show that Debby plays second base or she doesn't play second base. Look at the matrix on the worksheet [passes them out] and explain to your partner how it was made. Can you find the square that stands for Bill and second base? Debby and third base? Which squares stand for Art? Which squares stand for first base?

	Art	Bill	Debby
1st base			
2nd base			
3rd base			

Mrs. Wolfe checks in with different groups of students, asking them to explain to each other how the matrix is structured and what the different squares, sometimes called *cells*, represent. She reviews the terms *rows* and *columns*, which the class used previously when describing arrays. She does not bother to talk as a class about the design of the matrix because she finds that all of her students during small-group talk can explain how it is like an array and what the different squares represent.

16. Mrs. W: Now that we understand how to read a matrix, let's put some information into it. Remember how one of the statements was that Art doesn't play first base? Ken, explain to us how you showed this in your matrix.

17. Ken: I put an X in the box. The problem says Art doesn't play first base, so I put an X in that square.

	Art	Bill	Debby
1st base	X		
2nd base			
3rd base			

18. Caroline: I put a NO next to Art and first base. Is that OK too? [Mrs. Wolfe nods.]

19. Mrs. W: Alright. We have a couple of ways to show that Art doesn't play first base. Look at the problem again. Do we know anything else about Art? Zach?

20. Zach: I think we can put an X next to third base, too, because it says that Art and the third baseman went to the movies so Art can't be the third-base person.

	Art	Bill	Debby
1st base	X		
2nd base			
3rd base	X		

21. Mrs. W: Juan, can you put this into your own words? How do we know that Art doesn't play third base?

22. Juan: Art and the third-base player went to the movies together, so they have to be different people. We can put a NO next to Art and third base.

23. Mrs. W: Notice how the column for Art has two Xs in it. Art does not play first base or third base. There is only one base left, second base. So Art must be the second baseman. Let's put a check or a YES in that square.

	Art	Bill	Debby
1st base	X		
2nd base	✓		
3rd base	X		

We have just used the "process of elimination." We decided that Art plays second base not from a direct clue but because we eliminated the other options. The only base left for Art to play is second base. Talk to your partner and explain how we used the process of elimination to conclude that Art is the second baseman.

Notice how Mrs. Wolfe stops and goes to partner talk to make sure that every student engages with this idea of using elimination to draw a conclusion. When teachers present new material to students, no matter how clear and organized the presentation, many miss the salient points. However, by asking everyone to talk, Mrs. Wolfe forces them to consider the ideas. She calls on Yuree, who earlier in the conversation was confused by this idea, to explain how we know Art plays second base.

24. Yuree: The chart really helps see that all that is left for Art to play is second base. The other bases got eliminated earlier so this is the only thing left for Art to play.

25. Mrs. W: Here is another nice thing about using a matrix and the process of elimination. If Art plays second base, can Bill or Debby play second base? [Students respond no.] OK, so we can eliminate them and put Xs or NOs along the row of second base. [Mrs. Wolfe fills in the chart on the board.] Fill in your chart like I have.

	Art	Bill	Debby
1st base	X		
2nd base	✓	X	X
3rd base	X		

26. Mrs. W: Now we are ready to go back to the problem and find other information. Who can read another fact? Elise?

27. Elise: "Art and the third baseman went with Debby to the movies yesterday." This is like before. If Debby went with the third baseman, she can't be the third baseman.

28. Mrs. W: Talk with your partner and put this information into your matrix. Use the process of elimination when possible.

	Art	Bill	Debby
1st base	X		
2nd base	✓	X	X
3rd base	X		X

This discussion continued, with the class coming to the conclusion that Debby was the first-base player. Then Mrs. Wolfe asked many students to explain how they eliminated certain options and used this process of elimination to come to the conclusion that Bill played third base. Students shared how they used the matrix and the process of elimination.

Notice how Mrs. Wolfe used a variety of talk moves to make sense of the logic statements. In Line 7 she asked students if they agreed or disagreed with Zach. When Yuree indicated that she was confused by Zach's statement, Mrs. Wolfe had Zach repeat it. Then in Line 10, Mrs. Wolfe asked Caroline to add her own ideas to Zach's comments. Throughout the discussion, Mrs. Wolfe asked students to explain the ideas under discussion to someone else during partner talk (Lines 15, 23, and 28). Finally, this vignette illustrates how teachers might use discourse to help students better understand content that they are introducing. Mrs. Wolfe was teaching students about a matrix and the process of elimination using direct instruction and talk. The discussions were all geared toward providing students with multiple opportunities to understand what inferences might be made from the statements.

One final note about this vignette: In the next chapter, we will discuss ways to use talk to develop definitions of words and symbols. However, in this case we see the teacher introduce a phrase that is important but very difficult to define in isolation: *process of elimination*. If Mrs. Wolfe had started out the lesson trying to define this term, she would have run into problems, and most students would not have followed her definition. But by having students engage in the procedures that actually constitute the process of elimination, and using the phrase again and again as they became more experienced with those procedures, Mrs. Wolfe built the experiential base they will need to eventually reflect on the meaning of the phrase and add it to their vocabulary.

Reasoning Inductively

Talk can help students develop their inductive reasoning ability. Many problems require students to find generalizations that hold for many different examples. Yet it's sometimes hard for students to recognize patterns when the examples are presented in different representational formats. Students may have trouble seeing the commonalities among examples presented in words, symbols, tables, pictures, and graphs. Extended discussion can help students come to understand that relationships among mathematical entities can be expressed in more than one form. Talk also provides ways to explore the limitations of inductive reasoning—sometimes a pattern does not generalize in a way that was expected, and students need models for how to reassess the situation.

Mr. Khoury is a kindergarten teacher who regularly presents problems using induction. He has his students play a version of the game "one of these things is not like the other." He presents many different examples that represent a rule, and then he asks his students how the examples are the same and what the rule might be.

NCTM Standard:
Reasoning and Proof

Grade K

  1. Mr. K: Look at these funny dolls. They live in a land where all the dolls have agreed to rules about some of the things they will wear. Let's see if we can find something that is the same for all of them.

A   B   C   D

So let's look at these four funny dolls. What do we see here? What are they wearing that's the same for all of them?

2. Giselle: Hats. They have hats!

3. Mr. K: OK, Giselle says they have hats. Thanks, Giselle. David, will you show us what Giselle means? Can you come up and point to what she's talking about and tell us in your own words?

4. David: [Pointing] This one has a hat, and this one has a hat, and this one has a hat, and this one doesn't have hats.

5. Mr. K: OK, thanks David. Giselle, is that what you were saying?

6. Giselle: Umm, I thought they all had hats, but that one [A] just has something else in her hair.

7. Mr. K: Oh, OK, so this one [A] has something else in her hair?

8. David: Yeah, a bow tie.

9. Mr. K: OK, so remember that in the land our dolls are from, they all agree to wear something that is the same. We're trying to find out what is the same for these four dolls. Ahmad, do you have an idea about something that's the same for all four dolls up here?

10. Ahmad: Their shoes! They all have the same shoes!

11. Mr. K: Sandy do you agree or disagree with what Ahmad said?

12. Sandy: Uhmm . . . [Fifteen seconds go by.]

13. Mr. K: Who can repeat what Ahmad thinks about all the dolls? Katrina?

14. Katrina: I think he said they all have shoes.

15. Mr. K: OK, Ahmad, is that right?

16. Ahmad: Umm, I said they all had the *saaame* shoes! I think they all agreed to wear the *same* shoes on their planet.

118

17. Mr. K: Oh, OK. So who agrees or disagrees with what Ahmad just said? Tell us whether you agree or disagree and why. Kylie?

18. Kylie: I think I agree? Because . . . umm . . . they all have shoes.

19. Mr. K: OK, let's look. [Points to all four in turn] This one has shoes, this one has shoes, this one has shoes, and this one has shoes. But do they all have the *same* shoes? Remember, in their land the dolls all agreed to wear some things that are the same. Did they agree to wear the same shoes? James?

20. James: Well, I noticed another thing that's the same. Three buttons.

21. Mr. K: Wow. Another thing that's the *same* for *all four* of the dolls up here? Who can show us what James means?

For teachers in higher grades, this conversation may seem a bit laborious, but there is important progress being made here. Mr. Khoury is working with ideas, phrases, and words that are important for inductive reasoning: *all, the same, all four,* and so on. It is not enough to notice properties of one or two or even three of the set of four dolls. By using the talk moves that are now familiar, Mr. Khoury is helping these kindergarten students focus their attention in ways that will support inductive reasoning.

Reasoning About Algebra

It's generally assumed that all students will study algebra in middle school or high school. Algebra is considered a pivotal course in a student's education because students must make sense of algebra if they are to be successful in many other mathematics courses. Lack of success in algebra sometimes translates into lack of opportunity for future schooling and careers. Algebraic reasoning is an important topic for elementary students because the experiences students have in grades kindergarten through 6 can help prepare them for success in a formal algebra course. Activities and discussions that revolve around patterns, equality, properties, generalizations, and symbolism are the precursors to the formal study of algebra. When we have students talk about these topics and how they make sense of problems, we help them develop an understanding of algebra.

Mrs. Malloy is currently teaching sixth grade but has also taught algebra to eighth-grade students. She knows that her students often have difficulty making sense of the concept of equivalence. She remembers that many of her eighth-grade students could solve equations for unknowns by memorizing rules, but they didn't understand what they were doing or why they were doing

it. Mrs. Malloy's goal this year is for her sixth graders to solve problems that involve unknowns in ways that make sense to them, by reasoning rather than following rules. She wants them to realize that in some situations there is only one value for a specific unknown, but in other situations a variable can represent a set of numbers. She also wants to help students gain a deeper understanding of equality so that they don't interpret the equal sign as a "do an operation" cue.

Mrs. Malloy has been using balance-scale problems as a means for reasoning about variables and equality. At the time of the following discussion, students have learned that in order for a scale to balance, the objects in each pan must weigh the same amount. They have had experience drawing balance scales to represent equivalent quantities. Mrs. Malloy wrote the following problem on the board and gave the students about five minutes to solve it on their own.

> *Three apples weigh the same as one orange and two plums.*
> *One orange weighs the same as four plums. How many plums*
> *equal the weight of one apple?*

1. Mrs. M: Andrea, would you share with us your solution process?

2. Andrea: First, I drew two scales to show the information. On the first scale, three apples weigh the same as an orange and two plums. Then on the second scale I put an orange on one side and four plums on the other. [See Figure 6–1.]

3. Mrs. M: I'm going to interrupt you for a minute, Andrea. Did anyone show the relationships between the weights of the fruit in a different way? Amira?

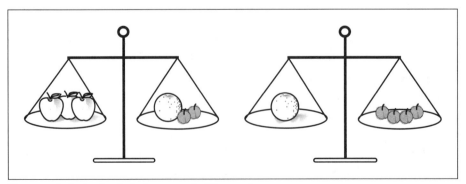

FIGURE 6–1 Andrea's balance-scale illustration.

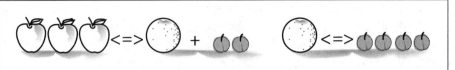

FIGURE 6–2 Amira's representation of the balance problem.

4. Amira: I drew pictures of the fruit and used arrows. I remembered that the equal sign is used with numbers. [See Figure 6–2.]

5. Mrs. M: Are both of these representations OK? Does the balance scale and the picture show the same relationships between the weight of the fruit? Talk to your partner about these questions. [A minute elapses.] OK, Vicky?

6. Vicky: Yes, I think both are the same. When a balance scale is level or balanced it shows that the objects weigh the same. I think you can show that they weigh the same with a picture and arrows, too.

7. Mrs. M: Good. When we have numbers, we also can use an equal sign to show that weights are the same. An equal sign also implies balance, like $8 = 6 + 2$. Is that clear?

8. Students: Yes.

Uh, huh.

9. Mrs. M: OK, Andrea, go ahead. Please continue with your solution.

10. Andrea: On the first scale I took two apples away from one side and two plums away from the other side. I also took two plums away from the second scale. So we now have one apple and three plums left, so one apple is equal to three plums. [See Figure 6–3.]

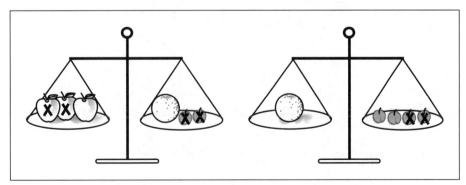

FIGURE 6–3 Andrea's attempt to solve the problem using her illustration.

Mrs. Malloy knows that Andrea's answer isn't correct, and she isn't sure how Andrea arrived at this incorrect solution. In addition, Mrs. Malloy is unsure if she should correct Andrea or not. To give herself some time, she might revoice Andrea's statement and then ask her to elaborate. Another tool Mrs. Malloy might use is to set up a discussion in which she presents two or three possible answers, not indicating acceptance or rejection of any. The subsequent discussion of the solutions requires students to reason about the statements their peers have made. Mrs. Malloy decides to use this approach.

11. Mrs. M: So here is one solution. Andrea is saying that the weight of one apple is equal to the weight of three plums. Does anyone else have a different solution? Ben?

12. Ben: That second scale says that the weight of one orange equals the weight of four plums, right? So I can use that to say that three apples equal six plums.

13. Mrs. M: Remember, we are talking about the weights of the fruit. Who can explain where the plums fit in?

14. Ben: [Ben comes the to the board and draws pictures to illustrate his explanation.] Three apples weigh the same as one orange and two plums. But one orange weighs the same as four plums so the three apples have the same weight as six plums. [See Figure 6–4.]

15. Mrs. M: Then what?

16. Ben: I just divided each side of the balance scale by three, and then I know that the weight of one apple equals the weight of two plums.

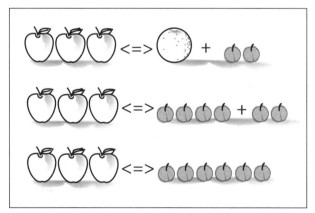

FIGURE 6–4 Ben's representation of the balance problem.

17. Mrs. M: OK, so we have two different solutions here. One is that three plums weigh the same as one apple and another is that two plums weigh the same as one apple. Which is correct? Discuss these two solutions with your partner. [Three minutes elapse, and Mrs. M resumes the discussion by calling on the partner team of Nick and Elizabeth.]

18. Elizabeth: Nick and I think that two plums equal the weight of one apple because you can't just cross off apples and plums—maybe they don't weigh the same amount.

19. Brian: I agree with Elizabeth. You can't do what Andrea says because we don't know if the objects weigh the same.

20. Carlos: My partner and I think that Ben's method makes sense. We think one apple equals the weight of two plums. Because you trade the orange for four plums so that makes six plums.

21. Mrs. M: A number of you are using a technique in algebra called *substitution*, where you substitute one value for another. Since one orange weighs the same as four plums, we can substitute the value of one orange by crossing it out and writing four plums. Talk to your partner about this. Does this make sense?

Students in Mrs. Malloy's class are starting to reason algebraically. Some of them are realizing they can use substitution to find the number of plums that equal the weight of three apples. Others do not yet realize that they can't remove unlike objects from both sides of the equal sign or balance scale. Talk, however, makes students' reasoning visible and helps Mrs. Malloy assist everyone in interpreting and solving problems. As the students share their insights and misconceptions, she is able to make instructional decisions to further their learning. In addition, talk helps students sort through multiple interpretations of algebraic situations and settle on common ground.

When Andrea presents her solution strategy in Line 10, a teacher or other listener might have an immediate sense of confusion. How did Andrea get there? Could that method possibly be right? Should we take the time to work through her reasoning? Here the teacher chooses to focus on Andrea's solution rather than her reasoning, first eliciting another solution path from Ben and then letting students talk about the two possible answers. She could also have chosen to go into more detail with Andrea's reasoning, asking her to spell out her thinking in more detail. When using classroom talk to deepen mathematical reasoning, teachers frequently encounter puzzling or incoherent contributions from students. We return to this issue in Chapter 10.

One of the most important and difficult parts of trying to improve students' abilities to reason mathematically involves helping them extend their knowledge about reasoning to new problems. Often when students encounter a new strategy or tool that helps them reason through a particular problem, they seem to understand it well. However, often their understanding is limited to the context of that particular problem, and their teacher watches in frustration as students fail to see how to apply or extend the strategy to solve a slightly different problem. We have found that talking about the reasoning involved in a problem helps students generalize problem types and solution strategies and apply them to new situations. To help them in this process, it's important to encourage students to look beyond the specific details of problems to the underlying mathematical relationships, to talk about the similarities and differences among problems, and to reflect aloud on how what they learned from other problems can be used in the solution process.

DISCUSSION AND REFLECTION

1. National organizations and reports have highlighted the importance of algebra and algebraic reasoning. In the vignette, what did Mrs. Malloy do to focus the discussion on important algebraic concepts and skills?

2. Why talk about reasoning? Can students in grades K–2 reason about mathematical ideas? Explain.

3. Mrs. Wolfe spent a lot of discussion time analyzing the matrix. What are the benefits of spending time discussing representations?

4. Students often have difficulty understanding negations. Find another matrix logic problem in which some clues involve negations (e.g., the use of the words *none, no, not*, etc.). Describe the problem as if you were running a class discussion with students. What should you tell students? What should they figure out on their own?

7

Mathematical Terminology, Symbols, and Definitions

If students are to become competent mathematical thinkers, able to work with and communicate about mathematical ideas, they must become familiar with mathematical words and symbols, such as *multiply, perimeter,* =, *square unit, prime number,* and so on. In our work, we have learned that simply providing students with a definition for a mathematical term or symbol doesn't result in students gaining a deep understanding of that term or symbol. Understanding a term or symbol entails understanding the concept or action that term or symbol refers to, and the relationships that exist between that concept and related concepts and ideas.

Carefully guided talk—multiple opportunities to discuss aspects of the meaning of words and symbols—can help students develop this kind of understanding and can also provide them needed practice in using terminology precisely and effectively. As we guide students in talking—clarifying and discussing the complexities associated with the appropriate words, phrases, and symbols—we are helping them clarify their own thoughts and understandings.

For some mathematical terms, like *rectangle,* learning the definition is more complex than learning the definitions for everyday words that name concrete objects. Consider first how as children we learned the meaning of words that name ordinary objects, such as *chair.* Most of this learning takes place as we encounter instances of the category, gradually learning which things other humans label as *chairs,* and making inferences about what kinds of objects the label *chair* might refer to. Now consider how we learn the meaning of a word like *rectangle.* First we encounter examples of rectangles and learn to recognize and label them, in part by paying attention to which things other humans label as *rectangles*. But even once we can recognize examples, our work is not over: To really understand what the term means in mathematics, we must know that it names a closed figure with two sets of parallel, congruent sides, and four internal ninety-degree angles. In other words, understanding the concept *rectangle* means understanding its formal definition. This second stage of learning is difficult for students. If we ask elementary students to identify a rectangle, most of them will pick out the shape of a typical rectangle. When asked to provide a definition of rectangles, however, very few will list all of the criteria that define what a rectangle is. Only by explicitly talking about the formal definition of a rectangle can we get at the real nature of the mathematical concept.

In general, words and symbols used in mathematics tend to have stricter or more precisely stated definitions than everyday words. If someone says, "Bring me a chair; I need to sit down," you are unlikely to be considered a failure if you bring them a stool or a bench. But if you are asked to construct a rectangle, you will fail unless it meets the criteria listed here. Mathematical terms carry "high stakes" definitions; there is less room for interpretation. As your students go on in school they will encounter such precisely stated "technical terms" in a wide range of content areas. The precise use of technical terms is difficult for many students, because it departs from their ordinary ways of using language. Talk about the exact meanings of mathematical terms can help them make the transition. Their discussions of definitions in your classroom may be their first encounter with the very important academic practice of using technical terms.

Another of the challenges of mathematical language arises from the fact that some mathematical terms also have everyday meanings. For example, the word *difference* can be interpreted mathematically as meaning the value we get when one number is subtracted from another number. But *difference* has nonmathematical meanings as well, such as *dissimilarity, disagreement in opinion*, and *distinction*. Students must be aware of the various meanings of words in order to decide which meaning makes most sense in a specific context. They must also be able to choose the word they want to use so as to achieve clear communication. Classroom discussion can help develop students' awareness of the meanings of mathematical terms, symbols, and definitions.

In this chapter, we will provide examples that show how teachers can help students begin this process of learning the meanings of words and symbols through discussion, even in kindergarten or pre-K settings. And at higher grade levels, we will see that students continue to benefit from talking about definitions, symbols, and other conventional kinds of representations.

Sorting Out Different Word Senses

Why is it important to talk about definitions of words, phrases, and symbols? One aspect of being an educated person is having a broad vocabulary and being able to choose words that exactly express what you are trying to say. And one of our jobs as teachers is to help students learn to use correct vocabulary to express themselves clearly and articulately. In the past, many teachers felt that it was not necessary to worry about language arts issues in mathematics class. Yet it is clear that if we want students to use specific words and phrases correctly, they must have opportunities to discuss word meanings and to practice correct word usage.

For example, in studying the concept of similarity, Ms. Lee, a sixth-grade teacher, had reviewed with her class the definition presented in the textbook: *Two figures are similar if and only if the corresponding angles have the same measure and corresponding sides are in proportion.* The next day during the mathematics lesson, Ms. Lee noticed some confusion and posed the following question, "What does the term *similar* mean in geometry?" One student replied, "Similar means that the shapes are like each other." Not sure what the student meant by the phrase "are like each other," Ms. Lee responded, "Could you give us an example?" The student's response indicated her partial understanding, "Two rectangles are similar because they are both rectangles. They both have ninety-degree angles and parallel sides."

NCTM Standard:
Geometry

Grade 6

Notice that this student is using a nonmathematical definition of similar—having characteristics of likeness—rather than the mathematical definition—having corresponding angles with the same measure and corresponding sides in proportion. However, the student is not completely incorrect, as angle measurement is important when considering similarity. This is a case where the mathematical meaning of a word is more restrictive and precisely stated than its everyday meaning, and yet they overlap, creating confusion.

To push the student's thinking, Ms. Lee drew two rectangles on the board, one long and narrow and one a square. (She chose a square to remind students that a square is a rectangle with the special characteristic that its sides are all the same length.)

Then she redirected the question to the entire class: Are these rectangles similar?

As students contributed to the discussion, some agreeing and others disagreeing that they were similar, the class as a whole was required to reflect on the mathematical meaning of the word *similar*. Guided by Ms. Lee, the term was linked to many examples, some of which did fit the mathematical definition and some of which did not. The students discussed each one in turn.

The discussion then returned to the task of determining a definition of the word *similar*. One student stated, "I think similar figures have the same shape but are different sizes." Another student added, "And to have the same shape they have to have the same angle measures." In order to further assist students in understanding the mathematical use of *similar*, Ms. Lee directly addressed the confusion with everyday language by suggesting, "Let's compare the meaning of *similar* in everyday life with its meaning in math." She organized student responses on the blackboard into two columns, mathematical meaning and nonmathematical meaning, and asked a number of students to summarize the class responses.

Ms. Lee often relies on the technique of calling attention to the everyday meaning of a word and contrasting it with its mathematical sense by writing two columns of examples on the board. This type of careful consideration of vocabulary not only helps students heighten their awareness of the differences between technical terms and everyday language, but also helps them broaden and deepen their understanding of concepts like *similarity*. In effect, she is using the everyday meaning of a word—something most students will know—as a tool in helping students focus and reflect on its distinctive mathematical meaning, which may be new for many students.

NCTM Standard:
Measurement

Grade 2

We know that misunderstandings can be caused by a student's shallow understanding of the mathematical meaning of a word, and an overreliance on its everyday meaning. Discussion about mathematical definitions can clarify these misunderstandings. For example, in a second-grade classroom the teacher, Ms. Bajwa, asked her students to write down the numerical expressions for different times of day. For the time "quarter past ten," a number of students wrote *10:25*. At first, Ms. Bajwa thought that the students did not know how to tell time. She asked the students to tell her the meaning of *quarter*. One student replied, "Twenty five of something." When she probed further, asking other students for meanings of the word *quarter*, several gave the definition "a piece of money that is twenty-five cents." Since a quarter has a value of twenty-five cents, the students had assumed that a quarter past ten was twenty-five minutes past ten.

This is a common misunderstanding, particularly in the lower elementary grades. For many children, the first meaning of *quarter* they encounter is the meaning related to money. Once students learn about fractional parts of a whole, they can start the process of connecting the facts they know into a more coherent conceptual understanding. A student with a full understanding of the word *quarter* will know that the quantity it names depends upon the quantity of the whole: A quarter of 100 is 25, but a quarter of 60 is 15. Ms. Bajwa's students, like others you may have encountered, thought it referred to a specific quantity rather than a fraction of a whole.

Getting students to understand the fractional meaning of *a quarter* is not easy; it takes time. Teachers who have already introduced concepts like one half and one fourth might schedule a discussion in which they talk about how *one-fourth* and *one-quarter* are two ways of saying the same thing. In this context, discussion of the meaning of *quarter* in the case of money versus time can move students closer to this understanding. If you, like Ms. Bajwa, are not ready to enter into a discussion of fractional parts of a whole, you can nevertheless be prepared for misunderstandings based on some students' limited understanding of the word *quarter* as a name for the quantity 25.

Extending Students' Knowledge Through Talk About Words

A further reason to talk about definitions of words and phrases is to extend students' knowledge. In Ms. Lee's classroom, the discussion about the word *similar* led to another discussion about the meaning of the word *congruent*. Logical relationships between the two words were introduced: If two shapes are congruent, are they also similar? And if two shapes are similar, are they also congruent? What started out as a short explanation of the word *similar* resulted in students learning more than was presented in the textbook. Definitions can play an important part in extending students' general knowledge when discussions about definitions require students to think about networks of underlying concepts.

NCTM Standard:
Geometry

Grade 6

Sometimes teachers must also monitor students' understanding of nonmathematical terms! When students do not know the meanings of words and phrases in a problem, they may have difficulty making sense of the content under discussion. For example, in the case in Chapter 2 in which the fifth-grade class was working on a problem about the number of peach tarts that could be made using a set number of peaches, a few students did not know what a peach tart was. They mistakenly confused it with the popular breakfast food Pop-Tarts. This confusion, though minor, made it difficult for them to follow other students' explanations of their solution processes. The students wondered why their classmates were representing the peach tarts with round circles since Pop-Tarts are rectangular. Unfortunately, students often focus on irrelevant features of problems, in part because they are trying to make sense of those features they find confusing. By discussing vocabulary and phrases, and by providing background information, teachers can help students understand the context of a problem (which will improve problem solving), and they can also extend students' overall knowledge of the world.

Building and Monitoring Common Understandings

Whenever talk is used as an instructional tool in the classroom, it's important for students and the teacher to be in agreement on definitions. They must work at maintaining what is sometimes referred to as "shared meaning" or "common ground" so that everyone can follow a discussion as it develops. Central to the use of mathematical discourse is the premise that students and teacher will work toward common understandings that are satisfactory to all. The greatest value of this practice becomes apparent after a short time: When all students and the teacher have explicitly agreed upon facts, definitions, and procedures, this shared understanding becomes part of the ongoing discourse and helps move the whole class forward. Time invested in building a solid common ground of understanding pays off in multiple ways.

NCTM Standard:
Geometry

Grade 3

What do shared understandings look like in practice? Not surprisingly, they take time to build. Mr. Radulfo asked his third graders to sort into two groups a variety of solid figures— pyramids, cones, cylinders, rectangular prisms, triangular prisms, spheres, and cubes. Then he held a class discussion regarding the sorting characteristics that students used. Here are a few student responses:

- My group sorted them [solids] by looking at how all of these are flat [points to flat faces of prisms, cubes, and pyramids] and all of these are curved [points to curved surfaces of cones, cylinders, and spheres].
- We used the flat sides too, but we sorted them by a flat base or not a flat base.
- I separated the blocks by the roundness or flatness of the faces.

Students used a variety of words to describe the same idea—*side, face, base, flat surface*—but because they were able to point to a physical feature on the actual blocks, everyone was able to make sense of each individual student's contributions. If there had been confusion about the different terms for the side of a prism, Mr. Radulfo would have needed to shift the discussion in order to clarify the meaning of each word. Note that this discussion was not intended as a discussion of vocabulary. Students were describing the basis for their sorting of shapes. The teacher intended to address solid geometry vocabulary *after* the students were familiar with the solids and their characteristics. Nevertheless, he had to carefully follow the words that students used, in order to make sure that everyone was following the meaning of the discussion. He also had to monitor whether all students had access to what those words referred to. In this case, he had to ascertain whether all students could see what the speaker was pointing to when using a word like *side* or *face*.

When the discussion is not about common physical objects, this monitoring process can get more challenging, but it becomes even more important. In some cases, teachers have to briefly stop a discussion in order to make sure that everyone agrees on the meaning of a word or phrase. During the discussion in Mr. Radulfo's class, one boy, Armin, kept calling a *cube* a *square*. Pointing to a collection of cubes, Armin said, "These squares are all different sizes." Mr. Radulfo decided to call attention to this in a sympathetic way.

1. Mr. R: Armin, let's slow down right here. It's hard to follow sometimes when people talk about these shapes. Let's take a moment to talk about the terms we're using. Armin is labeling these shapes as *squares*. Donna, do you agree or disagree? Is that what you call them?

2. Donna: Well, I was calling them *cubes*. But I don't know. . . .

3. Mr. R: I think a lot of people call them squares. Can someone tell me why people might call this shape [holds up a cube] a *square*?

4. Donna: I think people might call them a square because they're square.

5. Mr. R: Tell us what you mean when you say they're square.

6. Donna: Well, I mean the sides are squares. See? [She picks up a cube and points to a face.]

7. Mr. R: Does someone remember another word we used for *sides* here?

8. Felicia: *Faces*. We said faces are square. So a cube has square faces.

9. Mr. R: OK, so there's an interesting thing here: We said that
these solid shapes are three-dimensional, right? And
we talked about two-dimensional shapes, right? So
let's think about the words *square* and *cube*. Who can
tell me which is a name for a three-dimensional object,
and which is a name for a two-dimensional object? Talk
to your partner for one minute.

As he walked around listening to the partner talk sessions, Mr. Radulfo saw
that virtually all the students were able to make the connection between three
dimensions and *cube* and two dimensions and *square*. By using partner talk, he
had given extra time to the few students who were still trying to make this connection. In the discussion that followed, he called on those students with
weaker understanding and gave them a chance to demonstrate their knowledge
of the difference between names for two- and three-dimensional shapes in this
case. He then decided to extend the discussion to cylinders, another case where
students often use the more common two-dimensional term *circle* instead of the
infrequent term *cylinder*. In that discussion, he learned that some students did
not have a firm grasp of the term *cylinder* in the first place, calling it a "cyn-
daler" and "a silo shape." After using the discussion (and the blackboard) to
make sure that everyone knew how to say and spell *cylinder*, Mr. Radulfo
returned to the confusion that had started the whole discussion.

1. Mr. R: [Holding up a cylinder] So we just said this is a three-
dimensional object, right? And that its mathematical name is
a *cylinder*. But let's say we heard someone calling it a *circle*.
Why do you think they might be saying that?

2. Ben: I think somebody might say that because the ends of the
cylinder are circles. Like the sides of the cube are squares.

Mr. Radulfo was able to use this discussion of names for shapes and solids
to go beyond the original misunderstanding in a way that strengthened all students' understanding of two and three dimensions, and that helped them see
that language is part of what makes math complicated and sometimes difficult,
but interesting! It is worth giving some time and attention to the words and
expressions we use, discussing them in their own right. The words and expressions often provide the perfect entry point into better understanding of the
concepts themselves.

Sometimes teachers of kindergarten and pre-K students feel that an
extended discussion might be too much for their students. We think that it's a

good idea to start gradually, but you may be surprised at how well your kindergarteners respond. One good place to start is by focusing on getting students to use a common set of words to refer to the same things. In the higher grades this takes the form of getting students to use a word with its technical meaning: *denominator* or *relative frequency* or *slope*. In discussions, teachers can bring students to use a technical term in a consistent way. In kindergarten, teachers can bring students into the same practice and mind set by getting them to use a common set of terms in a shared activity. This helps very young students develop their ability to pay attention to the words used for different objects, actions, and concepts.

Mrs. Johnson introduced a classification game to her kindergarten: Guess My Object. In this game, sets of objects with different properties—colors, shapes, sizes—are set out on the floor in the middle of a circle. The teacher selects one object and puts it behind her back. She then calls on students to ask her a question, such as, "Do you have a blue star?" If the teacher does not have a blue star hidden, the students can take all the blue stars and remove them from the pile. Mrs. Johnson first introduces the students to the objects. She makes sure that everyone can label each object in the same way, including its color, shape, and size.

NCTM Standard: Geometry

Grade K

1. Mrs. J: So who can tell me what we call this? [Holds up a red star]

2. Students: It's a star! A star. A shape!

3. Mrs. J: I heard people say "a star." Can someone find another one like it? Jeremy? Can you find another star?

4. Jeremy: [Picks a blue star out of the pile.] This one.

5. Mrs. J: OK, Sandra, do you agree with Jeremy that that's a star?

6. Sandra: [Says nothing.]

7. Mrs. J: [Waits for fifteen seconds.] Jeremy, hold up the shape you picked again. OK, Sandra, here's Jeremy's and here's mine. Do you think we can call them both stars?

8. Sandra: Jeremy's is blue and yours is red.

9. Mrs. J: Good observation! Do other people agree? Who agrees that Jeremy's is blue and mine is red?

10. Karen: I agree. But yours is a star and his is a star too.

11. Mrs. J: OK, let's see how we can tell that each one is a star. Mine has how many points [gets students to count with her]? One, two, three, four, and five! Does someone think they can count the points on Jeremy's shape? Mina?

12. Mina: One point, two, three, four, five.

13. Mrs. J: OK, good. So Jeremy's has five points and mine has five points. Should we call them both stars?

14. Tony: A red star and a blue star!

15. Mrs. J: OK, let's call this a red star and this a blue star. OK, everybody say those together. [Holds up red star as all repeat:] RED STAR! [Holds up blue star as all repeat:] BLUE STAR! Great! Now can somebody find another blue star in the pile?

After the students have spent several minutes finding red stars and blue stars, Mrs. Johnson invites them to notice the different sizes of the stars. There are large stars and small stars. Next she invites the students to consider the other shapes, which are all triangles, blue and red, large and small. A similar discussion ensues. When she is finally ready to begin the game, the students are well practiced in referring to the classes of objects in a common fashion.

This kind of game, and the preparatory discussion, may look very different from those we describe in higher grades, but the principle is the same. Mathematical thinking and learning require students to use language in precise and coordinated ways. This is somewhat different from their everyday language use, so we can help them get used to it by gently engaging in discussion in ways that help them practice these things.

Discussing the Meanings of Symbols

Mathematics is sometimes referred to as a language, partially because of its symbolic notation. Symbols enable us to express ideas unambiguously and to form precise statements about quantitative relationships. But symbols can be misunderstood and used incorrectly, especially by young learners, just as words can. As a result, we also need to talk about the meanings and uses of a variety of symbols.

One of the most important symbols students encounter is often misunderstood. Researchers have shown that many students do not see the equal sign (=) as a statement of equivalence (Carpenter, Franke, and Levi 2003; Kieran and Chalouh 1993). Instead they interpret this symbol as a signal to "write the answer."

When students rely on this interpretation of the equal sign, they might respond to the following equation, $12 + 8 = \underline{} + 12$, by replacing the blank with 20 instead of 8. Further evidence of this misunderstanding of the meaning of the equal sign is seen in the common practice of writing a chain of partial calculations that are connected by the equal sign (Stacey and MacGregor 1997). For example, the expression $1 + 6 = 7 \times 4 = 28 \div 2 = 14$ may be written by a student as a "running record" of thinking: first add 6 to 1, then multiply the sum by 4, and finally divide by 2. However, as an expression out of context, it's incorrect and misleading because it implies that $1 + 6 = 7 \times 4$ and that $7 \times 4 = 28 \div 2$.

Just as words take on different meanings in different contexts, so do symbols. For example, a fraction bar can be interpreted in a number of ways. It can indicate a fraction ($\frac{2}{3}$—two parts out of three parts); a division ($\frac{2}{3}$—two divided by three); or a ratio ($\frac{2}{3}$—two items compared to three items). We need to find out what preconceived notions students have about symbols and orchestrate discussions that build on students' current understanding as we introduce them to new interpretations as well. One very useful practice we recommend is to call students' attention to the multiple meanings of a symbol or word. When we introduce a new meaning for a symbol, we explicitly ask students first to put into words their understandings of that symbol. Just as Ms. Lee did in the example concerning the term *similar*, we can ask students to give us examples of the meaning of the symbol they are already familiar with. We might ask them to remember a previous lesson in which it was used in the way they are familiar with. The class can organize these examples on the board into one coherent meaning for the symbol. The teacher can then introduce the new meaning in explicit contrast to the old meanings. Even young students are able to accept that there can be more than one meaning for a word. They are also able to accept that there can be more than one meaning for a symbol. But in order to do this, they need time to work through the meanings explicitly. Group discussion, conducted using the talk moves we describe, is an effective way to help students work through different meanings for words or symbols.

Sometimes teachers avoid introducing extra discussion of multiple meanings of words or symbols in mathematics, thinking it will only confuse their students. In fact, we have found that discussion of the kind we describe in this book actually reduces confusion and supports more robust understanding. Only after students have discussed and solidified their current understandings do we introduce the new meaning. Over time, we have seen real improvement in students' ability to monitor their own use of symbols and words. Their written and spoken expression becomes more precise, and they are more mindful of how they formulate their ideas in words. They also become more willing to exert effort to understand how others are using words or symbols!

Even young children can benefit from participating as active "meaning makers" in discussions of symbol meaning. Young children are just learning about using symbols as a form of representation. They often know less about the symbols used to represent a computational procedure than the actions associated with the procedure. Teachers can use young students' knowledge of the actions involved in a procedure to strengthen their understanding of the symbols. They may know, for example, that Julia has eight candies in all if she had five and her friend gave her three more, but they may not know that this situation can be represented with symbols as $5 + 3 = 8$. This should not be surprising—there is no intrinsic quality of symbols that signals their meaning. They are social conventions that children become familiar with over time and with much experience. Discussion, however, can help link young children's understanding of a computational procedure and the symbols used to represent it.

Mrs. Hartwig presented this problem to her first-grade class:

Julia has five candies. Her friend gives her three more candies. How many candies does Julia have in all?

NCTM Standard:
Connections

Grade 1

She gave the children the chance to work on the problem individually and encouraged them to record their calculations in any way that made sense to them. Some used manipulatives such as small trays of beans kept in the work area.

1. Mrs. H: Who wants to tell us how they figured out how many candies Julia had in all? Tim? What about your method?

2. Tim: I took five beans and got three more. So I said, "Five." And then I counted: "Six, seven, and eight."

3. Mrs. H: So Julia had eight candies? Is that right? [Tim nods.] Good. I noticed that Geri wrote something to solve the problem. Here's what she wrote.

$5 + 3 = 8$

Does anyone see any connection between Tim's actions with the beans and Geri's number sentence? Meli?

4. Meli: The five in what she wrote is the five beans that Tim started with. The little *t* means to add three beans. And then it equals eight!

5. Mrs. H: Does anyone know what we call the little *t*? Does it always tell us to add three?

6. Sierra: It's called a plus sign. It means to do something to the numbers.

The purpose of this discussion was to help students start to link actions on real objects with the number sentence that symbolizes them. Due to the complexity and variety of mathematical symbols, students will not likely make this connection on their own. Yet making this connection is crucial to success with computation. Mrs. Hartwig uses discussion to clarify both the identification and meaning of the addition symbol. She does this by asking another student to react to her classmate's suggested name and meaning. By having students offer both ideas and clarifications, Mrs. Hartwig is allowing them to develop their own shared, accurate interpretation of the symbols they'll use in future computations. This discussion could extend in a number of helpful ways, but even this short stretch shows that careful use of talk can help students make sense of new conventions using words or symbols.

DISCUSSION AND REFLECTION

1. Can you recall examples from your own teaching where the every-day meaning of a word seemed to cause difficulties with students acquiring the mathematical meaning of the word?

2. Can you recall examples where student knowledge of the everyday meaning of a word *helped* them understand the mathematical meaning of a word?

3. Consider the meaning of the equal sign in mathematics. How might you define *equal* for students at your grade level? What will your students say the symbol means? Are there particular problem contexts in which we use the term *equal* but perhaps shouldn't? If there are potential confusions at your grade level, how could you plan a discussion that might clarify these?

4. Reread the vignette about Mr. Radulfo's class discussing two-dimensional and three-dimensional shape names. Imagine that they continued talking about cylinders and a student asked how many faces a cylinder has. Mr. Radulfo suddenly realizes that he does not know how many faces a cylinder has! Is it the two ends only, or does the surface of the curved part count as a face? Math discussions sometimes lead to territory where the teacher is not sure of the correct answer. What could he do in this case? What would you do?

PART
III

Implementing
Classroom Discussions

8

Getting Started

Talk is productive in math class when it is used to strengthen students' mathematical thinking and reasoning. Student talk must be respectful, engaged, and focused on mathematics; only when both the social and the mathematical aspects of communication are in place do we find that classroom talk offers maximum support for learning. In this chapter, we first introduce five principles for you to keep in mind as you make plans to incorporate talk into your mathematics teaching. Following these are five approaches we have found helpful as you and your students start to talk during math lessons. Finally, we introduce some practical suggestions for tracking your own progress in making talk an integral part of your math instruction.

Five Principles of Productive Talk

Principle 1: Establishing and Maintaining a Respectful, Supportive Environment
Principle 2: Focusing Talk on the Mathematics
Principle 3: Providing for Equitable Participation in Classroom Talk
Principle 4: Explaining Your Expectations About New Forms of Talk
Principle 5: Trying Only One Challenging New Thing at a Time

The following five principles deal with the major issues you will encounter as you start to build this kind of productive talk in your classroom. You will recognize some of these topics from the discussion of ground rules for respectful talk and equitable participation in Chapter 2. Here they have been formulated into principles so that you may more easily incorporate them into your mathematics teaching practice.

Principle 1: Establishing and Maintaining a Respectful, Supportive Environment

It's common knowledge that learning takes place most easily within an atmosphere of respect and support. We have all had the positive experience of learning in a supportive environment, and have seen what it can do for us. Conversely, we have all experienced the feeling of being silenced or shut down, of not wanting to speak up because we are afraid of ridicule or criticism. Neither students nor teachers will engage in productive talk about mathematics if they are afraid that they will be laughed at, "dissed," or somehow made to feel stupid. Therefore, it's important to emphasize the positive and forestall the negative. A big part of the preparation for using talk in mathematics involves putting in place classroom norms that will ensure a safe and supportive place for people to talk about their thinking.

As we discussed in Chapter 2, setting the ground rules for a respectful classroom culture must come first. It's helpful to emphasize to students that each of them has a right to be heard and have their ideas considered with respect. Along with this right comes an obligation: the obligation to listen to others just as they themselves will be listened to. We think it's important to emphasize the positive aspects of respectful discourse—the good thinking and learning that can emerge in a civil and supportive environment, and the pleasure of thinking together with one's classmates. It's important, however, to make clear to students that this respectful discourse is not optional, and that there are sanctions for failing to maintain the norms of respect that you set up. In later sections of this chapter, we provide concrete suggestions for how to implement this principle in your classroom.

As your students become more adept at talking about mathematics, you will be able to discuss with them further ramifications of respectful discourse in mathematics. For example, in your classroom students will have a right to have their ideas taken seriously. This means, however, that they are obligated to try very hard to make their thinking available to others and communicate their thoughts as clearly as they can. To some extent, this happens naturally. As students have their ideas taken seriously, they begin to try harder to get those ideas across. They don't give up as easily, and they begin to pursue the consequences of their own ideas and those of others. Although this may happen naturally over time, it is nevertheless important to remind students from the start that they should try to communicate their mathematical thinking as clearly and explicitly as possible.

Principle 2: Focusing Talk on the Mathematics

As you establish norms for respectful discourse, you should simultaneously make sure that classroom talk is focused on the mathematical content and reasoning that is relevant to the lesson. Be sure to tell students that the role of talk in math class is to help them understand the mathematics they are studying, and that a thorough and solid understanding for everyone is the goal. To make sure that you and the students maintain this focus, you need to prepare lessons carefully, considering ahead of time how the mathematical topics and procedures might play out in the classroom talk. Using the categories of mathematics and ideas introduced in Part Two, Chapter 3–7, you can decide how to focus the talk in mathematically fruitful directions. In this way, a focus on talk can strengthen not just your students' understanding, but your own as well.

Principle 3: Providing for Equitable Participation in Classroom Talk

All students can benefit from the kinds of discourse practices we are describing, not just those who are actively speaking, but also those who are listening. Yet it's important to think carefully about equitable participation. This has two aspects: how to make it possible for all students to participate actively in the talk from time to time, and how to make certain that all students are listening actively all of the time. If a student rarely has an opportunity to talk, that student does not have full access to participation. If a student can participate in the talk but is not listened to seriously, again, there is a problem with equitable participation. Finally, if a student does not listen, that student does not have access to participation.

One of the core obligations of teaching is to provide equal access to learning for all students. However, in every class there are challenges to achieving this goal. Some students are eager to discuss mathematics and feel confident doing so. Others, however, may seem diffident, reluctant to participate, even resentful of being asked to talk out loud. Still others may seem not to understand, or may understand so quickly that you fear they will be bored as others talk. Dealing with the variety of personalities, knowledge, and attitudes that one finds in any classroom is always a challenge. While this challenge will not disappear when you use talk in your classroom, carefully orchestrated talk may help. It may allow you to bring more students into the excitement of thinking mathematically, students who may not have participated as enthusiastically in the more traditional forms of instruction. Patterns of participation may change in ways that surprise and delight you. Many teachers have reported to us that as they began to focus on giving all students opportunities to talk about their ideas, they were pleasantly surprised by what they learned about their students' thinking.

The traditional method of calling on students (whether or not they have raised their hands) gives the teacher maximum control of who talks in the conversation. Some teachers augment this with a variety of methods of assigning turns. For example, some teachers institute a "gender rule" for taking turns, in which boys and girls alternate. In a class where girls don't participate as actively as boys, or vice versa, this rule supports girls (or boys) by making every other turn in the talk an opening for them. Some teachers allow a student to nominate the next speaker after he or she has finished speaking. This can be useful when there are one or two students who tend to monopolize the floor. Some teachers institute a reward system whereby students receive points for volunteering a question or an explanation (not an answer!). (There should be a limit to the number of points that can be gained this way, as otherwise the "monopolizers" will be encouraged.) Each classroom and school has its own set of norms for taking turns, but we encourage you to think creatively about this important aspect of setting up the conditions for equal participation in productive talk.

Principle 4: Explaining Your Expectations About New Forms of Talk

Preparatory discussion is essential whenever you introduce a new form of instruction so that students understand your expectations. To this end, explain clearly how you want students to participate in talking. Students often find it helpful to hear your reasons for asking them to engage in this new form of talk. Help them understand what the talk will accomplish and how it might improve their mathematics learning. We suggest that you do this every time you introduce a new form of talk, and follow up with numerous refreshers at later dates as necessary.

It's very likely that there will be some students in your class for whom discussion of their ideas with adults is comfortable and familiar. But for other students, this form of activity will be completely new. Some students are from social or cultural backgrounds in which it's not typical for children to engage in talk on intellectual topics with adults. These children may be more used to listening attentively to what adults say, or to learning through careful observation. These students may need to hear that this type of talk is expected in school. Furthermore, some immigrant students may come from countries where students are never allowed to talk in school and the very idea may be confusing and even upsetting. For several reasons, then, it makes sense to first discuss what you are expecting students to do, and to make explicit why you think talk is a good idea. You may have to repeat this reasoning more than a few times, as students gradually get used to this new way of interacting.

Principle 5: Trying Only One Challenging New Thing at a Time

Creating the conditions for productive talk is a complex task that involves coordination of several different things at once. Therefore, to keep things manageable, try one challenging new thing at a time. When introducing a new talk format or move, make sure that the mathematical concepts or procedures you are talking about are familiar to all of the students in the class. Conversely, when you are introducing challenging new mathematical content, make sure that the talk routines you are using are familiar and can be used comfortably by all the students in the class. As the examples in the following section will illustrate, you may wish to introduce the key talk moves described in Chapter 2 only one or two at a time.

It's important to give yourself and the students adequate time to use these new tools. Consider the first time you tried to type a document using a new word processor, or the first time you tried to take a train in another country where the language was not your first language. Skills and abilities that you usually take for granted can easily grind to a halt as you try to add on the challenging new behavior or skill. Not surprisingly, the same thing may happen as you begin to incorporate talk into your mathematics teaching. Some teachers report that they feel like they are juggling plates, or that they go blank at unexpected moments because of the new demands of trying to orchestrate student talk while thinking about mathematics. If this is true for teachers, imagine how much more challenging it is for students!

Therefore, it's important to think through how you plan to introduce the new talk format or routine. You want everyone to be able to participate in the still-unfamiliar talk, so everyone should already understand the mathematics to a great extent. These principles are designed to work together, and to interact in positive ways. For example, introducing only one new thing at a time (Principle 5) and being explicit about what you expect (Principle 4) will support participation by all students (Principle 3). If students must figure out the rules of the talk at the same time as they are being asked to think about mathematics, their performance will not be optimal and participation is likely to be uneven.

Five First Steps

Step 1: Practicing Two Talk Moves on Your Own
Step 2: Introducing Students to Talk-Centered Instruction
Step 3: Beginning with a Whole-Class Discussion
Step 4: Using Partner Talk
Step 5: Building and Supporting an Argument

Some of the practices and moves we describe here will now be familiar to you. Nevertheless, as you start the work of instituting productive talk in your mathematics class, they may serve your purposes in new ways. The following suggestions present several different ways to begin teaching mathematics in a talk-intensive fashion.

Step 1: Practicing Two Talk Moves on Your Own

Two of the talk moves we have introduced, revoicing and wait time, are moves that are primarily used by the teacher. They are under your control—students do not have to be aware of what you're doing. But just as you should "try one new thing at a time" with your students, you should allow yourself to ease gradually into using these moves. Even before you begin the process of introducing your students to talk in math class, you may want to spend several lessons trying out these two moves without fanfare, using them yourself to get the feel of how they can help you support student understanding.

You might set up a lesson in which students must present their solutions for a particular problem. It can be a problem that is new to them. You are not going to present them with any new talk moves that they must execute, so they can focus on the mathematics. You will be using revoicing and wait time to help them.

Revoicing

If you have asked students to present their solution strategies for a challenging problem, it is very likely that students' responses will be unclear. Sometimes it seems as though *all* students' responses are unclear. As soon as a student says something unclear, you have a perfect opportunity to try a revoicing move. Recall the discussion about peach tarts from Chapter 2. Imagine that you have asked for a solution strategy and a student has said, "I just drew it and then I drew lines for the things." Respond to the student: "So you're saying that you drew a picture of a peach tart and then you drew lines for things?" Or perhaps, "So you're saying you drew lines for things . . . ?" Let the student respond to your question. If the response is still unclear, you may want to formulate a further question: "So can you explain what you mean when you say you drew lines for things?" This is a good point of entry to a deeper discussion of the student's meaning. Using this very simple tool of revoicing, you're on your way to getting students to respond more thoughtfully, carefully, and clearly than they might otherwise. You are letting them know that you welcome their elaboration of their reasoning.

Try to use this move with several different students during the lesson. Practice it for several days until you feel completely comfortable using it. Remember that it's very important not just to repeat what the student said and then move on; rather, you must repeat or rephrase, but then ask the student whether that is the correct interpretation of what he or she was trying to say. You can do this with a rising intonation—"So you're saying you think it's thirteen?" Or you can make it a statement followed by an explicit question—"So you're saying you think it's thirteen. Is that what you said?"

Early on you may find yourself using revoicing when it's not needed. You may feel slightly silly as you start to overuse it: Many teachers have told us that they hear themselves using it when the student has said something quite simple and clear. "So, you're saying that two times three is six? Is that what you're saying?" "Umm, yes", the student may say, eyeing you warily. You will soon become better at using it when a student is really vague or unclear, and avoiding it when it's not needed.

What if a student has produced an important and clear contribution, but you don't think everyone has heard it? You may want to "rebroadcast" it for others to hear by using revoicing. You may also want to use the revoicing move to help students expand their reasoning. Consider again this student response from Case 3, Episode 2 in Chapter 2. Recall that the students are trying to clarify their representation of the peach tarts problem.

24. Tyavanna: I drew ten peaches? And . . . um . . . like . . . um, I think that's what you have to do because you have to show the thirds of the peaches? 'Cause that's what you have to figure out to make the tarts. Not the other way around.

At this point the teacher might have chosen to revoice Tyavanna's contribution by expanding and clarifying it, then asking her if this expanded version was in agreement with her intention:

Ms. Stangle: So Tyavanna, you're telling us that if we want to know how many tarts we can make, we have to use the fact that each tart takes two thirds of a peach? And so we have to figure out how many sets of two thirds we have in our ten peaches? And so that means we have to *draw* the ten peaches so we can work with those? Is that what you're saying?

Tyavanna: Yes, because if we drew the tarts instead, that wouldn't tell us anything about the peaches. We don't even know how many tarts to draw, because we don't know how many we can make.

In this case, Ms. Stangle's use of revoicing to clarify and expand Tyavanna's answer actually motivated Tyavanna to clarify even further. By the end of this interchange, the entire class could follow Tyavanna's logical reasoning about her choice of what to represent in her problem solution.

Revoicing in small-group discussion   If you feel unsure about using revoicing in a large-group discussion of problem solving, there is an even more low-key way to begin trying it out. Most teachers use small-group work to allow students to work together on solving problems. Small groups have advantages and disadvantages. Many researchers have found that they give shy or less advanced students a chance to participate that is not available in large groups. On the other hand, small-group work can sometimes put such students at more of a disadvantage, unless the groups are carefully structured and monitored. For example, low-status students may especially suffer in small-group work. Also, teachers obviously cannot be everywhere at once, so small-group talk may not yield consistent results. Nevertheless, it can be a particularly good venue for you to begin to practice the revoicing move. Give the students a problem, selected according to the same criteria as we have discussed for a whole-class discussion. Make sure it's a problem that is familiar to the students, and for which most students will be likely to find some solution. Make sure that multiple solution strategies are possible. Ask the students to take ten minutes to solve the problem in groups of three or four.

Focusing on understanding, not correcting   As students discuss the problem in their small groups, circulate around the room, listening. After a few minutes, start to interact with different groups. Ask: "What solutions are you coming up with?" Or: "Can you explain to me what you all are doing to solve the problem?" When they tell you, repeat their solution back to them to check if you understand it. You can say, for example: "So you're saying that [fill in with their solution]. Is that right?" This will get them to start realizing that they are responsible to put together a coherent explanation of their strategy. Just as important, it gives you time to process what they are saying. As students see you struggling to really understand what they are saying, they will start to try harder to communicate clearly with you.

There will be times when you cannot understand what students are saying to you. Resist the temptation to avoid the situation and move along. Both students and teacher can feel embarrassment when a student cannot be understood, but unless you persist in trying to get clarification, students will not learn that you intend to take their explanations seriously. One strategy is to draw on others in the group. If one student has given the explanation and you cannot follow it, first ask the student to clarify. If you still cannot understand, ask another student, saying: "Well, this is complicated, and I'm still not sure I understand. Can you put what he said in your own words, Jamal?" Try to get each student in the group to explain it in their own words.

It is important in small-group discussion, just as in whole-class discussion, that you focus the talk on promoting understanding. Many students have the habit of simply waiting for the teacher, or another student, to show them how to solve a problem. Resist the urge to show a group how to solve the problem. Instead, say: "Repeat the problem to me so that I'm sure that we both have the same understanding of what it is." Or: "Tell me what you know about the problem so far." Or: "What do you think you might do first?" Put the responsibility on their shoulders to make the effort of working on the problem. Also, refrain from telling groups whether their solutions are correct or incorrect. Instead, tell them that their solutions and explanations are the material you will use in a whole-class discussion.

Some groups may finish solving a problem well before other groups are done. A common technique that teachers use is to ask the group to solve the problem in another way. You might also suggest that the students who are finished talk with one another about how they will present their solution strategy: Who will introduce it and describe it? What should they write on the board? They might even practice delivering their explanation out loud.

Waiting

Another move to practice on your own, without fanfare, is wait time. During a large-group session, practice using wait time. Many of us think we are very good at waiting for students to answer. But if you actually time yourself, you may find that your average wait is only about two or three seconds. How can you time yourself if you are in the midst of teaching? Some teachers discreetly hit a stopwatch in their pocket and look at it later. Others make an audiotape of their class and listen to it later. Still others ask a friendly colleague to help them by observing and timing. Most people are surprised with the results, but self-knowledge is the first step when we are trying to change something.

Try to use wait time in your class in two ways. First, when you ask a question of the whole class, don't wait for just a few seconds and then call on the one or two students who have their hands up. Decide how long you will wait. Ten seconds is a good place to start. Then make your students see that you are willing to wait. (It may take ten or fifteen repetitions of your determined waiting before they will actually believe that you are willing to wait for them to think through the problem and come up with an answer.) Second, use wait time when you finally call upon an individual. When you run across a student who needs extra time, surprise the student by giving him or her thirty or forty seconds. Although it may seem excruciatingly awkward, it can take students that long to formulate an answer to a complex question, particularly if they are English language learners. If the student seems embarrassed, you can support his or her effort by saying: "These are complicated questions. It can take a long time to put something into words. That's OK. In this class we'll always wait for you to put your thinking into words."

Many teachers have the habit of skipping over students when they seem reluctant to answer questions. When a student doesn't answer after ten seconds or so, most of us move on to someone else. None of us likes to be viewed as "mean" or as teachers who put students on the spot. Nevertheless, in Project Challenge we have found that many students respond very well if we tell them, "OK, I'll come back to you in a few minutes." Then, after calling on one or two other students, we return to the student who could not answer previously. The additional time, plus the support of hearing the other students talk, often allows the reluctant student to put together an answer. This practice, along with the determined use of wait time, lets students know that you expect them to keep trying and to be able to participate eventually, even if they are stymied at the moment. It sends a message about your expectations for them, a message they will eventually hear.

Step 2: Introducing Students to Talk-Centered Instruction

After you have gotten a bit of practice using revoicing and wait time, begin to explicitly introduce your students to talk-intensive work in mathematics. How should you introduce your students to talk? As the first principle suggests, your first step should be about establishing the norms—the ground rules—for respectful and courteous discourse. In some classrooms these may already be in place. In other classrooms, teachers may need to introduce these separately, as the first step in the process. In addition, you need to introduce the actual talk moves that will require students to talk in new ways:

- Repeating: Can you repeat what [another student] just said?
- Reasoning: Do you agree or disagree with what [another student] just said? Why?
- Adding On: Who else would like to make a contribution?

In our view, the most effective way to introduce these moves is to tie them to your goal of supporting students' mathematical thinking, reasoning, and problem solving. This means that first you will introduce students to the idea that talking about mathematics can help them become better mathematical thinkers. Then you can discuss the conditions that have to be in place for this kind of talk to succeed. Finally, you can introduce the specific talk moves, explaining to students why each is worth doing.

For Pre-K Through Grade 2
You can use variations of the following phrases to introduce talk moves to your students. Adapt these to your students' needs and backgrounds:

- Thinking together about math can help us all understand math better.
- Each person's thinking is different and unique, and we can all learn from one another.
- We can think together by talking together about our thinking.
- What does it take for us to understand another person's thinking?

  We have to be able to hear what they say.

  We have to listen carefully and try to understand.

  We have to ask questions when we don't understand.

  We have to take turns so everybody who wants a chance gets one.

Then you can introduce the talk moves during a whole-class discussion.

With young children, it's a good idea to start with the talk move of asking a student to repeat what another student has said in his or her own words. Tell students before you begin that you will be asking them to repeat what they have heard. Explain that this will help everyone make sure that they have heard what the speaker has said, and that they have understood it. It's a good idea to ask several students in a row to repeat what the same speaker has said. This lets them know that each student's listening and speaking are important. It reminds children that they are responsible for listening carefully to every speaker.

It's also a good idea to ask young children to support their own reasoning from early on. When a student provides an answer, begin with a gentle follow-up: "So can you tell us about your reasoning?" Or: "Can you tell us why you think that's the answer?" This will soon lead even young children to begin talking about their reasoning. You can use the technique of revoicing to make sure that other children can hear and begin to understand what the speaker is saying.

As previous sections have indicated, one very useful talk move is asking students whether they agree or disagree with another student's idea or claim. Teachers of very young children may want to introduce this aspect of the practice only after the children are comfortable talking about their own thinking and listening to others. However, this move is certainly possible for very young children.

For Grades 3 Through 6

Here is a list of more advanced phrases to introduce older students to productive classroom talk. Keep in mind that students in this age range vary greatly in their ability to take in complex explanations for instructional practices. Rely on your own judgment in using and sequencing these suggestions. Remember to be explicit in your explanations and leave time for discussion and clarification of this important first step.

- Thinking together about math can help us all understand math better. Difficult problems often require more than one person to solve them. Furthermore, we can all learn new ways of thinking about mathematics from listening to how others think. Talking through our thinking can also help us clarify our own thoughts. If we try to communicate clearly, our thinking may get better as a result of our efforts.
- Thinking usually seems to go on inside one person's head. However, we can share our thinking by talking together about our ideas.

- What does it take for us to understand another person's thinking?

  We have to be able to hear the speaker. Everyone has a right to be heard.

  Everyone has an obligation to listen and to try to understand what the speaker is saying.

  We are obligated to ask questions when we don't understand.

  The speaker has an obligation to try hard to be clear.

  Everyone has a right to participate. How can we make sure that everyone has a chance to participate? [Here you might discuss your current methods of taking turns and ask your students to make suggestions.]

  What might keep people from participating? [Here a discussion of how people feel when others make fun of their thinking is a good idea. From this discussion you can derive your classroom's norms for courteous and respectful discourse, including agreements about what sanctions will be brought to bear on those who violate the norms.]

When you ask older students to explain their own reasoning, start by asking them to repeat what someone else said. This focuses the talk on clarification and shared understanding.

The "agree-or-disagree" move may best be introduced a bit later, depending upon your students' facility with this kind of interaction. When you introduce this move, it may be a good idea to emphasize the connection between Principle 2 (our talk is about mathematics) and Principle 1 (we practice respectful discourse). For example, when you ask students to agree or disagree with what another student said, it's helpful to emphasize that the agreement or disagreement is about the *idea* or about the *mathematics*, not about the *speaker*. In the social world of the classroom, people can be very sensitive to the interpersonal implications of agreeing or disagreeing with a position someone has taken. On the playground, disagreements may ignite an actual conflict or dispute. In mathematics, a disagreement is a way of moving forward, of getting closer to a mathematical understanding. But we should not assume that students will take to this norm with ease. In fact, we should expect, anticipate, and deal preemptively with the possibilities for hurt feelings and conflicts.

Project Challenge Rights

1. You have the right to make a contribution to an attentive, responsive audience.
2. You have the right to ask questions.
3. You have the right to be treated civilly.
4. You have the right to have your *ideas* discussed, not *you*.

Project Challenge Obligations

1. You are obligated to speak loudly enough for others to hear.
2. You are obligated to listen for understanding.
3. You are obligated to treat others civilly at all times.
4. You are obligated to consider other people's ideas, and to explain your agreement or disagreement with their ideas.

FIGURE 8–1 **Project Challenge chart.**

Some teachers have used such a discussion as an occasion to create a wall chart codifying the norms of respectful discourse and full participation. You can integrate your own concerns in this discussion, and the wall chart can be reviewed and changed as time goes on. Some teachers may want to introduce the first three principles to their students as a way to set up the classroom norms.

Teachers in Project Challenge distributed a version of this chart to all students to put in the front of their math notebook. (See Figure 8–1.) It was printed on green paper and became known as simply "the green sheet." When teachers encountered a problem with compliance or disrespect, they would simply say, "Take out the green sheet. Let's go over it again." You might want to construct your own "green sheet," adding to these rights and obligations and emphasizing issues that are of importance to your class.

A Detailed Introduction

An experienced teacher created the following passage to introduce her older students to many of the norms and moves we've described here. This introduction would probably be overwhelming for younger students, and many teachers might want to break it into smaller sections, introducing different parts at different times. Nevertheless, we include it here to give you an idea of the kinds of issues that should be explicitly addressed, either all at once or over time.

> You may be used to the kind of math class where the teacher asks the questions, you give the answers, and then the teacher tells you if you're right or wrong. If you're right, your turn is over. If you're wrong, the teacher then explains

to you what the right answer is. This math class is going to be different. Although I'll still ask you questions, when you give me an answer I'm going to ask you why you think what you think.

But being asked to explain your reasoning will probably not be the biggest difference between this class and others you've had in the past. In fact, a lot of you may be used to this. Here's what I think will be really different for you: When you give your answer and the reasoning behind it, I am usually not going to tell you whether you're right or not. Instead, I am going to ask your classmates to respond to your comment. I may ask them to restate the comment in their own words. Or, I may ask them to state whether they agree or disagree with your comment and explain why. In this class, when you speak, you're speaking to everyone in the room, not just me. When you're not speaking, you need to be listening.

By now, you may have two questions. Why am I making you do this? And how are you going to learn how to do this? I'll talk about the why part first. There are lots of reasons why I want you to learn math this way. The most important one is that I truly believe you'll learn more math more deeply this way. When I ask you to explain your reasoning or why you agree or disagree with a classmate's idea, you may at first say to yourself, "Oh, that's easy to explain." But when you try to put the right words together, you may find that there are some things you're still confused about. When you know what's confusing you, you can then get the help you need. The second reason is that one of the goals I have for you is to become better at communicating mathematically. You live in a world where being able to communicate what you know is just as important as knowing it. One day, you'll each have a career where you'll be asked to solve problems; maybe they'll be math or science problems; maybe they'll be other kinds of problems. You'll also be asked to present your solutions in a way so that others understand them and believe that they make sense. This class is going to prepare you to do just that.

Now on to the how part. Well, the first thing you need to do is talk. I know it can be scary to speak in public but trust me, the first few times are the hardest. If you're nervous, make your first few comments only one or two sentences in length just to get over the jitters. Next, you need to talk loudly enough for others to hear. Pretend as though every time you talk you are talking to someone seated on the opposite side of the room. Third, the content of each comment must be mathematical. Use mathematics vocabulary. Talk us through what you think, reason by reason. Talk us through your actions, step by step. Explain to us the mathematical sense behind your methods, strategies, and procedures. You don't have to say everything perfectly every time, but do strive to make each of your comments as clear and thorough as possible.

You also need to listen to what your classmates are saying when they speak. And when I say *listen*, I mean *really listen*. I'm not talking about the kind of listening where you hear the words but let them go in one ear and out the other. What you need to do is listen so that you can figure out what the other person thinks and why. If you listen like this, you'll be ready to respond in a meaningful way so that the discussion keeps moving forward toward the mathematical truth.

The last point I want to make is that we are in this together. You have my word that your ideas will be respected by your peers and by me. I will do everything I can to make sure that you feel safe to talk about what you know and don't know. So, as we get started with this endeavor, remember what's expected of you: Talk loudly and clearly when it's your turn. When it's not, listen so that you are ready to respond in a way that brings us closer to the mathematical truth.

Step 3: Beginning with a Whole-Class Discussion

After you have explicitly introduced the norms for respectful discourse, and have talked about the ways you will ask your students to talk about mathematics, you will want to introduce the norms and talk moves in an actual lesson. A good way to begin is to present the class with a math problem that supports multiple solutions. You will then ask students to present their solution strategies to the class. As they talk through their reasoning, you can introduce the talk move of asking students to repeat in their own words what someone else has said. You can ask them to explain why they chose a particular solution path. And you can practice the now-familiar revoicing move and the use of wait time to make sure that all students have been heard and understood.

Asking students to present multiple solutions is something that many teachers do already. As students talk through their reasoning over many such sessions, they learn the importance of communicating clearly and being understood by others, and begin to use language in precise and explicit ways. Often, students will recognize flaws in their reasoning or computational procedures as they make their solution strategies public. Finally, of course, students will get access to solution strategies beyond their own.

A good way to begin is to choose a problem that lends itself to being solved by several different strategies, or that can have multiple correct answers. In the early grades this might be a problem that relies on fairly simple computation, such as, "Jane is looking for three numbers that add up to thirty-seven. What three numbers will work?" For older students, you may present a multistep problem that they can solve using a variety of forms of representation and different computational steps, such as the peach tart problem presented in Chapter 2.

Keep in mind Principle 5: Try only one challenging new thing at a time. Make sure the problem is one that all of the students in your class can do. It helps to choose a type of problem with which they are familiar. You can make sure that the difficulty of the problem is manageable by choosing numbers for the problem that are "friendly" numbers. For example, in second grade, you can use the problem about Jane's three numbers, but instead of 37, choose 20 as the target number. After the students are comfortable with reporting out their solution strategies, you can make the target number more difficult. In a fifth-grade discussion of the peach tart problem, use one-half of a peach per tart instead of two-thirds. The type of problem is still the same, and it will still elicit multiple solutions. However, more students are likely to participate if the computational aspects of the problem are not made more difficult by using "unfriendly" numbers.

After all the students have discussed and understood the solution strategies, let them practice both the talk and the mathematics by introducing a slightly harder version of the same problem—move from one-half of a peach per tart to two-thirds of a peach per tart. If you have time, and if your students are ready, you can introduce harder numbers: seven-eights of a peach per tart, or one and two-thirds of a peach per tart. This is one way to smoothly integrate new talk formats while not losing sight of the mathematical content.

Starting Off
To start, introduce to your class what you expect them to do. As we mentioned, this serves Principles 1, 3, and 4. It helps ensure that all students can participate, as they will understand what you are doing. It also helps to ensure that students will feel safe making public contributions to the discussion. An

effective way to start off is to actually model what you expect students to do. For example, you might begin this way.

> Today as we go over this problem, I'm going to ask a number of you to explain your own solution strategy. I want you to tell us what you did to solve the problem. Now, there are lots of ways to solve this problem, but everyone tends to have their own way, the way that seems most natural to them. Today we want to hear about as many solution strategies as we can. If we can do that, we'll all learn new ways to think about problems like this. I'll go first and show you what I mean.

You would then slowly work through an explanation of one solution strategy, using the board as appropriate, going slowly enough that everyone can follow. You might then ask: "Does anyone else have a *different* way of solving the problem? Let's take some time to solve the problem. You can work with your partner to find a solution that's different from the one I just presented. Then I'll ask partners to present their solutions."

Slowing It Down and Asking for Repetitions

It is likely that many of the students' contributions will be hard for others (and possibly for you) to understand. Resist the urge to pass quickly over the unclear explanations. As students make their contributions, take the time to ask them to clarify their ideas so that they are as understandable as possible. For example, you might revoice what students say and then check with them to make sure you have correctly paraphrased their idea: "OK, Gloria, so you're saying that you first added ten and ten, and then you saw that you still had a long way to go to reach thirty-seven? Is that right?" When Gloria assents, you might then record that part of her solution on the board: *10 + 10 = 20.* Then say: "So what did you do next? You said that a little bit quickly, so I want to make sure that everyone understands."

In addition to your own revoicing, ask students to repeat what others have said. You can ask for exact repetitions ("Solange, can you repeat what Donny just said?") or you can ask for paraphrases ("Donny, can you put what Michael said into different words?"). If a student offers a particularly interesting or complex explanation, you can ask several students to put it into their own words. This will give all students a chance to hear it and think about it several times. You can also ask the original speaker whether the new renditions of his or her contribution are in fact what he or she intended to say ("Michael, is that what you intended to say?"). As students realize that their contributions are actually being listened to and understood by their classmates, their motivation for participating increases.

Encouraging Many Contributions

As students continue to add their solutions, at some point you may feel that there are no other distinct solution strategies. But recall that in this session, your purpose is to give students practice in talking out loud about their mathematical reasoning. So don't stop just yet. Ask the students: "OK, we have four different solution strategies up here on the board. This first one is Gloria's. Did anyone else use a strategy that is similar to Gloria's? Solange, can you tell us what you did?" If Solange says that her solution is just like Gloria's, ask her to put it into her own words. Continue to elicit solution strategies from students in this way. You may find that some did add a new twist that you didn't anticipate. Mathematically, this practice is valuable for several reasons. Not only do students get a chance to hear new strategies that differ from their own, but also they begin to develop a sense of classes of solution strategies, and of what is mathematically the same and different.

You may end up spending one entire mathematics class on a whole-class discussion of solution strategies for one problem! It may feel strange, but it's time well spent. If this is the first time you have used this practice, it might be enough to simply go through all the solution strategies in the class. If you have time, you may want to let the students try another, mathematically more challenging version of the problem, as described earlier. In either case, what is most important is that the talk is aimed at deepening the understanding of each student.

Keeping the Discourse Respectful and Keeping
Everyone Focused

As you go through the process of letting all students get the feel of making their reasoning public, you will be presented with a number of opportunities to reinforce the classroom norms that will support respectful and engaged talk. To create an environment of respect, you must first make sure that students actually attend to one another's contributions. Of course, it is appropriate and wise to remind students that you expect them to listen to one another. But there are several other ways that you can push students to internalize their own responsibility to abide by these norms. One is to remind students, when they make their contributions, that they must speak loudly enough for others to hear them.

At first this may seem intrusive. A quiet student is struggling to make his or her reasoning clear, and you are asking him or her to speak louder! For many of us, this strategy may even seem cruel—in many settings, it's not considered polite to force someone to speak up if they don't want to. However, one of the purposes of schooling is to gradually, over a span of years, enable students to do things that they would not be inclined to do on their own. We have seen some remarkable results come from years of gentle prompting to speak up so others can hear. Gradually, students gain the confidence to communicate their thoughts and eventually, as their confidence grows, their desire to communicate and think with others also grows.

This is a very rewarding outcome, but it doesn't happen overnight. So you must persist and be flexible. After you ask a student to speak up, if he or she gives it a try but is still too quiet to hear, you revoice what the student said, making sure that everyone can hear. As that student's contribution is taken seriously, with your help in making it available, the student will begin to gain the confidence that his or her contributions really do matter.

Asking students to repeat what another has said has several benefits. It lets all students know that they are responsible for listening to and understanding other students' ideas. It allows all students to hear the solution strategy more than once, and it keeps the discussion going since it gives everyone more time to reflect on what is being said. As you practice this consistently, reminding students that you will call on them to repeat in their own words what others have said, they come to expect your request and, miraculously, begin to pay closer attention to what their peers are saying. Finally, this move helps you avoid the common situation in which students are partially tuned out, simply awaiting their turn to talk, rather than listening to or building on what others have said. Your goal is for students gradually to come to treat one another as partners in mathematical thinking and reasoning.

NCTM Standard:
Number and Operations

Grade 5

The following example illustrates some of these problems and strategies in a whole-class discussion in which Mrs. Cardello is eliciting multiple solutions from her fifth-grade class. The teacher posed a question for the students: "Which is larger, three-fourths or seven-eighths?" The teacher asks Juan to give his answer and explain how he got that answer.

1. Juan: So first I thought about a rectangle and how if I divided it into four pieces then three would be colored in. And then I thought about the same rectangle, but cut into eight pieces, and I thought about what it would look like if seven were colored in, and I just knew that that one would be more.

2. Mrs. C: So who can put what Juan said into their own words for us? How about Gina?

3. Gina: Well, Juan said that he compared how each one would look if you colored in the parts that are the numerator.

4. Mrs. C: OK, that went by kind of fast for me. Let's see if we can put Juan's solution on the board. Gina, can you go over again what Juan did? Tell me what to draw up here.

5. Gina: OK, first he took the three-fourths and drew a picture of a rectangle and cut it into fourths.
[Mrs. Cardello draws a rectangle and divides it into fourths.]
Then he colored in the three-fourths.
[Mrs. Cardello colors in three-fourths of the rectangle.]
Then he drew the same size rectangle and cut it into eight pieces.
[Mrs. Cardello draws a rectangle and divides it into eighths.]
Then he colored in the seven-eighths of that rectangle and he saw it was more.

6. Mrs. C: [Finishes coloring in the seven-eighths.] OK, I see, so Gina said that you colored in the number of parts corresponding to the numerator. Juan, is that right? Is that your solution strategy?

7. Juan: Yes, but I didn't draw it, I just pictured it in my mind.

8. Mrs. C: OK, good, but we need to picture it up here so we can be sure we understand you. Did anyone use a different approach? Sheila?

9. Sheila: Well, I changed both of them into the same denominator, so three-fourths became six-eighths and seven-eighths became just what it was, and then seven is bigger than six.

10. Mrs. C: Patty, can you repeat what Sheila said in your own words?

11. Patty: [Looks embarrassed] I wasn't listening.

12. Mrs. C: OK, remember that it's really important to pay attention to what's going on; otherwise you'll miss the explanation and you won't be able to use that knowledge in your own work. Patty, go ahead and ask Sheila to repeat what she said. I'm sure she won't mind.

13. Patty: Can you repeat what you said please?

14. Sheila: I said that I took both the three-fourths and the seven-eighths and I changed them into the same denominator. That

way I could compare them. So three-fourths became six-eighths and seven-eighths stayed the same, so I could see that seven-eighths is bigger than six-eighths.

15. Mrs. C: OK, Patty, can you put that in your own words?

16. Patty: Um, so Sheila converted the two fractions to the same denominator and then she compared the numerators to see which one was bigger.

17. Mrs. C: OK, so Juan used a strategy of visualizing the two fractions as parts of a whole and comparing them, and Sheila used the strategy of finding a common denominator for both fractions and comparing the size of the numerator. Did anyone else use a different strategy?

Notice that in this example, in the final turn, Mrs. Cardello repeats the strategies used by both students, summarizing for the class what they have seen so far. She then asks for additional contributions. This helps keep everyone focused on what has been shared so far.

Step 4: Using Partner Talk

Many teachers are familiar with the general idea of this talk format, and often ask their students to "turn and talk" or "talk to your neighbor." This format has several benefits. It allows students to practice their ideas—to put them into words—before they face the entire class. It allows students to hear how one other student is thinking about the problem, perhaps giving them confidence that they too have a workable idea or giving them an idea of how to proceed if they are stuck.

Imagine that you are returning to a lesson from a previous day, in which students were solving a difficult problem on their own. You noticed on that previous day that some students were shy about presenting their solution strategies. You also noticed that because of the difficulty of the problem, students talked quite incoherently the first few times they tried to describe their strategies. You now want to give students a chance to practice talking about their solutions with one other person before you ask them to talk to the whole class. You can begin the lesson by reminding students about where you left off. Then tell them that you will be asking them to report on their solutions, but first they will have time for three to five minutes of partner talk. Tell them to refresh their memory and practice describing their solutions clearly by talking to their partner for a few minutes. Also tell them to ask questions whenever they're not sure about what their partner is saying.

During the three to five minutes in which they are talking to their partners, circulate and listen to their strategies. Listening to partners as they share strategies and solutions helps you identify students who have hit on the solutions that you think are mathematically important or interesting. Later, as you begin a whole-class discussion, you can use this information to call on particular students whose solutions you think will push the content of the discussion forward in mathematically important ways.

An example of this partner talk format is given in Chapter 2, Case 4, when Mr. Harris works with his students on division of fractions. You might wish to reread that case before going on.

Step 5: Building and Supporting an Argument

All teachers are proficient at asking questions, calling on individual students, and then evaluating whether the answer is right or wrong. Consider a sequence like this:

"Sarah, what is ninety-nine divided by eleven?" (Teacher initiates a question.)

"Nine?" (Student responds.)

"Yes, that's right . . . " (Teacher evaluates the answer.)

The teacher knows the answer to the question, and the student is aiming to get the right answer. While this method—called "quizzing" by some—has many legitimate uses, it has its limits. What is missing from the quizzing sequence? There is no place for the student to do more than supply an answer to a closed question. The focus is on the right answer and not the thinking process, and there is no opportunity for other students to agree or disagree. In other words, there is no way for deeper thinking to evolve.

Teachers can foster deeper thinking by adopting moves that address these missing pieces. In a situation in which the teacher is asking a question of students, she still initiates a question, and the student still tries to respond. But instead of offering an evaluation—a "yes, that's correct" or "no, that's not correct"—the teacher then asks the student a further question, a question aimed at getting the student to give evidence or offer a rationale for his or her answer. Finally, instead of evaluating or moving on, the teacher builds on the student's answer by asking another student if she agrees or disagrees with that answer, and why.

If you have introduced norms for respectful discourse, and students are now used to externalizing their reasoning, you can work toward this emphasis on argument and reasoning. Hold a discussion in which you make extensive use of Move 3, the "agree or disagree" move, and consistently follow it up with a request that students explain the basis for their agreement or disagreement. With older students, you may be able to adopt this practice almost from the beginning. With younger students, or with those who are less used to this kind of discourse, it may take somewhat longer.

NCTM Standard: Number and Operations

Grade 5

To start, the teacher should select a problem that offers rich potential for different solution paths, and complex reasoning. Students may or may not come up with different answers. If they do, the teacher will want to address that eventually, but the purpose of this session is to focus on the development of arguments and connected reasoning. A sequence may run something like this session in a fifth-grade classroom:

1. Ms. F: So which is larger, one-third or three-tenths? Edwina?

2. Edwina: I would say three-tenths.

3. Ms. F: OK, so what makes you think that? Give us your reasoning.

4. Edwina: Well, tenths are bigger than thirds, so three-tenths is going to be bigger than only one of thirds.

5. Ms. F: Denaldo, do you agree with what Edwina said? And tell us why you agree or don't agree.

6. Denaldo: Well, I don't agree with her answer because I think thirds are bigger than tenths. So I would say that maybe one-third is bigger, or maybe three-tenths. I'm not sure.

7. Ms. F: So you're not sure which is larger, but you would say that tenths are not larger than thirds. Is that right? [Denaldo nods.] Serena, do you agree or disagree? What's your view, and tell us why.

8. Serena: I agree with what Denaldo said about thirds are bigger, but I did it a different way. One-third is more than three-tenths, because if you draw a picture of ten-tenths, and then you shade in three of them, that won't be equal to cutting it up into thirds. You'd still need another tiny third of a tenth.

9. Ms. F: Denaldo, do you agree with what Serena said, and could you put it into your own words?

10. Denaldo: Umm . . . I don't understand what Serena is saying.

11. Ms. F: Serena, could you draw a picture on the board so we could understand better what you're saying?

Notice that as the students make their contributions, they are required to give a reason for their answers. Ms. Fields does not say "right" or "wrong" at this point. There are, of course, many times during a lesson when the teacher is focused on checking for right or wrong answers and is explicitly correcting students, but here she has a different set of purposes in mind. She wants students to

- talk through the problem and struggle to make their thinking clear to others;
- get into the habit of giving reasons for their answers and evidence for their claims, a crucial part of mathematical, scientific, and logical reasoning;
- get into the habit of listening to and evaluating one another's contributions; and
- reason aloud so she can gain information about the mathematical beliefs and understandings of individual students.

Ms. Fields will build on such sequences in helping students understand the truths and conventions of the larger mathematics community.

In the short term, such sequences can reveal to the teacher whether the majority of the students understand the current question or not, and if not, where the principal problems lie. This information is important for informing the teacher's further instructional decisions. This activity has a longer-term effect as well. Over time, students become less attuned to guessing the right answer, and more attuned to actually engaging in logical reasoning. They become more interested in being able to support their answer successfully rather than simply guessing what the teacher has in mind.

Evaluating Your Own Progress

How can you tell when what you are doing is working? It may take months or even a year to see really striking changes in students' abilities to use classroom discourse to learn mathematics. But this is a long time to wait. What can you do in the meantime to help yourself see what is working and what isn't? We suggest that you find a way to keep track of your use of the principles that we introduced at the beginning of this chapter for each day that you intentionally use extensive talk in your mathematics instruction.

Perhaps the best place to start is with Principle 4, providing a clear and explicit discussion of what you expected from students in their classroom talk. If you have not already done this, your best course is to remedy the situation and have a talk with your students about what you plan to do and what you expect.

Next, look to Principles 1 and 2. Did your class maintain the norms of respectful discourse, and was the talk consistently about mathematical reasoning, with an emphasis on understanding? It will be obvious to you if the norms of respectful discourse were not met. You will probably also be able to tell if the talk in your classroom was not primarily about mathematical reasoning. But over time, it is important to keep track in a consistent fashion, so you can reflect on what has happened over a longer period than just a day or two.

Different teachers will find different ways to keep track of this. Some will take a moment after class simply to reflect on the checklist that follows this section. Others will instead spend five minutes later in the day discussing their class with a "buddy"—a colleague who is also engaged in the same effort. Other teachers who find keeping a journal helpful may use space in their journal to remind themselves of what they intended, how it played out, and what they plan to do next.

Some aspects of the process are best observed weekly rather than daily. For example, Principle 3, providing for equitable participation, may not be best evaluated on the basis of one class. Imagine that you are discussing a topic on one day and most of the volunteers are boys—the girls just sit back, hands lowered. If you evaluated your progress on the basis of that one day, you might be discouraged, and outside visitors might be misled. Experienced teachers know that student participation varies from day to day for a variety of reasons. It may be best in this case to keep track at slightly longer time intervals. If a whole week goes by and you see that mainly boys are responding, or mainly the Anglo students in a diverse classroom, or mainly native speakers of English in a classroom containing many second-language learners, then it may be time to reevaluate the strategies you are using to call on students. To start out, you might keep a class list to use during the discussion or later, adding a check mark for each student who participates. (See Figure 8–2.) At the end of the week, review the list for patterns and reflect.

IMPLEMENTING TALK IN THE CLASSROOM

Self-Evaluation Checklist

Principle 1: Establishing and Maintaining a Respectful, Supportive Environment
Principle 2: Focusing Talk on the Mathematics
Principle 3: Providing for Equitable Participation in Classroom Talk
Principle 4: Explaining Your Expectations About New Forms of Talk
Principle 5: Trying Only One Challenging New Thing at a Time

Principle 1: Establishing and Maintaining a Respectful, Supportive Environment

- ☐ Did you consistently require that students respect one another's contributions by asking them to listen, and to speak loudly enough so that others could hear?
- ☐ Did you emphasize that we agree or disagree with what others say, not with the speakers themselves?
- ☐ Did you enforce the norm that students may not ridicule others or make derogatory comments about others?
- ☐ As the weeks pass, do you see students opening up to the possibilities of talking about their ideas in a supportive environment?
- ☐ Do you see evidence that the norms for respectful discourse are having an effect outside of math class?

Principle 2: Focusing Talk on the Mathematics

- ☐ Did you consistently monitor to make sure that the preponderance of classroom talk was about mathematical ideas and reasoning?
- ☐ Did you plan sufficiently well that you could guide the talk in mathematically productive directions?
- ☐ As the weeks and months pass, do you see a change in your students' level of sophistication in talking about mathematical concepts, definitions, representations, and forms of reasoning?

(continued)

FIGURE 8–2 **Implementing Talk in the Classroom: Self-Evaluation Checklist**

Principle 3. Providing for Equitable Participation in Classroom Talk

☐ Did you succeed in paying consistent attention to whether every student is benefiting from your uses of classroom discourse?

☐ Did you succeed in eliciting participation from most, if not all, students this week?

☐ As the weeks and months pass, do you see a change in the participation of students who started out only as listeners?

☐ Do you see increasing participation from students who are learning English as their second language?

Principle 4. Explaining Your Expectations About New Forms of Talk

☐ When introducing something new, or reviewing a practice or activity, did you explain clearly what you want students to do, and did you give them reasons for engaging in this kind of talk?

☐ Did you make sure that all students understood what was expected of them?

☐ As the weeks and months pass, do you notice that students are secure in their knowledge of what you want them to do during mathematics talk?

Principle 5. Trying Only One Challenging New Thing at a Time

☐ When introducing a new talk move or format, did you try to make sure that the mathematical concepts or procedures you started with were well understood by all the students in the class?

☐ Conversely, when you introduced challenging new mathematical content, did you try to make sure that the talk routines you used were familiar to all the students in the class?

☐ Over the weeks, do you find yourself improving in your ability to integrate talk moves and formats with increasingly challenging mathematics?

FIGURE 8–2 *continued*

DISCUSSION AND REFLECTION

1. Ensuring equitable participation is not always easy. Discuss some of the major obstacles that you face in getting everyone to participate in your classroom, within your school. What kinds of practices or routines could help mitigate your particular set of obstacles?

(continued)

2. If you are reading this book, chances are that you have tried to use discussion in your classroom before this. Can you recall students who had trouble participating in the past? Discuss personal, cultural, social, psychological, or medical issues that might lead to some students not talking at all, or talking too much. Discuss your attitudes and feelings about these things. Identify one or two of the most difficult situations and think about ways to deal with them if they should arise.

3. We have stressed in this chapter that students must feel safe from ridicule or they will not participate. What if you begin to use classroom talk in the ways described here and some students do not cooperate? Do you and your school have a behavioral system in place that will support you in instituting a zero-tolerance policy for disrespectful behavior? What are the procedures? Is it clear how you would use them in your classroom?

4. It is sometimes more difficult to implement a change in your pedagogical practice if you do not have support from your fellow teachers. If more than one teacher at your school is working on using classroom talk to support math learning, how can you work together to support one another, given your time constraints and resources? What aspects of the five principles covered in this chapter could you help one another implement? Can you involve your principal or department head in your efforts? How?

9

Planning Talk-Based Lessons

Now that you have started thinking about how to use productive classroom talk in mathematics, you probably have lots of practical questions about incorporating talk into your lessons. The first thing you must consider when planning a unit or a lesson is the mathematics that students will talk about. In order to maximize students' understanding, you have to be extremely clear about what mathematics you will stress or highlight. It helps to list ahead of time the key concepts, problem-solving strategies, vocabulary, forms of representations, reasoning, and computational procedures that are at the heart of the topic. Once you've determined the mathematics, consider discussion questions and anticipate possible answers that might be used to help students develop understanding and proficiency.

Some curriculum materials do not provide any guidance for using discussion to help students understand key ideas. However, other curriculum materials state the mathematics in the lesson and provide questions to ask students. This is a great starting place, and we suggest you use these prepared questions. However, we also have found that even excellent curricula do not provide all the questions that you will want your students to consider. In many cases the questions provided are low-level, single-response questions rather than questions that force students to analyze, synthesize, or generalize. Furthermore, you have worked with the individuals in your class and are aware of your students' knowledge of related topics and their strengths and weaknesses. Thus, you can pose pertinent questions for your students. Whatever your curriculum, this section gives guidance on how to plan lessons to get the most out of classroom talk in terms of student learning of mathematics.

Four Components for Effective Lesson Planning

Just as there are many aspects to using talk, there are also many components involved in effective lesson planning. The lesson plan we suggest has four different components:

Four Components for Lesson Plan
1. Identifying the mathematical goals;
2. Anticipating confusion;
3. Asking questions;
4. Planning the implementation.

Component 1: Identifying the Mathematical Goals

In this part of your lesson plan you need to identify the mathematics that is most important in the lesson. In Chapters 3 through 7 we described the mathematics to be talked about: mathematical concepts; computational procedures; solution methods and problem-solving strategies; mathematical reasoning; mathematical terminology, symbols, and definitions. This is a useful list to review when writing your lesson plan, but keep in mind that most lessons do not include all of these math topics.

Component 2: Anticipating Confusion

This section of your lesson plan is where you list the particular aspects of the mathematical content that may be potentially confusing or misconstrued by students. It helps to identify possible incorrect notions as well as common errors that might occur. By highlighting in your lesson plan the mathematics that may be problematic for students, you are more likely to make sure that students think carefully about these ideas and procedures during class.

Component 3: Asking Questions

You want to generate questions that will engage students in talking about what they understand or that will reveal misconceptions. These questions do not elicit single-word responses. (For example, avoid questions that can be answered by "yes" or "no.") Rather, ask questions that require students to ana-lyze a computational procedure or problem-solving strategy, connect skills to the underlying conceptual ideas, generalize patterns and relationships, and/or link new understanding to previous knowledge. Sometimes teachers write what they think some of their students' likely responses will be so that they can have additional questions and counterexamples ready for use.

Component 4: Planning the Implementation

In this section, outline the sequence and content of the activities that you will use to help students make sense of the mathematics.

Summary: The Value of Planning for Talk

The structure of this lesson plan may look a bit different from ones you have used before. Notice that it keeps the focus on using talk to learn mathematics. It is easy to get caught up in a discussion that sounds great and then realize at the end of the class that students probably did not learn any new mathemati-cal content. Thoughtful lesson planning will enable you to keep the discussion focused on students' understanding of the mathematics that you want them to learn. It helps move the talk forward so that the mathematical goals of the les-son are addressed. Since students' comments in math class are largely a result of their current understanding, it's important to anticipate what ideas they might have that are and are not mathematically sound. Likewise, it is essential for teachers to consider possible questions, examples, and counterexamples that will push students to reflect on their reasoning.

As explained in Chapter 2, you have a choice of moves and formats to use during instruction. Plan ahead of time which talk formats and talk moves you'll use during the lesson, choosing moves and formats that you think will lend themselves best to the mathematical ideas in the lesson. In addition, certain parts of a lesson, such as the introduction, the exploration, or the summary, are best suited for particular formats and moves. Thinking about which formats and moves to use, and when to use them, saves valuable time during class and strengthens the productivity of the talk. Finally, it is helpful to identify princi-ples, such as building a respectful, supportive environment, that you want to address.

Planning and Projecting: A Sample Lesson Plan

Let's start with a lesson that Ms. Wong is planning for her second-grade students on area. This is the first formal lesson on area but students have had previous

NCTM Standard:
Measurement

Grade 2

experience covering drawn figures with different-shaped blocks. Ms. Wong knows that the students have little knowledge of the topic and thus have little vocabulary associated with the topic.

In past years, Ms. Wong has filled out lesson plans with descriptions of the introduction, the exploration activities, and the summary for each lesson. In order to increase the amount of talk in this lesson, Ms. Wong adopts the talk lesson plan format discussed in this book. However, to save time, she simply incorporates her notes from previous years into this new lesson plan, below. The plan is followed by some commentary to explain her reasoning.

Grade 2 Lesson Plan: Geometry and Measurement

IDENTIFYING THE MATHEMATICAL GOALS

- Students will learn that the surface of an object can be covered with no holes or gaps. This is called the area of the surface.
- Students will discover that some objects cover a surface more completely than others (e.g., square tiles versus circular disks).
- Students will learn that to measure area, you can count the number of square units covering the surface.
- Vocabulary: *area, covering, surface, square unit*

ANTICIPATING CONFUSION

- Students might not realize a surface must be covered completely—they may leave holes in the surfaces, simply cover the borders, or overlap tiles.
- Students may not understand the meaning of the vocabulary.
- Students should be able to cover objects with units but may not connect this action to the idea of determining the area of the object.

ASKING QUESTIONS

- What does the word *surface* mean? Can you show me?
- What does it mean to cover something?
- Which objects cover the surface completely? Which do not? What do you notice about the shapes of objects that cover the surface completely?

- If students are not covering the whole surface, just the border, or are leaving holes in the surface, be sure to ask these questions: This surface has a big hole in it. Why do you think I would say that it's not completely covered? When you cover a surface with tiles and leave a hole, why would I say that it's not OK?

PLANNING THE IMPLEMENTATION

- Introduce the task: Student pairs estimate the number of square tiles, circular disks, and large paper clips that cover their reading books.
- Student pairs cover their reading books with square tiles, circular disks, and large paper clips. They count the number of objects used and write these numbers on sticky notes.
- Student post their findings in a class chart organized by type of object.
- Whole-class discussion: Have many students share what they discovered about covering the book's surface with different objects in terms of number of objects and completeness of covering.
- Introduce the term *area*. Link this term to the idea of covering a surface with no holes or gaps.

Let's examine the kinds of things Ms. Wong was thinking about when she wrote this lesson plan. What assumptions did she make, and what did she purposely leave out?

In the *Identifying the Mathematical Goals* section, Ms. Wong lists the concepts and vocabulary that she wants to develop during the lesson. At one point in her planning, Ms. Wong had two additional mathematics objectives in the lesson, but then realized that if she addressed all of the objectives, there would not be time for students to talk about any of them. She is working diligently to plan lessons that give students time to talk about fewer mathematical ideas in depth rather than many ideas on a superficial level.

When writing the *Anticipating Confusion* section, Ms. Wong relies on a number of resources to help her. First, she uses her experience as a classroom teacher to reflect on difficulties students in prior years had with the topic. She also examines her teacher's manual for information about possible errors or misconceptions. Ms. Wong sometimes refers to reference books that help her think about the mathematics and potential problems students will have with the topic.

Finally, if the lesson is brand-new to her, after teaching it, she records her own errors and confusion as a way of gaining insight into students' minds.

The *Asking Questions* section is very important because it forces us to think about the purpose of our questioning and to consider questions that go beyond recall of knowledge. Some questions help us learn whether or not students comprehend the content of the lesson; some questions help us determine whether or not students can apply knowledge to new situations; and many discussion questions engage everyone in connecting mathematical concepts and procedures and in generalizing mathematical relationships. Ms. Wong looks back at the first two components of her lesson plan when writing this section. First, she writes comprehension-type questions that she thinks might reveal students' accurate knowledge, misconceptions, or confusion about the mathematics. Second, she writes questions that might cause students some cognitive conflict—ones that she thinks will force them to reconsider any incorrect, preconceived notions. Third, she writes questions related to the mathematical objectives she identified that will lead the class to relate knowledge from several areas, to predict, or to draw conclusions. Ms. Wong saves her lesson plans from year to year and plans to note which questions were especially powerful in helping everyone make sense of the mathematics. Not surprisingly, she expects that she will drop questions that were not helpful in making the talk productive or ones that she did not use.

In the *Planning the Implementation* section, Mrs. Wong summarizes the key elements of her lesson. She plans on using two talk formats: partner talk and whole-class discussion. She has students use partner talk as a way for everyone to share their interpretation of the meaning of *surface*. She uses whole-class discussion when she wants students to draw conclusions that everyone has agreed upon. In addition, during the whole-class discussion she wants to remember to ask a number of students the same question. In the past, Ms. Wong did not ask more than one student to respond to the same math question, but she realizes that her second graders often are confused when ideas go by too quickly. She believes that this approach will give her students more time to process the key ideas and will acclimate them to talking in mathematics class.

Making Decisions About Talk Formats

When planning a lesson, how do you decide when to use each of the three talk formats? We have found small-group discussion to be effective when the problems or tasks presented to students are quite difficult. The benefit of four minds instead of two focused on one problem cannot be underestimated! Also, tasks that lend themselves to a division of labor are also good for small groups because students can share the results of their individual subtasks. And small-group talk can be used when students need to practice talking and listening to each other. Ms. Wong didn't use this talk format this time but could have incorporated it into her lesson when students were working in groups.

However, sometimes when small-group discussion is used, teachers become frustrated with the outcome. When students work in groups of three, four, or even five students, there are situations when some of these students do not contribute to the group work or participate in the group talk. For example, a student might sit quietly and let others solve and discuss the problems and then copy down the answers. Or a student might be totally off task, engaged in other activities, and cause problems for the group by making productive talk nearly impossible. Finally, some small groups are more interested in social talk than mathematical talk. In order for students to benefit from small-group discussion, you must construct the groups carefully, taking into consideration both the social and cognitive dynamics among students. Furthermore, you can keep changing the groups until you get groups who talk and work cooperatively. Chapter 10 offers additional suggestions on how to maximize the effectiveness of small-group discussions.

Partner talk can be used in almost any situation: talking about vocabulary, interpreting a word problem, describing the steps in a computation, or solving a problem. In Project Challenge we used it regularly. During partner talk, the two partners must talk to each other and are forced to think and talk about the mathematics because there is no one else to do it for them! When students are engaged in trying to make sense of a situation, it is more likely they are learning. We also used partner talk whenever students were confused or unsure of a response. If a question posed to the class did not elicit much response, we stopped the whole-class discussion and asked the students to turn and talk with a partner to discuss the solution, the word, or whatever was the issue at hand. The room would burst into talk as students shared their ideas. Partner talk provides a venue for students to try out, refine, and revise their ideas prior to presenting them to the whole class. Following partner talk, students may still be confused, but they are typically more willing to voice their confusion once they know they aren't the only ones who don't understand.

We found that it was important to choose partners carefully and to let them work together for extended periods of time—anywhere from two to eight weeks. This enabled the partners to develop some shared practices and to grow into a team. We considered the processing speed of students when partnering them—we put students who processed and computed quickly together, and we paired students who regularly needed additional time to compute and solve problems. We did not place the top-achieving students with those students working at or below grade level. Constructing partner groups by achievement levels enables you to give extra challenges to some partner teams and provide more content support for other teams. It also helps avoid the situation where only one student does all the talking and thinking. As with small-group talk we moved partners around until we got the right combination: students who willingly talked together and were respectful and kind to each other.

Whole-class discussion is the talk format that can be used at the beginning of a lesson to set the stage for what is to come and to clarify the parameters of the instructional task. Whole-class discussion can also be used during the last third of the lesson as a forum for students to share what they have discovered and then both summarize and generalize the important ideas. Sometimes a full math class is spent discussing one question! One reason that whole-class discussion is used regularly is that it allows all students the opportunity to consider everyone's ideas and thoughts about the mathematics. Specifically, by listening and contributing, students are building their own understanding. The class as a whole also is developing shared meaning for whatever ideas are under consideration. Finally, whole-class discussion provides the teacher with a way to assess students by asking specific students to repeat a statement or opinion, react to another student's statements, or provide their own solution methods.

Generating Good Questions

At the heart of using productive talk in instruction are the questions we pose. Our questions are the catalyst for students' thinking and talking. So how do you come up with questions that further students' mathematical knowledge? Almost every question-categorization scheme that exists, starting with Bloom's famous taxonomy, makes a distinction between low-level, cognitively undemanding questions, and high-level, cognitively challenging questions. The simplest, lowest-level questions ask students to recall knowledge that they already know. The most challenging questions ask students to explain a complex situation, evaluate the usefulness of a method, or synthesize a set of findings. At the far ends of the spectrum, it is fairly easy to tell the low-level question from the high-level question. For example, everyone knows that "yes/no" questions are less challenging in general than more open-ended "why" questions. There are many kinds of questions, however, where it is not so easy to tell what the "level" of the question really is.

Mary Kay Stein has spent many years thinking about the cognitive demands of tasks in mathematics instruction—what makes a low-level versus a high-level task. After many years of working with mathematics teachers, she has concluded that it is not always easy to tell how a question or task will pan out. Will it evoke high-level intellectual activity, a good discussion, or a conceptual breakthrough? Or will it devolve into a routine and unexciting activity? The answer depends upon the task, the teacher, and the students. If you are interested in thoughtful discussion on this matter, we recommend reading *Implementing Standards-Based Mathematics Instruction* (Stein et al. 2000).

In the meantime, though, we can suggest a strategy: *Plan for high-level questions—the low-level questions tend to take care of themselves.* In other words, as you plan your lesson, try to come up with several big questions that will move students' thinking forward, questions that will require them to explain, synthesize, and make connections. You may not get all of these questions answered in one lesson, but at least they will help you define the trajectory you want to be on. The low-level questions that you must ask to check whether students remember, comprehend, or follow the discussion will emerge naturally as you pursue your larger, more complex questions.

For example, Ms. Wong asked questions to help her students generalize the fact that rectangles and squares cover surfaces more completely than circles and, in general, shapes that fit together with no holes or gaps cover a surface better than shapes that are curved, rounded, or include holes. As you write questions for each lesson, you should refer back to the mathematical goals you have defined. Make sure you are not just asking low-level questions about facts, since they usually are not conducive to discussion or debate. When asking a low-level question, consider how you can extend it so it has more than one purpose. For example, a discussion about estimating the number of beans in a jar might start out with a question designed to check students' number sense. But by asking students to explain how they decided upon their estimate, or asking them to compare their estimation technique with another student's technique, you have moved the instruction to a higher level of cognitive challenge.

Finally, when you hit upon a higher-level question that really stimulates productive talk—talk that results in student advances in mathematical thinking—write it down! Share it with your colleagues! Tell your colleagues how the discussion proceeded after you introduced the question. These questions are among the valuable tools you will discover as you become more adept at using this type of instruction.

Improvising and Responding: In the Midst of a Talk Lesson

Sometimes the lessons we design do not translate directly into practice. In fact, teachers more often than not are revising, modifying, or improvising on their

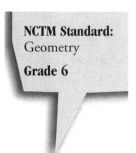

NCTM Standard:
Geometry

Grade 6

lesson plans because students either know more or less than was expected. Talk lessons can sometimes lead us down paths for which we did not plan. In the following example, we see how Mrs. Carlson, a sixth-grade teacher, improvises and thus changes the direction of her lesson because of student responses. Mrs. Carlson's lesson focuses on understanding the formula for the area of a circle. Her students know how to find the area of squares, rectangles, parallelograms, and triangles. In this new lesson, students are to take a circle, cut it into small wedges, and then rearrange the wedges into a shape that approximates a parallelogram. Estimating the area of the parallelogram-like shape is intended to help the students make sense of the area formula of a circle. Following the activity Mrs. Carlson plans to have students talk extensively about their findings.

Mrs. Carlson began the lesson by going over a few homework problems from the night before, reviewing previously introduced content such as how to find the circumference of a circle and the area of a parallelogram, and finally introducing the topic of the area of a circle. Students were seated at tables in groups of three, four, or five students. Paper circles (all the same size), protractors, and scissors were on the tables. Mrs. Carlson posed the following task to the class:

> *In order to determine the area of these paper circles, each of you is to take one, divide it into equal-size wedges, cut out the wedges, and then reconfigure the wedges into a shape that approximates a parallelogram. Without using a ruler, work together to determine the base and the height of your parallelogram-like shape and use this information to find its area. Later we will all talk about our results.*

1. Anna: How many wedges are we supposed to make?

2. Mrs. C: That is up to you. How many wedges do you think you should cut?

3. Anna: Four?

4. Ryan: I don't think that'll be enough for the new shape to look like a parallelogram. Look. [Ryan takes a circle and cuts it into

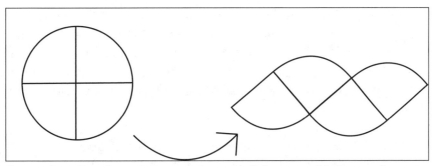

FIGURE 9–1 Ryan's attempt to make a parallelogram with four wedges cut from a circle.

fourths and puts them together for everyone to observe. See Figure 9–1.] I think we should try to cut lots of wedges.

5. Mrs. C: How many wedges could you possibly cut? Talk to the people at your table about this for a minute or so.

At the time, Mrs. Carlson didn't think her question was anything special. She thought students might agree that eight or ten or sixteen wedges would be a good number for the task. She went over to one group of students and heard these suggestions:

6. Arjun: I think we can make an infinite number of wedges.

7. Kasey: No, I think three hundred sixty.

8. Alan: Wouldn't the number be one hundred eighty?

9. A. J.: I'm confused. I can't figure out how to make more than thirty-six wedges.

Mrs. Carlson now has to make an instructional decision. Does she ignore some of the ideas that students are talking about in their small groups and just focus on an answer to how many wedges the students need to cut for this task so they can go on and complete the lesson? Or does she shift gears and have students explore through discussion the idea of determining the number of possible wedges? This is a forty-five-minute math period and with the review time at the start, about thirty minutes are left. Talk will often take classes down unanticipated paths, and it's not always clear whether or not to pursue the unexpected. In Project Challenge we tried to base our decisions on whether we felt the mathematics was important to know versus just nice to know.

We often made mistakes and followed a discussion that, in retrospect, could have been skipped. However, we also had situations where we and the students learned a great deal by shifting gears. Making these types of instructional decisions is not easy. In Mrs. Carlson's case, she decides it is worth pursuing the idea of an infinite number of wedges. She calls the class back to the whole-class discussion.

10. Mrs. C: Listening to you talk in your groups I heard a number of possibilities for the number of wedges we might cut. I heard one hundred eighty, thirty-six, infinite, and three hundred sixty just from one group [writes *180, 36, infinite,* and *360* on the board]. How many wedges are in a circle? Does anyone else have a suggestion?

11. Tania I think one hundred should also be added.

12. Mrs. C: Why?

13. Tania Well, we know that a circle is one hundred percent, so then we can cut it into one hundred wedges, one for each percent.

14. Mrs. C: Are you thinking of a pie chart when you say that a circle is one hundred percent? [Tania nods. Mrs. Carlson adds *100* to the list on the board.] Now we have five different suggestions for how many wedges there might be. Which, if any, is correct? Talk to your partner. [Partners talk for a few minutes.] Andrew?

15. Andrew: I think that there are an infinite number of wedges possible because you can just keep making the wedges smaller and smaller, like decimal amounts big.

16. Mrs. C: Andrew, could you explain what you mean by "decimal amounts big"?

17. Andrew: I mean we can pick a decimal amount like millionths and cut the circle into that many pieces. We could do that for every piece—just keep cutting it into smaller pieces.

18. Swetha: I agree with Andrew. I think the number of possible wedges is like infinity. You can just keep cutting more and more wedges.

19. Mrs. C: Paul, do you agree or disagree with Swetha's idea?

20. Paul: I think I disagree. Because we, like, we can't cut that many. I think it's probably three hundred sixty or so. There are three hundred sixty degrees in a circle so that means one wedge for each degree.

21. Mrs. C: A. J., can you repeat what Paul just said?

22. A. J.: I agree with Paul. His explanation of three hundred sixty makes sense to me. Degrees are really small so the wedges will be tiny. It will be hard to cut so many tiny wedges but I think we can do it.

23. Mrs. C: Sarah, do you want to add something?

24. Sarah: I agree with Andrew's idea. If you took each degree and cut it in half or in quarters or in eighths or any small fraction you would keep getting smaller and smaller wedges. I think there are just zillions of wedges in a circle but they are so small we could never actually cut them out.

25. Sterling: Yeah, you can't really do that. You can't cut the wedges that small. So there are so many wedges but I don't know what to do with this problem.

Notice that two questions are being addressed: the number of wedges that can actually be cut and the number of wedges that are in a circle. It takes Mrs. Carlson a while to sort this out. As she listens to her students, she starts to understand their confusion. Furthermore, she understands that she has inadvertently posed both questions during the class period. She continues to respond to the direction of the discussion, not totally clear where this might lead.

26. Mrs. C: Sarah and Sterling bring up a point for us to consider. What is possible in our minds and what is possible in reality? Namely, how many wedges are possible if we only think about it in our minds and don't try to cut them out? Talk to your partner about this.

Following more discussion, the consensus is that there are an infinite number of wedges that can be imagined. Mrs. Carlson asks everyone to summarize the points made about the number of possible wedges in their math journals. She thinks to herself that this slight diversion was well worth the discussion time. She is ready to return to her original plan. Then A. J. raises his hand and says, "I still don't understand this infinity stuff."

27. Mrs. C: OK. Who thinks they have an explanation that will help A. J. make sense of this idea? Arjun.

28. Arjun: A. J., you can first imagine cutting the circle into three hundred sixty wedges. Now blow up one of those tiny wedges

in your mind. If you had a laser or something could you cut
each of the one-degree wedges up into smaller fractions?
Yes, we could cut them into smaller and smaller wedges.
You just have to imagine doing it, not it really happening.

29. Mrs. C: [Andrew is waving his hand wildly.] Andrew, do you want to
add anything?

30. Andrew: Think of all the tiny decimal numbers there are. We can cut
each degree into tiny decimal amounts like hundredths or
thousandths or ten-thousandths. We can just keep doing this
forever and if we do, the number of wedges will never end.

In many talk situations it is not the teacher who is the authority on the
correctness of an answer. Instead the mathematical logic that students present
is used to support answers, drive decisions, and justify conclusions. In this
case, Arjun, Andrew, and others made contributions that helped A. J. better
understand infinity and that supported the idea that there are an infinite number of wedges in a circle.

Mrs. Carlson realizes the period is almost over. The final thing she does
before the end of the class period is to set the stage for tomorrow's lesson.

31. Mrs. C: We concluded that there are an infinite number of wedges
possible in a circle, but we still have the area problem to
address tomorrow. So take one of the paper circles at your
table and for homework please cut it into wedges that we
can use to find the area. Does it make sense to cut these
circles into one hundred or three hundred sixty wedges?
No. So please pick a reasonable number and remember the
wedges must each be the same size. Put your wedges in an
envelope and bring them to class tomorrow.

Most of the discussion time was focused on the idea that there are an
infinite number of wedges in a circle. Based on her knowledge of students'
understanding of previous lessons, Mrs. Carlson believed that most of the
students in her class understood that if they cut the circle into a large number
of wedges and rearranged them into a parallelogram, the shape would closely
approximate a parallelogram. Thus she did not spend any time on this idea
and instead adjusted the lesson to respond to the question about the number
of possible wedges in a circle. In general, teachers should try to have discussions about ideas that students do not grasp. If it becomes clear that a concept
or procedure is well understood, a shift in emphasis is warranted.

However, it is not always the case that teachers are clear on exactly what students do and do not understand. Mrs. Carlson may find when her students return that they do not understand how the wedges can approximate a parallelogram. Throughout this book you have read dialogues in which teachers did not follow the thinking of a student. You have also seen situations where teachers ignored certain contributions in order to focus on a particular point. There isn't a road map for making instructional decisions on the fly—for deciding when to improvise and respond and when not. Nor is there one "right" direction for a discussion. Choices made by teachers bring classes down different paths, and each path contributes to students' understanding of content. However, based on our experiences with classroom discourse, we suggest that if you find that a discussion has stalled or is not producing the kinds of insights you had expected, it may be time to move on.

Summarizing and Solidifying: So Where Are We Now?

There are two distinct types of summarizing and solidifying that occur when using talk in lessons. One type is when either the teacher or the students summarize what occurred during the lesson. Remember that many discussions include contributions that are inarticulate, unclear in purpose, or unrelated. One job that the teacher has is to sort out the worthwhile comments (those that will help students make sense of the content) from all that was said during the discussion. Teachers often need to solidify what has been discussed in the lesson by clearly summarizing key points. Sometimes this happens in the middle of a class, sometimes it happens at the end of the class period, and sometimes it occurs first thing the next day. When lessons take two or three days, a summary might not occur until the lesson is brought to closure. The importance of summary cannot be overestimated. It is through this process that conclusions are drawn and shared meaning among the students is developed.

Notice that Mrs. Carlson had students summarize the discussion in their math journals. The next day she will call on a few students to read what they wrote. Other times, Mrs. Carlson summarizes or asks one or two students to briefly go over the main points established in class. This does not have to take a lot of time but it is important to include.

Just as there is a need to help students summarize the important information gleaned from classroom discussions, it is also important for teachers to summarize the questions and talk moves they used in their lessons in their own notes. Teachers refine their lessons from year to year. Thus, when you make changes to a planned lesson (whether because of a question that came up or because you ran out of time), it's important to go back to your original plans and add extensive notes. Mrs. Carlson's original plans did not involve talking about the number of possible wedges in a circle. However, because of what occurred in her class, she wants to include a discussion about infinity in regards to wedges in an even more focused way next year. She made notes in her lesson plans about the ideas and misunderstandings that came up regarding the concept of infinity. She also wrote down the questions that helped her students develop understanding of this concept.

Planning talk lessons follows a cycle similar to lesson planning in general. First, you must plan ahead and project what will happen. We do this by analyzing the mathematics in the lesson, anticipating confusion with the mathematics, and then asking questions that will lead to either clarity or further confusion! Second, teachers must be willing to adapt portions or whole lessons as they respond to what students know and don't know. They may have to improvise, slow down, change gears, or regroup. Finally, teachers need to remember how important it is to include summaries, both of small points and of major conclusions during and after their lessons. The summaries should help both their students and the teachers themselves.

DISCUSSION AND REFLECTION

1. Some teachers find that the *Asking Questions* part of planning is the most challenging became they aren't sure what questions to ask. Describe what is meant by high-level questions. What resources are available to teachers to help them determine the mathematical goals and related high-level questions when planning?

2. If you have tried using discussion in your classroom, describe what you found was most helpful in planning the use of talk. If you have not yet tried to use talk with students, write a talk lesson plan using the components described in this chapter.

3. In the discussion about the degrees in a circle, Mrs. Carlson did not tell A. J. the "right" answer. She was not the authority on the correctness of the answer. Instead the mathematical logic presented by Arjun and Andrew was used to explain infinity and justify conclusions. It can be unsettling for a teacher to not be the person who tells students they are right or wrong. What are the benefits of using students' reasoning to justify the correctness of a solution?

4. Write a talk lesson plan that could be used to continue the lesson in this chapter on deriving the area of a circle from the area of a parallelogram.

10

Troubleshooting

As experienced teachers know, any class can present obstacles or unexpected difficulties. This is particularly true when you, the teacher, decide to try something new. In our experience, students may or may not take to all of the methods described in this book. Some may easily begin to participate in talk, while others may not seem to want to participate at all. As you monitor your progress, it's a good idea to keep track of the difficulties you encounter. In this section we'll talk about the most common problems and what teachers have done in the past to improve things.

Common Problems and Concerns

My students won't talk.
The same few students do all the talking.
Should I call on students who do not raise their hands?
My students will talk, but they won't listen.
"Huh?" How do I respond to incomprehensible contributions?
Brilliant, but did anyone understand?

(continued)

I have students at very different levels.
What should I do when students are wrong?
This discussion is not going anywhere . . . .
Students' answers are so superficial!
What if the first student to speak gives the right answer?
What should I do for English language learners?
I'm falling behind in my curriculum.
Students are off-task while working in small groups.

My students won't talk.

Many students are used to a traditional classroom, in which the teacher normally does most of the talking and occasionally asks students to answer questions. It's a big change to ask them to talk about their thinking and respond to other students' contributions. In some classrooms, the teacher will be met with silence at first. This can be unnerving, and even demoralizing. So the first thing to do is to ask yourself a few questions.

First, are the students silent because they have not understood a particular question? Make sure that whether the question comes from you or from another student, they have heard it a few times and have had time to think about it. If it's your question, ask several students to restate it; if it's a student's question, either revoice it yourself or ask another student to repeat it. Be sure that any question is repeated and clarified.

Second, do the students understand why you are asking them to repeat what others have said, or to explain their reasoning? If you have given an introductory lesson about the reasons for these talk moves, you might revisit that. You might ask: "Why do you think I'm asking you to repeat what the previous speaker said?" Or "Why do you think I'm asking you whether you agree with another student's reasoning?" This will give students an opportunity to review the reasons that everyone must understand what is said, and everyone must pay attention so that they can understand.

If you have clarified questions and there is still no answer, it may be that your students are having an attack either of mass shyness or mass confusion! Sometimes it's hard to tell the difference. Early on in the process of starting to use talk, students may be hesitant to think out loud in front of their class-mates. If you are confronted with silence from the whole class, have your students use partner talk for two minutes to clarify their thinking and practice their answers with one another. If they still don't seem to be able to talk about the ideas, you may have to step back and pose a simpler but related question. Don't give up!

If many of your students seem reluctant to speak, make sure that it is not because of a pattern of discourteous or disrespectful comments or noises. Even the presence of one or two students rolling their eyes at the contributions of others may be a deterrent to participation.

In some cases reluctance to talk may be a function of an individual child's personality. In other cases it may be a family or cultural norm. In some families or communities, children are encouraged to observe and to learn through quiet apprenticeship. Children in these families or communi-ties are not supposed to hold forth about their nascent ideas. It may be particularly frowned upon for girls to actively speak out. When you ask such children to explain their mathematical reasoning, that behavior may be in conflict with what they are used to, although they may not be able to explain this to you. It will take time and patience to encourage quiet children to speak up voluntarily.

One teacher we know had a group of fourth-grade girls and boys from Puerto Rico and Central America who were particularly quiet. They were eager and cooperative students but she could not get them to volunteer, and when she called on them they were so quiet that no one could hear them. Repeated requests for them to speak up did not seem to result in louder contributions. Finally, after several months, the teacher spoke to them outside of class as a group. She told them that their contributions were very valued and that they needed to learn to participate, even if it might seem challenging. To help get the process started, she said, she expected each of them to raise his or her hand at least once every lesson: to ask a question, to answer a question, or even just to ask "Could you repeat that?" The students looked relieved, she said, to have the decision to participate made for them. After that, each one began to enter into the conversation and eventually even started to speak loudly enough for everyone to hear. For these particular children, however, the process took the better part of a year.

The same few students do all the talking.

Most teachers find that when they begin the process of asking students to talk, there are a few who immediately blossom into really big talkers! Just as with the quiet students, this can be an individual personality trait, or it can be a family or cultural norm. In some families and communities, children who talk a lot, who freely offer their opinions, are considered bright or personable, and their talk is encouraged. When these students are asked to talk in school, they have an advantage. Just like children who have played baseball since age two have an advantage on the playground, when these children get into the game of academic talk in elementary school, they will be way ahead of others in their skills. If you have such students in your class, they will usually jump to answer your questions. Other students will quickly decide that they don't need to force themselves to do the work of participating: These two or three "monopolizers" will do the work for them!

The teacher then has a problem: The few will gladly take the floor and discuss whatever needs discussion, and the "silent majority" will become less and less willing to participate. If you see this pattern starting, it's a good idea to nip it in the bud. How? First, be determined: Use your wait time. When you ask a question, and those same two or three hands go up first, keep waiting. Be explicit with your students about your use of wait time. Sometimes when teachers begin to increase their wait time, students are taken aback and wonder why the teacher is not calling on them right away. You might say: "All good mathematicians need time to think. So, I'm trying really hard to make sure that I give you time to think about the question before we hear one person's answer."

You may decide to repeat the question in order to provide additional thinking time for students who may want to participate, but who don't feel ready to do so. When other students finally do raise their hands, call on several of them and have them repeat one another's contributions. If you wait ten, twenty, or thirty seconds and still only the usual two or three hands appear, don't give in. Use partner talk to solicit more participation. You might say: "This is a tough but important question. Turn and talk with the person next to you for thirty seconds about this question." Many teachers report that when they do this, the room erupts with talk. In this case, call the students back together, and once again ask for volunteers to speak. Usually, the number of raised hands is much larger than it was initially.

Just as we suggested meeting individually with students who are hesitant to talk, we would encourage you to meet privately with students who monopolize the floor. You might say: "I see your hand up a lot. I'm not ignoring you, but my job as the teacher is to make sure all students participate. So since your hand is up almost all the time, you might want to think about this. Decide before you raise your hand whether this is something you really want to comment on. Remember, you can always come and talk to me after class about the problem."

Another tool you may want to consider is your inventory of turn-taking strategies. If the people who do all the talking are all boys, or all girls, you may want to introduce the "gender rule" in taking turns and have boys and girls alternate turns. You might decide to allow students to choose the next speaker, instead of choosing them yourself. This sometimes helps by getting students to speak because their friends called on them. (You will probably not want to rely on this turn-taking strategy all of the time, but it can be useful in some circumstances.)

Small-group discussion time offers a great opportunity to increase the number of students who speak during the whole-class discussion. As you circulate among students working in small groups, listen in on their conversations. If you hear a particularly quiet student articulate an insightful idea, ask an important question, or describe an effective solution strategy, ask that student if she or he would be willing to share the contribution later with the entire class.

You may also consider assigning random speakers as representatives of their small groups. Notify these students in advance that they will speak during the whole-class discussion. For example, in a discussion about solution methods, say: "In a moment, I'm going to call on several small groups to tell us how they solved the problem. The person in each group with the birthday closest to today will speak for each group. So, in your small groups, determine who that person is, decide what you want that person to say, and have that person practice what he or she is going to say."

Sometimes you may feel that the few who raise their hands early and often are the most able, and that you want to use what they have to say. Their contributions may be the most dynamic, the most illuminating in terms of getting other students to understand the issues. We encourage you to use the insights of those students. Build on their contributions. Just make sure that you don't fall into the habit of relying on them to support your use of talk to the exclusion of other, less clear or less confident students. Your goal is to build a classroom community in which everyone can participate.

Should I call on students who do not raise their hands?

For many teachers, one of the toughest parts of using student talk in the class-room is deciding whether to call on students who never volunteer. In every classroom there will be one or two students who are truly reluctant to say anything. Are they benefiting from the use of talk in the classroom if they never talk and only listen? The little research that exists on the question seems to indicate that students certainly can benefit by listening. They can learn without talking. However, as we argued in Chapters 1 and 2, there are benefits to participating in talk, from attention and motivation to clarification of understanding and improvement in language facility. So, how should you handle the few cases where you get the distinct feeling that you are torturing the students by waiting for them to answer a question?

Some teachers feel that if they call on such students they may actually harm them. In our view, if you are sensitive and supportive, you will actually help such students, rather than harm them. Once again, we recommend talk-ing to the student privately. Ask the student about his or her concerns and reluctance. Try to come up with a plan that will let the student dip a toe in the water, so to speak. A few planned contributions can build confidence, and the student may overcome a barrier that will help him or her in other areas of life as well. Your efforts with such students may continue over a number of months. You can use a variety of strategies to help them start to participate. Call on these reluctant students right after partner talk, when they have had a chance to practice with a partner. Ask: "What did you and your partner come up with?" You may even wish to work with such students during partner talk to help them prepare what they will say.

Remind students of their right to "pass" when you call on them. The obli-gation to participate in a discussion does not equate to an obligation to give answers on demand. Rather, it means that students are expected to communi-cate about what they are thinking and what they need to help them learn. So, students who need more time to help them learn have the right to this time. You might say: "Remember, if I call on you and you need more time to think about your answer; that's no problem. Just say, 'I need more time.' Or, 'Can you come back to me?'" When a student does ask for more time, be sure to remember to revisit with this student later in the discussion.

A more general issue related to this is how we call on students every day. Should we call only on those students whose hands are raised, or should we try to distribute the turns equally throughout the class? This is a difficult issue, and different teachers will have distinct views on it. In our view, the most effective approach is to try to get all students to make a significant contribution at least once every few lessons. And in order to get them over the hurdle of speaking out loud in a group, it may also be a good idea to have each student say at least one thing every day, even a minor request for clarification.

This topic bears on your adherence to Principle 3, creating the conditions for full participation, and thus will involve your choices of turn-taking strategies. Some teachers formally incorporate a requirement that all students participate at least some of the time by using a list of student names, choosing at random from the list until everyone is called upon. While this has the advantage of making sure that a few students don't dominate all the talk, it has disadvantages as well. Some days certain students may have very valuable contributions to make about a particular topic. If they cannot contribute at will when they have something important to say, the entire enterprise may become less interesting for them. In general, you will want to strike a balance that allows equitable participation but that also allows students to retain as much sense of self-determination as possible.

My students will talk, but they won't listen.

You may be fortunate to have a class full of students who are willing to talk and share their reasoning. However, these same students may have another problem: They may be so involved in talking that they don't listen well. Instead of listening to one another's contributions and building on the idea of the preceding speaker, they may interrupt, talk over one another, and contribute ideas that all but ignore the previous contributions. Sometimes small groups of friends may talk together while others are talking in the large group. There may even be some discourteous or disrespectful talk about others' contributions. How can you get students to listen respectfully to one another and think together as a class?

Start by having a talk with the whole class. Remind them that each of them has the right to be heard, but that this means they have a corresponding obligation to listen. Start to rely more heavily on the move of asking students to repeat what the previous speaker has just said. If they are not able to do this, use whatever classroom sanctions you have in place to let them know that this is a serious obligation.

One teacher had students in fourth grade who were not very good at making their contributions connect with those of the previous speaker. He ended up with lots of disjointed talk, where one student's turn had no obvious connection to the next. For a while he tried to draw the connections for them, but finally he decided to ask them to start each turn by saying either of two things: "I agree/disagree with what [the previous speaker] said because . . ." or "I want to add on to what [the previous speaker] said . . ."

We think you will find that if you are consistent, asking students to respond specifically to one another's contributions, students will begin to internalize the obligation to listen to others and think about what they have said.

"Huh?" How do I respond to incomprehensible contributions?

As we have shown in some of the examples in previous sections, students' responses are sometimes almost impossible to understand. What should one do when a student produces a really unintelligible utterance? What if it is so incomprehensible that you cannot even begin to rephrase it because you just haven't understood any of it? The temptation is simply to say, "Oh, I see. How interesting," and quickly move on to another student. This way we can avoid embarrassing ourselves and the student at the same time! However, in the long run, this will really undermine your purposes. You want students to practice at becoming clearer in their thinking and talking. What better place to start than with a student who is very unclear? You want students to learn that it is worth the struggle to try to clarify one's meaning. If you pass over unclear students, other students will learn that it's better to avoid embarrassment than to engage in the struggle for clarity.

If you are working hard to engage students in challenging mathematics, you will not be able to avoid this problem. People—whether adults or children—who are talking about something new and complicated tend to sound unclear. As comprehension gets more difficult, fluency and clarity decrease. In our experience, when teachers introduce a new and challenging mathematics topic, up to half of all contributions in a class may be very difficult to comprehend. So what can be done?

First, use the tools of revoicing and repeating. Try to repeat even a few words the student has said. If you can't do this, ask another student to do so. Unlikely as it seems, we have often seen students give wonderful renditions of what we found incomprehensible. In a way, this makes sense. You are up at the front of the class, trying to keep track of twenty-five different individuals and the contents of the lesson as well. Students can afford to sit at their desks listening. They may have understood something that got by you. Keep trying until you get at least a partial insight into what the student was saying. Remember to ask: "Is that what you said?" when either you revoice or another student repeats the original speaker's idea. In an effort to understand a contribution, listeners can often misinterpret what was said, and the student's original point can morph into something quite different in intent from the speaker's original statement.

Also ask unclear students if they would like to come up to the board to show the class what they are thinking. Even in classroom discussions, a picture is still worth a thousand words. It is important, however, not to let the students' written representation (e.g., equation or picture) supplant their verbal description. Once students record the representation on the board, ask them to explain what they have shown. Then, ask several other students to explain what the representation shows and repeat what their classmates have said.

There will occasionally be times when neither you nor anyone else can understand what a particular student is saying. If you need to move on, you can say to the student something like this: "Well, I guess we haven't really understood your contribution. See if you can work on it, and if you want to give it another try later, I'll come back to you." The student may or may not want to pursue it later, but at least you have conveyed the message that each student's ideas are worth struggling with.

Brilliant, but did anyone understand?

Occasionally a student will make a mathematically brilliant contribution, or one that at least has the potential to open up some important issues for everyone. But as you look around the room, you wonder whether you and the student are the only two people in the room who have understood what the student said. What are you to do?

First, start by asking the student to repeat. Say something like: "Wow, that sounds really interesting, but I got lost in the middle. Can you repeat that?" Next, ask several other students to repeat. This alerts them that they all have to pay attention to what has been said. Make sure that you ask the originator of the idea whether he or she agrees with the other students' interpretations. If the originator does not agree, he or she will have to repeat and clarify the idea. Even if the originator does agree, have several students in succession try to repeat the idea. If the idea is really important, having multiple students repeat it will ensure that most of them understand it, and that many of them will appreciate its significance as the discussion proceeds. In fact, you may even want to use one to two minutes of partner talk here to give everyone in the class the opportunity to repeat and make sense of the idea.

If the contribution is a lengthy one, don't be afraid to interrupt the speaker so that the other students are called upon to repeat the statement in parts rather than in its entirety. After the speaker makes one key point or describes one step in his or her thinking, say, "Let me interrupt you for a moment. Torrence, can you repeat what Diane just said?" Many times students are unable to repeat a comment because the comment is simply too long. Asking the speaker to stop at key points gives students time to think so that they can continue to follow along with the reasoning step by step.

Should you pitch in at this point, attempting to give yet another rendition of what the original student said? In our view, although it's tempting to take over and revoice the student's excellent contribution yourself, we think you should refrain, if you can. By allowing other students to try first, before you step in, you focus everyone's attention on the contribution, and you allow the originator to get credit for the insight. It also reinforces the joint, collaborative nature of the discussion. You can play a role, however, in determining the extent that all students understand the contribution, and in moving the conversation forward to aspects that they still may not understand.

You may also use the board as a revoicing tool. You can scribe what other students say as they try to clarify the originator's idea. Students may also scribe or illustrate their points. Sometimes slowing down the process enough to write things down allows you to get a clearer idea of how to proceed. And getting across the importance of a difficult new idea or an original observation can take a long time. We once watched the important idea of one student slowly become clear to other students over the course of two different lessons.

I have students at very different levels.
Most teachers are confronted with a wide range of backgrounds and abilities in their classrooms. If you are trying to get the students to focus on the same problem, what do you do if some of the students do not understand the problem? How can you have a discussion when your students are at very different levels?

Many teachers follow the practice of grouping weaker students with stronger students, because they believe that high-achieving students can help the weaker students understand the material. In our experience, in talk-intensive classrooms, this often does not work well. What happens is that high-achieving students quickly come to an understanding and present a solution, and the talk ceases long before the weaker student can participate in thinking through the problem. Even when the higher-achieving student tries to explain his or her reasoning in a sort of expository or lecture style, there is no guarantee that the weaker student will benefit. Often the weaker student takes on a very passive role as a learner, and this is the opposite of what we are trying to foster.

Therefore, the practice we have adopted is to pair students of similar ability and of compatible personality. What do we mean by similar ability and compatible personality? This is something that a teacher can discover only through getting to know the students. It doesn't necessarily mean pairing boys with boys and girls with girls, but rather is based on your intuition of which students will be able to talk to one another in a productive way. This may sometimes mean that a weaker student is paired with a student on grade level. Or a student on grade level may be paired with one of the most able students in the room. The only real proviso is to avoid pairing the very strongest students with the very weakest students.

Some teachers randomly assign partners, and this can work as well. But even in this case, you want to think carefully to avoid problems. In our experience, if you want to get the most out of this model of using talk, you might do well to pair students of similar ability, at least part of the time. Finally, you can switch partners at regular intervals, and if you see that a partnership is not working, don't be afraid to intervene and change partners.

It's important to notice that this isn't equivalent to putting students into ability groups that are given different tasks. Everyone here is doing the same task, and when the talk begins in whole-class discussion, everyone will have taken on the same set of problems. However, it's possible to give students who understand quickly an additional question or challenge that they can do while other students work with the main assignment. This also allows the teacher to provide more scaffolding and support to groups and pairs that need it. What we are aiming for is flexible grouping based on what students know about a particular area, and based on what the teacher has perceived about their ways of interacting.

What should I do when students are wrong?

Discussions like the ones you will experience are often full of mistakes of various kinds. In the process of working through a problem, students may use a word incorrectly. They may use a computational procedure incorrectly. Their answers may be wrong, sometimes strikingly wrong. Your task is to figure out how to respond. Our suggestions here fall into two broad categories: how to handle students' feelings about being wrong, and how to allocate time to their mistakes.

First, we'd like to point out that this kind of instruction requires students to agree and disagree with one another at some point. Often, in this atmosphere of inquiry, students will notice when someone says something wrong, or two students will come up with different answers. For most students, being wrong is not pleasant, and not trivial. Many students will still have the idea that success in mathematics means being right, not being a strong thinker. It is helpful to explicitly discuss the value of wrong answers, and the unavoidability of mistakes and errors. Errors can be repositioned as a source of new knowledge. Teach your students to say: "I'd like to revise my thinking" or the phrase that often pops up spontaneously in a good discussion: "I disagree with myself!"

It's very important to monitor the norms of respectful discourse at points like these, when a student has come up with a wrong answer. You do not have to avoid calling attention to a wrong answer, but you do need to continue to reassure students that it's OK to be wrong, and that all students must be sensitive to the feelings of someone who has publicly made a mistake.

Second, it will sometimes be the case that you will be in the middle of a good discussion where a student is making an important mathematical point. In the middle of making this point, the student will say something incorrect, such as "five times eight is forty-eight." You might wonder: Should you stop the discussion to correct this error, at the risk of derailing a conversation where students are getting intellectually involved? We encourage you to be sensitive to the flow of discussion. If students are dealing with new and difficult ideas, and the point of the discussion is to get clarity about concepts and ideas, it might be perfectly acceptable to ignore a minor mistake. However, if you are in a review, or in a discussion in which you are going over something that has become familiar to students, that is a good time to insist on high standards of correctness.

This discussion is not going anywhere . . . .

Sometimes you may get the impression that although your students are willing to talk and listen respectfully, the conversation is slow, repetitive, and even dull at times. If this is happening consistently, ask yourself whether you are "beating a dead horse" and going over material after the majority of students have understood. If you feel that there is too much repetition, you may be asking too many students to repeat ideas that they have already made sense of.

Use the small-group time that typically precedes the whole-group discussion to do a quick, formative assessment of students' thinking. For example, if most student groups are successfully solving a problem using a particular strategy, there may not be a need to explore this strategy further during the whole-group discussion. Rather, look and listen for effective and efficient strategies that groups are using with limited success and use those as the focus of your whole-group discussions. Discussions around the mathematics with which students are not yet proficient have the greatest potential to increase understanding.

Another issue may be the level of your questions. If there are too many low-level questions, you may not have appropriate fodder for a high-level, exciting discussion. It helps to work with colleagues on this issue. You might ask someone to come in and observe you, to see if your use of the tools of talk could be sharpened.

Sometimes the problem is that students are introducing interesting but tangential questions, and although the discussion is lively, you are not making progress toward your mathematical goals. It's important to remember that you cannot follow up on every single point. In order to keep the discussion moving, you will have to ignore some things and move other topics to the forefront. This is why planning is so important—it's easy to lose sight of your goals and get off track with interesting but tangential questions.

Students' answers are so superficial!

At the beginning of this process, as you first begin to use talk intensively, students may not know how to respond. They will rely on the strategy they have used before, namely, to provide a one-word answer to the teacher's question, as in the following example:

1. Ms. G: So what method do you think you'll use to solve this problem?
2. Phil: Subtract. [No response from Ms. Glass] Yes, subtract!

This is a typical response from a student who has not had much experience carefully thinking through a problem and presenting reasons for his responses. What should Ms. Glass do here? One option is to ask Phil why he thinks the method should be to use subtraction. Imagine, however, that Phil responds: "I don't know." What next? Ms. Glass could refer him back to the problem, asking him again why subtraction seemed to him to be a good method. Or she may ask him to describe the features of the problem that helped him decide to subtract. Upon rereading the problem, Phil may actually think more deeply about the problem, rather than simply trying to supply a one-word answer that in another class would be sufficient.

The principle here is that the teacher must continue to focus on reasoning: Ask students to justify their decisions, whatever sort of decisions those are. Don't be afraid to press them for evidence or reasoning. Students we have worked with have told us that they appreciate the experience of being made to think more deeply. Although they do say that they feel pressured sometimes, they enjoy the fact that mathematics starts to make sense because they are forced to make sense of it.

What if the first student to speak gives the right answer?

Imagine you have posed a problem to your students and after giving them time to solve the problem with a partner, you then begin the whole-class discussion. You ask, "Who can tell us how they began to solve the problem?" The first student you call on gives a coherent, articulate explanation of the correct answer. What do you do? Put aside your plans for a discussion? Move on? Not yet.

First, recall what you observed and heard when students were working in pairs or small groups to solve the problem. Did most of them solve the problem correctly before the whole-class discussion began? If so, you may wish in the whole-class discussion to ask several other students to repeat the speaker's statement and explain why they agree or disagree with its reasoning. Then, ask everyone to turn and talk with the person next to them about whether they agree or disagree with the speaker's comment, and listen to see if most can do so successfully. If the students can, it is not necessary to continue the discussion of a comment that most, or all, students understand. After all, classroom talk is productive when it allows students to progress in their understanding, not simply reaffirm what they already know. (If you have time, you can capitalize on their understanding by posing a similar but more difficult problem or problem extension for students to discuss. This will allow you to reach the mathematical goals of your lesson while still engaging the students in productive discourse.)

If the students you call on to respond to the speaker's comment cannot do so successfully, you may wish to use the techniques described in the section "Brilliant, but did anyone understand?" Or, you may feel that this comment will have much greater significance if discussed later on. Perhaps students do not seem clear on the constraints of the problem, nor are they sure of which strategies to use. Maybe most have solved the problem incorrectly and need clarification of their misconceptions before discussing the correct solution. In this case you may say to the student, "You have given us a lot to think about. I know I need to back up a little bit and think more about making sense of the problem and deciding which strategy to use and why. I'm going to ask if you would be willing to say your comment again a little later on. I know it is going to be helpful to all of us."

Further, if you wish to avoid this scenario in future discussions, use the partner- or small-group discussion time to decide who you will call on and in what order. For example, you may wish to begin the discussion by calling on several students whom you heard restate the problem and question articulately and thoroughly, even though their solution strategies may have had problems. Then, you may wish to call on students who explored different ways to solve the problem, progressing in difficulty and complexity. Notifying these students in advance that you plan to call on them also increases the productivity of the whole-group discussion. The more you know about what your students understand and the more prepared they are to speak, the more strategically you can use their contributions in a whole-class discussion.

What should I do for English language learners?

Three-quarters of the students whom we worked with in Project Challenge were English language learners. Yet they all made tremendous progress in classrooms using intensive talk. Teachers with ELL students should not shy away from using this approach to mathematics, but it helps to think carefully about the demands of the talk moves and formats we have introduced here. First, make sure that you give students plenty of time. Use wait time consistently and patiently. Waiting up to thirty seconds may be necessary, and if you have many native English speakers mixed in with your ELL students, you will have to model for them the value of waiting. Second, it may take longer into the year before such students are ready to handle the demands of talking, repeating other students' contributions, or making their own. Think carefully about putting them on the spot. But as the year progresses, do not assume that you must simply leave them out of the discussion. Talk with students outside of class to encourage them to ask a question, or to ask for clarification.

We found in Project Challenge that the talk moves and talk formats introduced in this book actually support language learning as well as mathematical thinking. There are ideas and practices throughout the book that will help students who are learning English. In Chapters 3 and 7, the emphases on definitions, concepts, and representations are particularly relevant for English language learners. Use revoicing to help them make their contributions clear, and use repeating and revoicing to make others' contributions clearer to them. Over time, the experience of listening closely, repeating, and making their own contributions will push your students ahead in English as well as mathematics.

I'm falling behind in my curriculum.

Teachers who are new to using talk in their classrooms typically report falling behind in their curriculum as one of their concerns. They find that asking students to explain and clarify their reasoning and respond to and repeat each other's ideas turns a one-day lesson into a two- or three-day event. In the face of this dilemma, teachers often revert back to direct instruction techniques in order to "catch up" but then worry that their students aren't getting better at using talk to learn mathematics. These are all typical and understandable concerns. Unfortunately, there are no quick and easy answers to managing the time pressures of teaching mathematics using any form of instruction. However, we have found that teachers who stick with talk do get better at managing instructional time.

We suggest that you plan your discussion questions in advance. Choose two or three questions that focus on the mathematical objectives of the lesson. Make sure that these questions are open-ended in either approach or answer. Ask students to repeat the answers to these questions. Chapter 9 has more information about asking questions and other important components of planning talk-based lessons.

Teachers who use talk-based instruction with their textbook series sometimes find that the discussions allow them to make adjustments to their curriculum. Sometimes students' comments reveal that they know more than what the textbook lesson assumed. For example, if several student groups use a strategy that is not covered until later in the chapter, the teacher may decide to focus the entire whole-class discussion on this strategy. This allows the teacher to move forward in the curriculum by either combining or consolidating lessons. In addition, talk encourages students to connect new ideas to previous understandings. Review of important mathematical concepts and skills often occurs naturally. Thus, teachers sometimes find that they no longer need to devote entire class periods to review.

Students are off-task while working in small groups.

Human beings are inherently social. Any adult who has ever worked in a cooperative group knows that a certain amount of socializing in a group setting is inevitable. Nonetheless, it is serious concern when the social aspect of the group interferes with and prevents learning from taking place. While off-task behavior is detrimental to any type of teaching, it is particularly problematic with discourse-intensive instruction. Students who do not engage in small-group discussions will likely be unable to participate in whole-class discussions in a meaningful way. There are a number of reasons why small-group talk may be unproductive. First, the questions the groups are to discuss may not be complex enough to support talk from multiple perspectives. If a question (for example, "Identify the parallel and perpendicular lines in the diagram") can be answered with a one-word response, students will quickly answer and then start talking about nonmathematical topics. Another reason small groups get off-task is because a task or question (for example, "Explain your method for solving this problem") doesn't provide enough fodder for all group members to stay engaged. Often only one or two students share their ideas and methods and the other students state that they agree with them. In this case, the question may be a good one but the talk format has not supported all students articulating their reasoning. Thus the format should be changed to partner talk. We tend to use partner talk much more often than small-group talk for exactly this reason. Partner talk guarantees that both students will have a chance to share their thoughts, thus staying engaged.

But what if the question posed to a group is a good, complex one and students are still off-task? What should you do? One way to make sure that students work productively in their small groups is to be very explicit about their accountability to the whole class. This can be accomplished by assigning each group a specific question or one part of a multistep problem or task to discuss later with the entire class. Alternatively, you may assign each member in the class to be the designated speaker for a particular question or problem step. In reality, you will not call on every student to speak about every question or problem. But anticipating that you might call on them to speak will likely motivate students to stay on-task.

Reassurance from Project Challenge Students

As you begin these new practices, you may be sensitive to negative reactions from students. Many people respond to new practices with complaints or resistance. You may feel that requiring students to listen to each person's contribution is too demanding, or that waiting twenty seconds for a student's answer puts too much pressure on them. We have some reassurance from some of our students in Project Challenge, the project described in the preface. Recall that about 75 percent of the students in the low-income urban schools we worked in were second-language learners of English, as were the Project Challenge students. We had had concerns since the beginning of the program about the challenges they might experience in our talk-intensive classrooms. Although we had seen tremendous growth, we wanted to know how they felt about it. So at the end of the fourth year of Project Challenge, we took some class time to ask one hundred seventh-grade students for their reactions to our four-year focus on productive talk. The following examples reveal what students said and wrote about talking and listening.

When asked, "Was being required to listen to each other helpful or not helpful?" approximately 95 percent of the students surveyed responded "helpful." When asked why he thought listening was helpful, Anton made the following remark: "Sometimes [math] is confusing but when you listen carefully, you can figure out how to do the math slowly, or little by little, and you find out how to do it." Anton's comment is that of an experienced and effective listener. He knows that listening does not make understanding instantaneous or automatic. Rather, as he says himself, listening helps learning *slowly, or little by little*. And how does this happen? It happens when students have conversations about mathematics, often revoicing an idea over and over again, until peers reach a common understanding of an idea. The listening continues as students comment on why they agree or disagree with an idea. All the while, the listeners are learning from the students who are talking. Anton not only knows how to listen, but also sees its value in his learning.

Mel offers a perspective on how talking and listening go hand-in-hand in learning mathematics. He says, "It helped us when we got to hear other people's answers. We can add things to our answers to make them better than [the solution] we had originally from the question that we had to answer." Mel's comment targets one of the very core benefits of listening—helping us figure out what to say and how to say it. Mel knows that we listen not for the sake of listening, but so that we can broaden what we know about a subject and thus get better at speaking about it. He knows this because he has been encouraged and expected to listen to his classmates and then use their statements to form and articulate his own reasoning.

Brianna's comment mirrors Mel's remark. She writes: "Listening to each other is helpful because if we don't listen to each other, how can we understand what each of us has to say?" Aaron writes: "It's helpful because if it was not required [to listen] I wouldn't pay attention." Jan says, "You can see other people's points of view. People can correct their mistakes by hearing others." These comments are from students who participated in talk-intensive classes. But their comments show that they understand the benefits of listening. And that's what is required if students are going to use listening as a learning tool as they continue with their studies.

When asked, "Was having to talk to others about math helpful or not helpful?" approximately 88 percent of the students responded "helpful." Jan notes that it is important to explain yourself in math class because, "In real life, if you can't explain and don't have evidence, it doesn't count." Aaron, who writes that listening forces him to pay attention, thinks, "It's helpful [to talk] because I could ask questions." Barry says, "I like the talking to your neighbor or partner thing because if somebody doesn't really understand something and they talk to their partner, their partner can help them understand it so you get to go on without being confused or having trouble." These students can articulate the benefits of talk because they have experienced these benefits regularly and consistently in their mathematics classes. By talking about their reasoning and receiving the support to do so, students come to realize that it is important to be as clear as possible, provide supporting evidence, and use talk as an opportunity to get clarification and understanding.

During the discussion about talking and listening, Tina and Mrs. Anderson had an exchange that shows that even when students are uncomfortable with talk, they still see its worth. Mrs. Anderson asked Tina if she liked being called on in discussions. This is the conversation that ensued.

1. Tina: Sometimes you push me to say the answer and I really don't know the answer.

2. Mrs. A: What happens if I keep pushing you and you still don't know the answer?

3. Tina: I tell you I don't know.

4. Mrs. A: And then what happens?

5. Tina: You go to call on a different person.

6. Mrs. A: So how does that make you feel?

7. Tina: Better.

8. Mrs. A: And when I call on another person what are you doing?

9. Tina: Listening.

10. Mrs. A: And then do you usually raise your hand after that?
    [Tina shakes her head no.] Why not?

11. Tina: 'Cause you'll usually just come right back and ask me.

12. Mrs. A: And when I come back automatically, then how do you feel?

13. Tina: Better because then I would know the answer.

It is not easy or enjoyable for students, or anyone, to admit that they do not know something. But the fact remains that not knowing answers is a normal part of life. And because it is, saying so should be a part of talking in math class. Students should be allowed to say when they do not know or cannot explain something. Some teachers are surprised when we push to revisit a student after he or she admits to not knowing an answer. They think that it puts too much pressure on a student who already has admitted that he or she lacks understanding. Tina's comments indicate that the opposite is true. Tina admits that she feels better when Mrs. Anderson goes on to speak with another student; it takes the pressure off of her. But while the other student is speaking, Tina is listening. So, instead of the discussion continuing without a contribution from Tina, Mrs. Anderson comes back to her. This gives Tina a chance to show what she has gained from listening, and she gets to contribute to the discussion. This, Tina says, makes her feel better. Tina's comments suggest that students appreciate being revisited since it gets them past the discomfort of "not knowing the answer" and on to being a contributor to the discussion.

When asked how she felt about the expectation to contribute to class discussions, Kara responded that she didn't like it. She said, "Some girls don't really know the answer or are shy and don't want to speak." When asked whether she felt that there was a payoff to speaking despite being shy or unsure, Kara said, "Sometimes it's worth it because you end up knowing the answer but you didn't know it before." Ryan told us that he did not like being called on to talk because when he was not paying attention, it was embarrassing. He then went on to say, "If I got called on and wasn't paying attention, I was afraid I would get called on again so I started paying attention." Both Kara and Ryan are quite honest in their feelings about required participation—they don't like it. But both also name benefits to it—it helps them pay attention and learn new information.

We end this chapter with one last striking example that convinced us that classroom talk was a difficult but rewarding endeavor. This example centers on Gayle, a Project Challenge student. When Gayle began Project Challenge in fourth grade, she did not say much at all in class. Watching Gayle and her partners complete a project, her fourth-grade teacher remarked, was like watching a silent movie. Gayle struggled on her weekly quizzes and did not seem to be benefiting from this instructional approach.

Yet over the course of fifth grade, Gayle began to change. Her fifth-grade teacher worked hard to get Gayle to speak in class. When called on, Gayle would often respond with a short to long period of silence, which was then followed by a short, barely audible response. Her teacher continued to call on Gayle, and each time her responses got a little louder, a little longer, and a little more sensible. While her evolution was slow but steady, one particular example of her emergence comes to mind. Gayle's class was discussing the sum of angles in a triangle. The question posed to the class was whether or not it was necessary to measure all three angles in order to determine the measure of each. Many students maintained that it was necessary when Gayle spoke up with this comment: "You don't need to measure all the angles because the sum is one hundred eighty degrees. So if you know that two of them are one hundred twenty degrees, you just ask yourself, 'What plus one hundred twenty is one hundred eighty?' and that gives you the answer." After she made this comment, Gayle's classmates were asked what they thought of her idea. As they were speaking, most in support but some still dubious, Gayle's teacher looked back at Gayle and saw her straighten her posture, throw her shoulders back, and while maintaining a serious look on her face, beam with quiet confidence. At the end of the program, Gayle was described by her seventh-grade teacher as still quiet but articulate, responsive, and engaged. Of talking and listening, Gayle writes: "It was helpful to listen and talk to each other because I got to listen to how people thought about problems and why they agreed or not, and I got to talk to people and tell them what I thought about certain things."

Gayle's transformation occurred because she had teachers who were determined to get their students to talk productively about their mathematical understanding. None of those teachers said it was easy. All said, without hesitation, that it was worthwhile. As you begin to use talk in your own class, you will help students change like Gayle did.

DISCUSSION AND REFLECTION

1. Which of the challenges described in the first part of this chapter have you experienced? Which of the authors' suggestions helped you overcome these challenges? What other strategies have worked?

2. Calling on students is a particularly emotional and complex issue. What do you think about calling on students who have not raised their hands to speak? Do you think calling on them is an effective instructional strategy? Why or why not?

3. The authors describe what happened when they asked their students to react to the use of productive talk in math class. Ask your students what they think about talking in math class. Specifically, ask them to describe how they think talk has or has not helped them learn math.

Case Studies

1

Grade 3: Looking at the Shape of the Data

This chapter presents a case study of a talk-based lesson in Mrs. Robert's third-grade class. Before we begin looking at her lesson and its plan, we want to make it clear that Mrs. Robert and her students are fictional characters. What happens in this lesson, including the students' successes, trials, and tribulations with classroom talk and the resulting teacher actions and reactions, are a compilation of our experiences with dozens of teachers and hundreds of students over the course of many years. We have heard students discuss this topic just as Mrs. Robert's students do in the dialogues presented here, and we have observed teachers act and react in ways similar to those of Mrs. Robert. We pulled from all of these experiences to bring you the events in this classroom example. We offer this case study as a realistic picture of what sometimes happens when you first strive to use the talk moves described in this book. You will see that Mrs. Robert's lesson does not go

NCTM Standards:
Data Analysis and Probability, Measurement

Grade 3

well. We have observed and experienced our own fair share of disappointing talk-based lessons and want to help you avoid some typical pitfalls. We hope this case study provides insights into how to use talk effectively and strengthens your willingness to persevere with using talk when a lesson doesn't quite work the way you had predicted.

Mrs. Robert's nineteen third-grade students are in the early stages of a unit on linear measurement and data analysis. The lesson at the focus of this case study is on interpreting and analyzing data about the length of students' feet. (This lesson is adapted from Economopoulos et al. 1995.) In this lesson, data are displayed in a line plot. The goals of this instructional sequence include using various units to measure lengths, discovering relationships among units, and analyzing measurement data using graphic representations. In previous lessons students measured distances by pacing. They compared and contrasted their pace sizes, and explored the relationship between size of the unit (i.e., their pace) and number of units (i.e., the number of paces) needed to measure a given length. They recorded the number of paces needed to measure a given distance in a line plot. In this lesson, Mrs. Robert planned to have students use a twelve-inch ruler to measure foot length in inches and then determine the typical foot length in their class.

Mrs. Robert is a third-grade teacher in a suburban school system that has just adopted a standards-based curriculum. Due to budget constraints, however, there has been little opportunity for professional development on how to use the new curriculum effectively. As a result, many teachers are confused about the philosophy, implementation, and goals of the new curriculum. Mrs. Robert recently attended a regional mathematics conference where she participated in a workshop on mathematical discourse. In this workshop she learned about many of the talk moves described in this book. She immediately sensed that mathematical discourse fit hand-in-hand with the mathematical investigations of the new curriculum. After attending the workshop, Mrs. Robert was inspired. She felt that she had found a way to teach math that would be engaging and rewarding for both her and her students. She knew, however, that one workshop would not be enough to become proficient in mathematical discourse. Nonetheless, she took copious notes during the workshop and began to make changes in her teaching the week following the conference. A dedicated and experienced teacher, Mrs. Robert is determined to have success using talk in her mathematics class. Her lesson shows, however, that just as she predicted, determination does not necessarily equal success.

We pick up the lesson about fifteen minutes after its start. Mrs. Robert first reviewed with her third-grade students what they had learned about linear measurement and data representation so far. Then Mrs. Robert launched into the day's main lesson.

1. Mrs. R: We are going to measure the length of our feet to see if we can find the typical foot length of a member in our class. So the first thing we have to decide is whether or not we are going to take our shoes off when we measure our feet. I'd like you to talk to the person next to you about this for a moment. [There is silence in the classroom. Many students look confused. So, Mrs. Robert explains again.] Maybe I was not clear. Since we are going to measure our feet we need to

216

know whether or not to take off our shoes. Talk about that with the person next to you. [Students begin to talk. Mrs. Robert walks to another part of the room to gather the rulers. She then calls on students to share what they talked about.] OK, Leigh, what do you and your partner think?

2. Leigh: We don't know.

3. Mrs. R: What do you mean, you don't know?

4. Leigh: Well, we didn't really know what we were supposed to be talking about.

5. Mrs. R: You could have asked another student. Who can tell Leigh and her partner what you were supposed to be talking about? Joe?

6. Joe: I think we should take our shoes off . . .

7. Mrs. R: Hold on, Joe. I didn't ask you that. I asked if you could repeat the question I asked you all to discuss with your partners.

8. Joe: We were supposed to talk about taking our shoes off.

9. Mrs. R: Sort of. I wanted you to discuss whether or not you thought we should. [At this point, the other students seem restless and disengaged. Some are writing on a paper that was handed out earlier but was intended for homework. A few are talking. Some others seem to be daydreaming.] Go ahead, Joe.

10. Joe: OK, so I think you should take your shoe off because, like, my toe is not touching my shoe so that would be wrong.

11. Mrs. R: Lara, do you agree with what Joe said? [Lara looks bewildered.] Joe, can you say what you said again? And everyone else, you should be listening too. [Some students seem to focus in at this point but not many.]

12. Joe: Um, I forgot what I said.

13. Mrs. R: Does your partner remember?

14. Dana: Actually, I thought we should leave our shoes on. See my shoe? It's exactly the same as my foot.

15. Mrs. R: What do some other people think?

16. Barb: I think someone maybe doesn't want to take their shoes off. They shouldn't have to if they don't want to.

17. Mrs. R: Do you agree with that, Bianca?

18. Bianca: What?

19. Mrs. R: I said, "Do you agree with what Barb said?"

20. Bianca: Well, I have something else to say. My partner and I had rulers already so we measured and it was the same.

21. Mrs. R: OK, but I didn't ask you to measure yet, did I? I wanted you to talk about whether the shoes on or off mattered. Did you hear what Barb said? [Bianca shakes her head.] Barb said that people should have a choice about leaving their shoes on or off. Do you agree with that?

22. Roberta: Yes, because it doesn't matter. [Mrs. Robert notices that Andrew seems very upset and is shaking his head no.]

23. Mrs. R: Andrew, do you have something to say?

24. Andrew: Yeah, they're wrong.

25. Mrs. R: Andrew, if you don't agree, you need to say, "I disagree with your idea." And tell us why you disagree.

26. Andrew: They're wrong because look at my shoe next to my foot. [Andrew stands up with his shoe off and lying next to his foot. Few of the other students can see so they clamber around to get a view. In doing so, there is some chatter and pushing.] See the difference? So it does matter.

27. Mrs. R: Martin, do you agree or disagree?

28. Martin: He should put his shoe back on. His foot smells. Peeeuuuu! [The students burst out laughing.]

29. Mrs. R: Martin, that was inappropriate. Please apologize.

30. Martin: But it does—smell it!

31. Mrs. R: Please apologize, now!

32. Martin: Sorry. [He rolls his eyes as he says this.]

33. Mrs. R: I want everyone to go back to their seats and sit quietly for a minute. [Mrs. Robert tries to regain her composure. She decides to try partner talk again.] Please turn and talk to your partner again about the decision to leave our shoes on or off. [As students talk, Mrs. Robert sees that many are still giggling about Martin's comment.] So, Tonya, what do you think?

34. Tonya: It doesn't matter.

35. Mrs. R: Do you agree, Raul?

36. Raul: Yes, it doesn't matter.

37. Mrs. R: Well, since we can't seem to decide, I'll decide for you. You are going to take your shoes off to measure.

Clearly, this is not what Mrs. Robert had planned for this part of the lesson. Her students are not listening to her or each other, do not know what to say or how to work together during partner talk, and do not seem to be treating each other with much respect. In addition, most of the students' comments are shallow, disjointed, and inarticulate. This part of the class took slightly over ten minutes and the lesson is going nowhere. What did Mrs. Robert envision for the lesson? Did she anticipate that this part of the lesson would take so much time? Let's take a look at her lesson plan.

Planning and Projecting

Mrs. Robert's Lesson Plan

IDENTIFYING THE MATHEMATICAL GOALS

- Students will make conclusions about the class foot lengths by looking at the shape of the data when organized in a line plot.
- Students will determine the typical foot length in their class by looking at the value(s) with the highest frequency or where the data clumps.
- Vocabulary: *data line plot, range, typical*

ANTICIPATING CONFUSION

- Students may think that the range of a set of data is the difference between highest and lowest values written on the line plot rather than the difference between the highest and lowest recorded pieces of data.
- Students may think that the highest value in the data shows what is most typical. They may think the word *typical* means *biggest* or *most*.

ASKING QUESTIONS

- Should we leave our shoes on or take them off?
- What do you notice about the shape of our line plot? What does the shape of the line plot tell us about the data set?

(continued)

- What is the range of our foot lengths? How do you know?
- What does *typical* mean? Explain.
- What is the typical foot length in our class? How do you know?

LESSON OUTLINE

1. Review what students have learned about linear measurement and displaying data in previous lessons in this unit.
2. Explain the task. Students will measure their feet in inches and then organize their data in a line plot.
3. Ask the students to discuss whether or not they think they should keep their shoes on.
4. Discuss how to use a ruler to measure lengths.
5. Students measure their feet and record the data on the line plot.
6. Have a whole-class discussion about the data.

Seeing Mrs. Robert's lesson plan reveals just how much the beginning of the lesson went awry. Her lesson plan mentioned that she would ask students to talk about whether they should leave their shoes on or off, but this was certainly not a goal nor a major focal point of the lesson. Yet, it consumed a significant amount of time during the lesson. Mrs. Robert's plan suggests that she thought students would be able to talk about the shoe issue coherently and briefly and then move on to exploring the heart of the lesson, collecting and looking at the data. This is not what happened.

Now that we have seen the discrepancy between the plan for the introduction and the implementation, let's explore possible reasons why the students' use of talk was unsuccessful. We will also show Mrs. Robert's reactions to the lesson as revealed in a conversation she had with her mentor teacher, Mr. Brown, who has more experience using talk in math class. We will also share our ideas about this based on our own experiences using talk.

Troubleshooting with a Colleague

Mrs. Robert sought out Mr. Brown after the lesson because she was distraught at how the lesson had gone. She began by explaining to Mr. Brown how surprised she was at her students' inability to pay attention to what others were saying in the shoe debate. She was surprised because "the class started with a good discussion about what students remembered from previous lessons in the unit." But when Mr. Brown asked Mrs. Robert for details about this part of the lesson, it became apparent that this review was not a discussion at all. Students volunteered things they remembered, but they were not required to restate each other's remembrances, question each other's statements, or connect their ideas to one another. Mrs. Robert realized that she had no idea whether or not her students were even listening to one another as they spoke. Their performance in the shoe discussion would suggest that they were not. Mr. Brown suggested that during lesson introductions, when students are asked to think about things they've learned, they should be required to relate their comments to the comment of the previous speaker. Mrs. Robert thought this was a good idea. She also decided she would try using repeating during future reviews in order to find out if they were listening.

When Mrs. Robert asked her students to talk with the person next to them about the shoe decision, the students were silent. When she restated the question, they did start talking to their peers, but not very productively. Leigh said that she and her partner did not know what to talk about. Joe and his partner, Dana, did not reach an agreement as partners.

Sometimes problems with getting students to talk productively together are due to the questions posed. If a question (for example, "What type of graph is shown on page 7 in your book?" or "What is the difference between a tape measure and a ruler?") can be answered with a word or phrase or the answer is obvious, it will not support discussion. But the appropriateness of questions must be considered in light of the age and sophistication of the students. Questions that are trivial for third graders can be very challenging for first graders. Other times the problem is with *how* a question is posed. A good question might not elicit discussion simply because students are confused by it. This may have contributed to the unproductive attempts in Mrs. Robert's classroom. Mr. Brown suggested that since Mrs. Robert's students were new to discussion that she use a more focused question to start. Her presentation might have been:

> Today we are going to investigate the length of our feet. Are our feet all the same length? Do third graders typically have feet this big, this big, or this big [teacher shows with hands three different lengths]? To find out we need to measure our feet. So our first decision is whether to measure our feet with or without our shoes on. Talk to your partner about

why we might want to leave our shoes on when we measure
and why we might want to take our shoes off. Come up
with at least one reason for both methods.

Why did Mrs. Robert's students have so much trouble with partner talk? They are inexperienced talkers. They may not know what to say or do when she says "turn and talk to your partner." After all, it's unfair to expect that students inherently know the procedures for discourse-intensive mathematics classes. Recall that when the students began talking, Mrs. Robert stepped away to gather the rulers for the lesson. It's very likely that if she had stayed and listened to what the students were saying (and not saying), she would have heard that they were not using partner talk productively. Mr. Brown suggested that she work with students during the partner-talk time. She would certainly not have time to speak with every pair, but if she spoke with two pairs each time she used partner talk, she would eventually have checked in with each group. During this time, she could observe and step in where necessary, making sure pairs were speaking to each other, responding to each other's ideas, and resolving any disputes by focusing on mathematical reasoning.

Mr. Brown also volunteered to come in to Mrs. Robert's class so that together they could model for the class how to talk during partner-talk time respectfully and productively. Realizing the key role that partner talk plays in productive discourse, Mrs. Robert asked him to come as soon as possible. Mrs. Robert also had an idea of her own. When she worked with a pair on using partner talk effectively, she would then ask them to briefly share with the whole class what they discussed.

Students' inability to agree or disagree with what each other said was also a distraction. Lara's bewildered look suggested she did not even know where to begin answering the question. Bianca either could not or would not state why she agreed or disagreed with Barb's comment. She instead wanted to give her own reason and eventually had to admit that she did not even hear Barb's comment. When Martin was asked whether he agreed or disagreed with Andrew's comment, he responded with an inappropriate, cruel remark. Raul, when asked if he agreed with Tonya's idea, could only repeat her three-word utterance.

Keeping in mind the students' lack of experience with classroom discourse, none of this is surprising. The ability to state why one agrees or disagrees with an idea is a sophisticated one. It requires listening to what was said, making an effort to comprehend it, and trying to see how it fits in with one's own level of understanding. Although some students may be able to start off at this level, this is certainly not an "entry-level" talk move for all students beginning to talk in math class. It's a talk move to aim for, but not necessarily one to start with. The talk move Mrs. Robert should start with is the repeating one to get students accustomed to listening to each other. Only when students have been taught to listen to each other throughout class can they be expected to move on to agreeing and disagreeing.

Another problem in this part of the lesson was the disrespect that Andrew and Martin exhibit. Andrew is not respectful in his disagreement with Bianca idea, beginning in Line 24. Mrs. Robert encourages him to be respectful by saying, "Andrew, if you don't agree, you need to say, 'I disagree with your idea.' And tell us why you disagree." But he ignores her, beginning his comment once again with "They're wrong because . . ." Then, his disrespect is met with further disrespect from Martin, whose comment is mean and distracting for the entire class. Andrew's comment seems to indicate that Mrs. Robert needs to spend more time setting the ground rules for respectful and courteous talk. Without this, students will not be willing to say much of anything. In her discussion with Mr. Brown, Mrs. Robert agreed that she needed to revisit the ground rules with the entire class and the consequences if they fail to meet the expectations. She also will insist that students like Andrew disagree respectfully when they speak. This means that she will stop students every time they begin to be disrespectful and not let them continue until they have amended their statements.

Mrs. Robert was upset about Martin's comment. She is a sensitive teacher who takes students' cruelty to each other as a sign that she has failed to create a safe environment for them. In our work, we have seen students use talk for malicious purposes. Reasons for this include students not knowing how to handle a discussion that isn't focused on their ideas, students' personal conflicts with other students, and students' desire for attention. Mrs. Robert thinks she knows why Martin made the comment about smelly feet. Martin is a very smart student. His hand is usually the first one up when she asks a question. At the beginning of the year, Mrs. Robert became accustomed to calling on him frequently. Having attended the talk workshop and having realized the importance of calling on many students, she has started to call on him less and less. Martin's reaction to this has been to fool around with friends when others are speaking, to call out, to wave his hand furiously in front of Mrs. Robert, and to yell inappropriate comments like "She never calls on me," when she calls on someone else. Mrs. Robert thinks that Martin's comment about Andrew's foot was his way of trying to regain some attention in math class.

We have met our fair share of students like Martin. However, we have been able to help them become active, positive contributors to class discussions.

Sometimes this change comes about by talking to the whole class in a very direct manner about what types of comments, gestures, actions, and sounds are and are not allowed in the class. Modeling how to speak coherently and respectfully also helps. Often we have to speak individually with the student about his or her behavior and about the class policy on respect. Finally we sometimes have to call parents and work together with them to help their child be respectful. Students like Martin usually change, but it takes intervention.

When Mr. Brown asked Mrs. Robert how she ended this part of the lesson, Mrs. Robert said that she decided for the class to take their shoes off. When asked why she did that, Mrs. Robert said she felt that the discussion was "dead" and that no matter what talk moves she might have attempted, she'd ultimately be unable to revive it. Besides, the clock was ticking and the data had not even been collected or analyzed. Mr. Brown agreed that her decision was reasonable.

The two spent some time brainstorming how she might have helped the students make the decision about measuring with or without shoes on. Before Mrs. Robert asked the students to talk with their partners again in Line 33, she might have helped the students pinpoint the positions students had taken so far, along with their reasons for those positions. This could have been done by writing the positions and their supporting reasons on the board. After partner talk, students would have had to defend one position and come up with a reason for it. These reasons would also have been posted. Mrs. Robert and Mr. Brown agreed that this may have helped the discussion progress further by giving students a way to build on each other's ideas.

The last idea that Mr. Brown suggested was for Mrs. Robert to take a more active role in discussions that did not seem to be progressing. For this example, she may have posed a question that forced students to realize that no matter which decision they made, they needed to be consistent. She might have said, "Suppose that Raul and Andrew have the same foot length but Raul leaves his shoe on to measure and Andrew takes his off. If Raul reports that his feet are eight inches long and Andrew reports that his are seven and a half inches, is this accurate data? Why or why not?"

Mr. Brown is skilled in using classroom talk. He regularly gives his students opportunities to explain their reasoning and for peers to argue for and against ideas with reasons based on mathematical evidence. But he knows that it is his job to make sure that students make mathematical gains in his class. He knows that ultimately he is the one who determines whether a discussion is mathematically meaningful. So, when he sees that a discussion is not progressing, he takes a more active role in it, such as asking questions (like the one he suggested to Mrs. Robert) that force students to reconsider their positions. These questions do not take over the reasoning process for the students. Rather, they give them the assistance they sometimes need to build strong mathematical arguments either for or against a certain position.

Not everything about this part of the lesson was a problem. Note that none of Mrs. Robert's students refused to speak. Certainly, many of their comments were neither meaningful nor connected, but they all said something when called on. Having seen classes where many students say nothing at all when called on, we know that this is a feature we should not undervalue.

Improvising and Responding: In the Midst of the Lesson

We wish we could say that Mrs. Robert's lesson went more smoothly when she returned to it the next day. But, as you will see, the rest of the lesson was problematic as well. After deciding for the class that they would take their shoes off, Mrs. Robert continued the lesson as follows.

38.	Mrs. R:	Tim is passing out the rulers. You will measure your feet in inches, and you should round off to the nearest half-inch. If you have any questions, you should ask me or a friend. Once you have your feet measured, you'll come up to the white board and add your data point to the line plot. We have used line plots in many of the lessons so far in this unit. [She draws the line.] What do you think will be the shortest foot length? Joe?
39.	Joe:	Three inches.
40.	Mrs. R:	OK. [She writes *3* at the left end of the line plot.] And the longest? Tina?
41.	Tina:	Twelve inches?
42.	Mrs. R:	OK. [She writes *12* at the right end of the line plot.] So, since we are measuring by halves, we would fill in from three to twelve by halves. So if you have a foot that is three and a half inches long, what do you do? Ralph?
43.	Ralph:	Put an X above three and a half?
44.	Mrs. R:	Yes. OK, you can start measuring and I'll stand up here to help you put these data on the line plot.

As students measure, Mrs. Robert waits at the board and looks around at the students who seem to be having no difficulty measuring. The first two students soon come to the board with their measurements. As planned, Mrs. Robert helps them put their Xs in the correct places, with the correct sizing and spacing. The third student says that she can't put her measurement up because it's 18 and there's no 18 on the line plot. Her partner has a measurement of 16; she complains that there is no place for her foot length either. While Mrs. Robert is asking them about how they got their measurements, another student asks, "What do I do if my number's not up here?" Mrs. Robert suspects that many students have measured in centimeters, so she decides that this is a perfect time to use talk to discuss the difference between inches and centimeters.

45. Mrs. R: Could everyone please stop measuring and take their seats. We seem to have a problem with our units. I asked you to find the length of your feet in inches and I think that some of you might have found your measurements in centimeters. Someone got eighteen units. Who can tell me why I think that's centimeters?

46. Jan: 'Cause the ruler only goes up to twelve on the side we were supposed to use.

47. Mrs. R: Mark, can you repeat what Jan said?

48. Mark: No.

49. Mrs. R: So ask her to repeat it.

50. Mark: Could you repeat it?

51. Jan: I said the ruler only goes up to twelve on that side.

52. Mark: She said the ruler only goes up to twelve on that side.

53. Mrs. R: And why is knowing that important?

54. Mark: [He shrugs his shoulders.]

55. Mrs. R: OK, let's back up then. Someone came up to the board and reported that their foot was eighteen long. I think that that person must have measured in centimeters. And why do I think that, Jan?

56. Jan: Because the inch side only goes up to twelve.

57. Mrs. R: Go on.

58. Jan: And there is only an eighteen on the centimeter side.

59. Mrs. R: Mark, can you repeat Jan's comment?

60. Mark: She said that there is not an eighteen on the inch side and that's why you think the person measured in centimeters.

61. Mrs. R: Jan, is that what you said?

62. Jan: Yes.

63. Mrs. R: Go ahead, Carla; your hand is up.

64. Carla: That side isn't centimeters, it's "mm."

65. Mrs. R: What do you mean "mm"?

66. Carla: It says "mm" on the end.

67. Andrew: That means millimeters. It's eighteen millimeters!

68. Mrs. R: So you think it's millimeters. What do some other people think?

69. Raul: It's centimeters.

70. Tonya: Mine doesn't say "mm" it says "cm."

71. Jeff: Where are you guys looking? I can't see. Mine doesn't say anything; it's just a bunch of lines.

72. Cindy: Wait, *which* side do we look at? This is confusing.

73. Jeff: Can I come up to the board now?

74. Katie: Do we line our heel up with the tip of the ruler or with the one-inch mark?

75. Mrs. R: Martin, stop spinning that ruler! [Martin has made a propeller out of his ruler and a pencil.]

Mrs. Robert looks around and realizes that students have different types of rulers. Some rulers do have "mm" written at the beginning of the metric side. Some others are only metric rulers! Mrs. Robert notices that with ten minutes left in the class, the students have neither filled in their data nor learned anything about what is typical. She is about ready to give up for the day. Feeling tired and discouraged, she is at a complete loss for how to save the lesson.

Before we reveal how, or whether, Mrs. Robert moved forward, let's explore what happened in this part of the lesson. First, let's recall what Mrs. Robert had planned for this part of the lesson. As she wrote in her plan, she was going to discuss how to use a ruler to measure lengths. What actually happened, however, was that she *told* the students to round off to the nearest half-inch and called on only one student to give a possible shortest foot length and another to give a possible longest foot length. She accepted their suggestions without asking them for explanation, justification, or feedback from their peers. The students did not discuss how to measure with a ruler or how to make sense of the two measurement systems displayed on the rulers. When reflecting about why her plan was so different from what took place, Mrs. Robert said that she was afraid that if she let the students discuss these issues about the ruler, it would take up too much time and, like the shoe discussion, go nowhere. So, she reverted back to an "IRE" (initiation, response, evaluation) technique, calling on her high-achieving students to make sure she got reasonable responses. She said that at this point in the lesson she was desperate to get the students measuring without any more delays.

We think that Mrs. Robert's reaction was both natural and reasonable. If the goal of the lesson is to measure the length of their feet, then efforts must be made to get students to reach this goal. Unfortunately, however, students were not able to reach this goal because some could not use the ruler accurately and others used metric rather than customary units. Possible reasons for this include misconceptions about linear measurement and a lack of experience using rulers to measure lengths. Furthermore, the rulers were not all of the same type. Had Mrs. Robert taken the time to discuss the ruler as she had planned, it is very likely that students' difficulties and misconceptions would have surfaced. Once on the surface, they could have been addressed and corrected. So, Mrs. Robert was faced with a discourse paradox: If she had stopped to talk about the ruler, the students might not have had time to measure. But by not talking about the ruler so that they could get to the measuring, they were unable to measure correctly.

Is there a solution to such a paradox? We think so. First, during the lesson, Mrs. Robert might have reminded herself why discussing how to use the ruler was in her plan. Had she stopped to think about this, she might have realized just how crucial this skill was to collecting, recording, and analyzing the data. Alternatively, the decision not to discuss the ruler wasn't necessarily a bad one. Because many students did not take the correct measurements, they disclosed what they didn't understand about linear measurement. Whether preventative or reactive, we believe that any time students reveal what they know and don't know about mathematics, it is beneficial to us as teachers. For Mrs. Robert, her decision not to discuss the ruler meant that students had to confront their own shortcomings with this instrument. Mrs. Robert can now use this as a "hook" for future discussion about using rulers.

Before going on, we want to point to talk moves in this part of the lesson that worked well. After Line 47, when Mark could not repeat what Jan said, Mrs. Robert had him ask her to repeat it. This is a good habit and an important expectation to set in the early stages of implementing classroom talk. If students are not listening, it is their job, not the teacher's, to ask another student to repeat it. Mrs. Robert could have asked Jan to repeat it herself but instead had Mark do it. In our experience, when teachers keep insisting that students ask each other to repeat, eventually they no longer need to be prompted, but instead do so on their own. After Jan repeated her statement at Mark's request, he was able to repeat it. But by then, Jan's statement had been taken out of its original context. As a result, Mark was unable to explain the importance of the statement. This is reasonable—if he wasn't listening to Jan, it's unlikely he was listening to the question, and thus he had no idea what significance "the ruler only goes up to twelve on that side" could possibly have. Mrs. Robert handled the situation well. Knowing that Jan's statement had lost meaning to Mark, it probably had lost meaning to others. But instead of taking Mark and the others off the hook by explaining to them why Jan's comment was important, she continued to hold the students accountable for this responsibility. She did this by "backing up" to the question to which Jan responded, giving the reason for asking this question, and having Jan restate her comment. At this, Mark was able to repeat Jan's reasoning in a meaningful way.

It is often important to "back up" the conversation to help students get back on board. Sometimes repeating just one statement is not enough for a student to contribute to a discussion. Recapping a segment of a discussion and then invoking the repeating move is a normal and necessary part of classroom talk, particularly in its initial stages.

So now we will end the suspense and reveal how Mrs. Robert's lesson ended.

76. Mrs. R: First I see that I have passed out some rulers that do not even have inches marked on them at all. I apologize for that. [She collects these rulers and gives students rulers that do have inches marked on them.] We need to figure out what happened because some people got measurements like eighteen nineteen, and twenty. Jan said that eighteen can't possibly be inches since the ruler is only twelve inches long. But we are not sure about the marks on the other side of the ruler. Let me give you this piece of information. The width of my pinky is about one centimeter. So, can you use

this information to identify the marks for centimeters on the ruler? While I go and check to make sure you know how long a centimeter is, talk to the person next to you about whether or not the length of eighteen is probably centimeters, millimeters, inches, or something else. [Mrs. Robert walks around the room checking to see if everyone can correctly identify the length of one centimeter on the ruler. This takes about three minutes.] OK, so who would like to tell us what you think? Is the eighteen millimeters or centimeters or something else?

77. Abel: It's centimeters since eighteen millimeters is way too small.

78. Mrs. R: Grace, what did Abel just say?

79. Grace: I couldn't hear him.

80. Mrs. R: So ask him to repeat it.

81. Abel: I said—

82. Mrs. R: Wait, Abel. Grace, you need to say, "Abel, can you please repeat it?"

83. Grace: Abel, can you repeat it?

84. Abel: I said that the eighteen is centimeters, since millimeters would be like . . . like this big. [He makes a gesture with his thumb and index finger.]

85. Grace: He said that it must be eighteen centimeters since eighteen millimeters is too small.

86. Mrs. R: And do you agree or disagree? And tell us why.

87. Grace: I agree because on my ruler there is no way someone's feet is this small. [Gestures to the eighteen-millimeter mark.]

88. Mrs. R: How did you know to point there?

89. Grace: Those little marks are millimeters, so I counted eighteen of them right to here.

90. Mrs. R: Nigel, how does Grace know where eighteen millimeters is?

91. Nigel: [Silence for fifteen seconds]

92. Mrs. R: Do you need her to repeat it?

93. Nigel: Yes.

94. Mrs. R: So, ask her.

95. Nigel: Can you repeat it, Grace?

96. Grace: I just counted the little marks until I got eighteen.

97. Nigel: There's eighteen centimeters there, which are those black marks.

98. Mrs. R: Is that what you said, Grace?

99. Grace: I couldn't hear him.

100. Mrs. R: So ask him to repeat it. And from now on, try to remember that if someone is speaking and you can't hear, you need to give me the signal. [Mrs. Robert demonstrates the signal—a hand cupping an ear.]

101. Grace: Could you repeat it, Nigel?

102. Nigel: There's eighteen centimeters at that mark you pointed to.

103. Grace: No, eighteen millimeters.

104. Nigel: Yeah, eighteen millimeters.

105. Mrs. R: OK, so we are out of time. Let's summarize where we are right now. We agree that the non-inch side on the ruler has marks that show centimeters and millimeters. The centimeters are about as wide as my pinky finger. The millimeters are the little marks that show the lengths in between the centimeters. We also agree that the eighteen must be eighteen centimeters since the ruler is only twelve inches long and it doesn't seem possible that someone had a foot that was almost two rulers long. Also, the eighteen is probably centimeters since eighteen millimeters is way too small. Tomorrow, we will talk some more about the ruler, continue to measure our feet, and make our line plot.

Mrs. Robert began this part of the lesson with a status report. She corrected the ruler situation and restated Jan's idea about a possible reason for the measurement of eighteen. She restated for the class what they were confused about—the meaning of the marks on the side opposite the inches—and gave them a benchmark measurement, the width of her pinky, to aid in students' understanding. Based on students' lack of experience exploring customary and metric units of measure, this piece of information certainly seemed to be a good way to help the students learn about the metric side of the ruler. It would have been futile to have continued a "what do you think they are" discussion about the unknown marks, since it seemed apparent that students had little previous knowledge of these metric units. In general, it makes sense to discuss mathematical ideas of which students have some foundational knowledge. While Mrs. Robert's decision to check to see if each student could identify a length of one centimeter on a ruler took a bit of time, it ensured that more students understood what the marks represented on the metric side. This allowed them to figure out why some of their classmates believed that a measure of 18 was likely centimeters.

Much of the time spent during this part of the lesson was used by students who had to ask each other to repeat what they had said because either they weren't listening or could not hear. Mrs. Robert lamented to Mr. Brown that she was very frustrated by this since it seemed to be such a tremendous waste of class time. Mr. Brown told Mrs. Robert that he too has been frustrated when students have used valuable class time having to ask someone to repeat something because they were not listening or because the speaker was not speaking loudly enough. But while the students who are not listening may waste time, Mrs. Robert's continued insistence that they ask each other to repeat is time well spent. Mr. Brown assured Mrs. Robert that her students would get better at listening if she continued to hold them accountable for it. Through her unyielding and consistent efforts to have students ask each other to repeat a statement that they did not hear, her students will learn that listening is required, not requested.

In Line 86, Mrs. Robert asked Grace to state why she agreed or disagreed with Abel's idea. Grace was able to do so coherently and reasonably. One may wonder why Grace could do so when so many other students could not. While two possible reasons include Grace's listening skills or her knowledge of linear measurement, another is found upon a closer examination of the dialogue. Mrs. Robert asked Grace to agree or disagree with Abel's idea after Grace had been able to successfully repeat the idea. This is a fine use of the reasoning talk move, as students can only agree or disagree if they have successfully heard and made sense of the comment in the first place. In the first part of the lesson, Mrs. Robert often jumped straight to the agree-or-disagree question without asking students to repeat. As a result of problems her students had with listening, they were not able to answer this question. While we would still recommend to Mrs. Robert that she focus on the repeat talk move, we would also recommend that when she uses a reasoning question, it only follows the successful repeating of an idea.

Summarizing and Solidifying

Mrs. Robert ended the lesson with a recap of what happened and an outline for what was to happen the next day. This is an important part of classroom talk. So much goes on during a class where students are using talk that it is important to leave students with focal points of the discussions. It is these focal points that allow students to see the significance of the talk, its relevance to past learning, and its linkage to future lessons. These focal points also allow students to reflect on their own learning by thinking about what they learned in the discussion and what they still have to work on. For example, a student listening to Mrs. Robert's statement may think, "I still don't know what those little marks are, but tomorrow I am going to get to listen to other people talk about it." This type of self-reflection, an essential component of learning, is one of the many benefits of classroom discourse.

When she talked with her mentor, Mr. Brown, Mrs. Robert learned a great deal. She learned first and foremost that the endeavor to use talk would be a long-term effort. She learned that she would have to take it step by step. She learned firsthand the value of principles discussed in Chapter 8. She had jumped into using talk without adequately setting up the conditions for a respectful and supportive environment (Principle 1). She had not explained her expectations about the new forms of talk she was introducing (Principle 4). And she had certainly not limited herself to one new thing at a time (Principle 5). Mrs. Robert learned that her students needed to work on using partner talk productively and on listening to each other when they spoke. Feeling back in control and with plenty of good ideas running in her head, Mrs. Robert sat down and made some notes about the next day's lesson, starting once more the process of planning and projecting.

We think that Mrs. Robert and her students are well on their way to using talk to support their learning of mathematics. Mrs. Robert has identified the elements of the lesson that caused her students difficulties, and more importantly, she has thought of specific ways to avoid such difficulties in future lessons. Further, Mrs. Robert's students are willing to talk and seem poised to learn how to talk effectively and respectfully. We would encourage Mrs. Robert to continue to try one new talk move at a time and stick to this goal during each lesson. We recommend that she continue to reflect on what worked and did not work after her lessons. By doing so, she can learn to use talk moves that have been effective for her class more frequently, and she can eliminate the decisions that are reducing the effectiveness of discussions. We would also encourage her to stay as motivated as she is, since the payoff for her efforts will likely be more than worthwhile.

Discussion and Reflection

1. This case study highlights the importance of setting up a respect-ful, supportive environment for mathematical discourse. What has helped you and your students create and maintain such an environment?

2. What strategies have helped your students get better at listening to each other during a whole-class discussion? What hasn't worked?

3. How have you reacted when a student (such as Martin) makes a disrespectful comment during a discussion? What has worked? What hasn't worked?

4. After teaching her lesson, Mrs. Robert wrote notes to prepare for the next day's class. If you were Mrs. Robert, what would you write in your notes? What strategies might she use to increase the productivity of the next day's discussion?

2

Grade 5: Algebra

We will now examine a lesson designed to develop students' algebraic reasoning that Ms. Nolan planned for her fifth-grade students. Like Mrs. Robert in the previous case study, Ms. Nolan is a fictional character. Also like Mrs. Robert, she is a character whose words and actions are similar to those of many teachers with whom we have worked. Her students are also a synthesis of many students whom we have seen use talk to learn mathematics. This lesson is similar to dozens of lessons we have taught and observed about algebra.

NCTM Standards:
Algebra,
Reasoning and
Proof

Grade 5

Ms. Nolan is an experienced teacher who has been using talk in her mathematics classes for two years. In addition, Ms. Nolan's school, which is in a suburb outside of a major city, has made a commitment to using talk to support learning in mathematics classes. So, by the time Ms. Nolan's students meet her in fifth grade, they are familiar with the rules of respectful, productive talk and with responding to classmates' mathematical reasoning through partner talk and whole-class discussion. This by no means makes Ms. Nolan's students perfect—or even proficient—communicators in all instances. But you will see that generally they are able to communicate their reasoning quite well.

Planning and Projecting
Ms. Nolan's students have worked diligently to develop fluency with multiplication and division of whole numbers. While instruction in earlier grades focused on developing students' quick and fluid recall of multiplication and related division facts, in fifth grade, the instructional goals are centered on concepts and skills of long division. Prior to this lesson, students have

explored how division is related to multiplication, including which properties of multiplication hold true for division. They have generated efficient strategies for dividing with both a single- and double-digit dividend, and they have solved a variety of contextualized problems that focus on the partitive and quotative interpretations of division. In particular, students have discussed how to use the context of a situation and the numbers involved to choose an appropriate computational procedure or problem-solving strategy.

Ms. Nolan knows that it is an important mathematical goal for her fifth graders to connect what they are learning about arithmetic to algebra. Specifically, she wants them to use their knowledge of multiplication and division to generalize relationships between quantities. She wants them to develop their abilities to use variables to express multiplicative relationships and to solve problems. Another of her instructional goals involves developing students' ability to represent a numerical relationship using different forms, including tables, graphs, and equations. (See page 237.)

To help her reach these goals, Ms. Nolan has found a problem that asks students to generalize about a multiplicative relationship.

> *Cell-Link USA: What's the Deal?*
>
> *Cell-Link USA is a new cell phone service provider. The company is trying to attract new customers with its offer of no monthly fee and the same cost per minute, no matter how many minutes a customer talks on the cell phone each month. The company's advertisement states that a 25-minute call costs $2.00 and a 45-minute call costs $3.60.*
>
> *Answer the following questions about Cell-Link USA's offer:*
>
> *A: What is the cost per minute at Cell-Link USA? Show or explain how you got your answer.*
> *B: Write an equation that a Cell-Link USA customer could use to find the total cost (c) for talking on the cell phone for any number of minutes (m).*

Ms. Nolan began the lesson by asking students to share their experiences with cell phones and cell phone billing plans. Students had a lot to say about this subject. A few of the students had their own cell phones, but most talked about their parents' cell phones and their complaints about their monthly bills.

Ms. Nolan passed out a copy of the problem "Cell-Link USA: What's the Deal?" to each student. She asked the students to read the problem silently on

Ms. Nolan's Lesson Plan

IDENTIFYING THE MATHEMATICAL GOALS

- Students will use multiplication and division to find a unit rate (cost per minute).
- Students will use a variable to represent a defined unknown.
- Students will write an equation that models a multiplicative relationship.
- Vocabulary: *variable*

ANTICIPATING CONFUSION

- Students may find the cost per minute using a "guess-and-check" strategy instead of division, making it difficult to write an equation.
- Students may use iterative thinking (e.g., $+0.08$) when they write their equations.
- Students may reverse the variables in their equations (e.g., $0.08c = m$ rather than $0.08m = c$).

ASKING QUESTIONS

- What patterns do we notice in the chart? How can we use these patterns to find an equation?
- What does $0.08m$ mean? (Does it mean eight cents per minute?)
- How do we interpret an equation that has variables? What do the numbers and letters in the equation represent?

LESSON OUTLINE

1. Make sense of problem together as a class.
2. Students work on problems in small groups.
3. Whole-class discussion: different methods for Part A of the Cell-Link USA question, agreeing on an equation for Part B.

their own. Then, she said, "OK, all good problem solvers work hard to make sure they understand a problem before they try to solve it. So, in a moment I want you to talk with the people at your table: What is the problem about? What's the situation? What is the important information we are told? I'm not asking you to share your answers or even strategies for finding the answers. I just want you to talk with each other about the problem. OK, go ahead."

As students talked in groups of two or three, Ms. Nolan circulated and listened to their conversations. When she heard a student state an important part of the problem in his or her own words, she asked the student to be prepared to share that statement with the entire class. So, before the whole-class discussion reconvened, Ms. Nolan had already assigned speakers to talk about each part of the problem.

After a few moments, Ms. Nolan called the students back together.

1. Ms. N: OK, thanks everyone. So, let's talk all together. Reanne, what is this problem about? Tell us what your group discussed.

2. Reanne: There's a company called, um, Cell—, Cell-Link USA, and they don't make you pay for the monthly fee. You just have to pay for what you talk. I mean for how long you talk.

3. Ms. N: What is a monthly fee?

4. Reanne: It's what you have to pay even if you don't use the phone. My grandmother got a cell phone once and she, like, never uses it. But she was mad because one month her bill was still $40 because it was a fee that she had to pay just for having the phone.

5. Ms. N: I hear you saying that it's important that the company does not charge a monthly fee. Is that what you are saying? [Reanne nods and Ms. Nolan writes *1: No monthly fee* on the board. She also underlines this phrase on the overhead transparency of the problem.] Don, what did you and your group talk about?

6. Don: Well, we thought it was important that it's the same price for all the minutes. It doesn't matter if the phone call is short or two hours; it's still going to be the same price.

7. Ms. N: So, a short phone call, say ten minutes, is the same price as a two-hour phone call? Is that what you're saying?

8. Don: No, the same price per minute.

9. Ms. N: And what does that mean, "price per minute"?

10. Don: That each minute, it is the same price for each minute, and then you have to pay for how many minutes you talk.

11. Ms. N: Emily, can you repeat what Don said about the phrase "price per minute"?

12. Emily: He said it means that each minute is the same amount. *Per* means *each* or *one*. So, it's the same amount of money for each of the minutes you talk.

13. Ms. N: [Writes *2: Same price per (for each) minute* on the board. She underlines this information in the overhead transparency of the problem as well.] What else is important?

14. Andy: A twenty-five-minute call costs two dollars, and a forty-five-minute call costs three dollars and sixty cents.

15. Ms. N: [Lists this information on the board and underlines it in the problem.] OK, so what is it that we are being asked to find out? Darnelle, tell us about Part A of the problem.

16. Darnelle: We need to find out the price per minute?

17. Ms. N: I thought we already knew that—it's *the same* price per minute.

18. Darnelle: Yeah, but we need to find out what that is. Like, is it ten cents or a dollar?

19. Ms. N: OK, good. So what about Part B? Alexa, what are we being asked there?

After agreeing on the questions and problems the students needed to solve, Ms. Nolan sets the class to work in their small groups.

For the first few minutes of the small-group work time, Ms. Nolan circulated and listened, watching for students who were relying on guess-and-check to find the unit rate. She was also listening and watching for students who were using the relationship between multiplication and division to find the cost per minute. One of the strategies her students had found helpful with similar but simpler problems was the use of a chart to double and halve quantities. She was curious to see if any student groups would use this strategy for this problem.

When Ms. Nolan noticed that one group was using guess-and-check in a rather haphazard way to find the cost per minute, she decided to intervene and speak with the group.

20. Ms. N: OK, everyone. Tell me what you are doing to answer Part A.

21. Latteisha: We are just trying different numbers. First we tried five cents a minute. But five times twenty-five is one dollar twenty-five cents, *not* two dollars. Then we tried ten

cents a minute, but that would be two dollars
fifty cents—that's too high.

22. Nick:	Yeah, so if five is too low and ten is too high, it's got to be in between. So, we are going to guess six, seven, eight, and nine.
23. Ms. N:	If we were to write a number sentence to show that a twenty-five-minute call at five cents a minute would cost one dollar and twenty-five cents, what might we write?
24. Latteisha:	Five times twenty-five is one twenty-five. [Writes *5 × 25 = 125* on her paper as she says this.]
25. Ms. N:	Andy, do you agree?
26. Andy:	Yeah, 'cause it's just five cents over and over again.
27. Ms. N:	So let's look at Latteisha's number sentence [points to 5 × 25 = 125]. For your other guess, we could write this [writes *10 × 25 = 250*], but like you said, that's not right either. What do we know for sure about a twenty-five-minute call?
28. Nick:	That it costs two dollars.
29. Ms. N:	So, in our number sentence, we want this number [points to *125* in the number sentence *5 × 25 = 125*] to be two dollars or two hundred cents, *not* one hundred twenty-five cents. So, go ahead and change that.
30. Latteisha:	[Crosses out *125* and replaces it with *200*.] But five times twenty-five *isn't* two hundred.
31. Ms. N:	You're right. So, we have to change the five. But what number do we put in its place?
32. Nick and Andy:	We don't know!
33. Ms. N:	So, what symbol can we put in place of five to show that we don't know yet?
34. Lia:	A question mark?
35. Ms. N:	Well, what do your group members think?
36. Latteisha:	If we put a question mark there, it would look like this [writes *? × 25 = 200*]. Then, we could do division. Oh, I get it! Multiplication and division are opposites, so we should divide.

37. Ms. N: OK, hold on a second. You have a couple of great ideas, Latteisha, but let's make sure your group members are on board. First, what does this mean [points to *? × 25 = 200*]?

38. Latteisha: It means what is the number that you have to multiply twenty-five times to get . . . to get to two hundred cents.

39. Ms. N: Talk to each other about Latteisha's ideas. When we come back together as a whole class, I want this group to share with us how we used these number sentences to help us answer Part A.

Ms. Nolan uses small-group discussions to prepare students to speak during the whole-class discussion. She wants to maximize the effectiveness of a whole-class discussion by asking students to share the solution strategies that are related to her lesson objectives. Notice how she builds off of their previous knowledge of guess-and-check to focus them on writing an equation to model the situation. In addition, one of her lesson objectives is for students to generalize the relationship between multiplication and division and then use division to undo multiplication to find the cost per minute. So, she encourages Latteisha's group to write a number sentence that includes an unknown ($? × 25 = 200$), which will also help them find the unit rate.

When money is involved in an equation, there is the added complexity of writing the equation using either dollars or cents. The equation $? × 25 = 200$ is written assuming that the 200 represents 200 cents. Many students will write the equation this way, even when they talk about the total being $2.00.

Ms. Nolan began the whole-group discussion by calling on Lia, who was in Latteisha's group. She knew that at least one other group (whose members were Danny, Rose, Sterling, and Nastia) had also used guess-and-check, so as Latteisha's group explained how they used their number sentences to answer Part A, Ms. Nolan used the revoicing and repeating talk moves to make sure that this other group made sense of Latteisha's group's method. Following is an excerpt from that discussion.

40. Ms. N: Lia, tell us what your group did to solve Part A of the problem.

41. Lia: Well, first we started to use guess-and-check but you told us to stop doing that.

42. Ms. N: You're right; I did. But let me explain. I knew you could solve the problem using guess-and-check. And guess-and-check is

one of our problem-solving strategies. But my job as your math teacher is to encourage you to get better at solving problems using more efficient methods. And your job as mathematicians-in-training is to push yourselves to use methods that, right now, seem a little new and challenging to you. So, go on, tell us about the method that I did encourage you to use.

43. Lia: So, we were trying five cents a minute, but we knew that was wrong since zero-point-zero-five times twenty-five equals one dollar twenty-five cents but we want two dollars.

44. Ms. N: [Writes $0.05 \times 25 = 1.25$ on the board.] Wait a minute. You wrote this [points to $0.05 \times 25 = 1.25$] but Latteisha wrote this [points to $5 \times 25 = 125$]. Which equation is correct?

45. Danny: We can use either one. Latteisha used pennies. There are one hundred twenty-five pennies or cents in one dollar and twenty-five cents. Our group wrote the money using dollar-and-cents notation. The zero-point-zero-five stands for five cents.

46. Ms. N: OK. That makes sense. Sterling, how did Lia's group know that five cents a minute was wrong?

47. Sterling: Because that would mean that a twenty-five-minute call was only one dollar and twenty-five cents. But the problem said that it was really two dollars.

48. Ms. N: Go on, Lia. What did your group do next?

49. Lia: Well, we were going to make another guess, but instead you helped us replace the one-point-two-five with two-point-zero-zero and the zero-point-zero-five with a question mark.

50. Ms. N: Come up and show this.

51. Lia: [Comes up to the board and writes the following information:]

$$0.05 \times 25 = 1.25$$

$$? \times 25 = 2.00$$

So, this is like asking "what times twenty-five equals two dollars."

52. Ms. N: Danny, why did Lia's group cross out the one-point-two-five?

53. Danny: 'Cause the cost is not one-point-two-five, it's two-point-zero-zero.

54. Ms. N: Rose, why did Lia's group cross out the zero-point-zero-five?

55. Rose: Because the five cents a minute isn't right. But they don't know what is the right rate.

56. Ms. N: What does this sentence [points to *? × 25 = 2.00*] mean?

57. Rose: It means, "What times twenty-five equals two"? And we can answer that by doing division.

58. Ms. N: So, you think it means what times twenty-five equals two? Is that what you said?

59. Rose: What *number*—it means what number times twenty-five equals two dollars.

60. Ms. N: And what do you mean we could do that by division?

61. Rose: Division is the opposite of multiplication, so we can do two dollars divided by twenty-five cents, and that's what goes instead of the question mark.

62. Ms. N: Everyone, turn and talk with the people around you about this number sentence. What does it mean, and how did Lia, Latteisha, Andy, and Nick use it to find the cost per minute?

Ms. Nolan used both talk moves and a visual recording of Lia's thinking to help others make sense of Lia's solution strategy. Ms. Nolan thinks that the talk coupled with writing will give students time to process each other's mathematical reasoning. Notice how Ms. Nolan asks other students to explain the rationale for each of Lia's steps. When teachers give students time to think about what their classmates are saying, and ask them to evaluate the logic of those statements, they develop their own understandings. They consider their classmates' ideas in light of their own and try to make connections between them. This can lead to new knowledge—in this case, how to use an open number sentence to find a unit rate. Or, it can lead to new connections between previous understandings. For example, here students are learning how to apply what they know about the operations of multiplication and division to identify an unknown quantity.

Improvising and Responding: In the Midst of the Lesson

In Line 62, Ms. Nolan asked everyone to talk about the open number sentence *? × 25 = 2.00*. She did this because writing a relationship between quantities using algebraic reasoning was one of her lesson goals. Ms. Nolan saw that several groups solved Part A quickly and simply by dividing 2.00 by 25. While this is an effective strategy, it is an *arithmetic* strategy. Ms. Nolan wants them to use this familiar, accessible math problem to develop their abilities to use *algebraic* strategies, such as writing an open number sentence.

Next, the class agreed on the value that should replace the question mark in the sentence $? \times 25 = 2.00$. The students reasoned that since multiplication was the opposite of division, they could divide 2.00 by 25 to get 0.08. Some students calculated $200 \div 25$ and had to interpret the quotient, 8, as representing eight cents. They discussed how they could write eight cents as *$0.08*.

Then, the class discussed their answers to Part B of the problem. Leo's group had created a chart, and during the small-group time, Ms. Nolan had decided that she would call on Leo's group to share their chart during the whole-class discussion. She has found that charts help students reason about proportional relationships. Students can use multiplication and division to scale quantities down to find unit rates or scale them up as needed to answer questions about a given situation. In this problem, where there is a proportional relationship between the quantities, the chart helps students focus on how the number of minutes and the cost of a call co-vary (e.g., if one quantity doubles, the other must double as well). Ms. Nolan called on Leo to tell the class how his group got their equation.

63. Leo: Well, we used a chart to answer Part A and that helped us with the equation. [Leo comes up to the board and writes the following:]

minutes	cost
25	2.00
45	3.60
50	4.00

We knew that a twenty-five-minute call was two dollars and a forty-five-minute call was three dollars and sixty cents. Since it's the same cost per minute, we doubled to get that a fifty-minute call was four dollars.

64. Ms. N: Meena, how did they get this information? [She points to the third entry in Leo's chart.]

65. Meena: They just doubled the first one. If the call is twice as long, it would cost twice as much.

66. Ms. N: Do you agree that that's true?

67. Meena: Yes, 'cause it's the same price for each minute.

68. Ms. N: Does that support your group's reasoning, Leo? [Leo nods.] OK, go on.

69. Leo: So, then Jocelyn noticed that for the extra five minutes, it was forty more cents.

70. Ms. N: Latteisha, can you repeat what Leo just said?

71. Latteisha: Can you come back to me?

72. Ms. N: Sure. Sterling, can you repeat what Leo just said?

73. Sterling: He said that it gets five minutes more when you go down to that next row, and the money goes up forty cents.

74. Ms. N: Latteisha, can you repeat that?

75. Latteisha: The time goes up five minutes and the cost goes up forty cents. So that means five minutes more cost forty cents more.

76. Leo: So, we knew five minutes cost forty cents and we filled that in our chart. [Leo fills in the first row in his table.] Then, we just knew that five times eight was forty. So, we checked that in our other rows and it worked. So, the rule is times eight.

minutes	cost
5	0.40
25	2.00
45	3.60
50	4.00

77. Ms. N: OK, let's stop for a minute. Everyone turn and talk with your tablemates. How did Leo's group fill in the first row? How did it help them find out the rule was times eight? What does that even mean—"the rule is times eight"? Go ahead.

Ms. Nolan used the "repeating" talk move to help ensure that students were listening to Leo's explanation and thinking about how his group used the chart to find the cost per minute. When Ms. Nolan asked Latteisha to repeat Leo's statement, Latteisha asked for more time. This is something that Ms. Nolan regularly emphasizes with her students: If she calls on them to answer, she does so because she wants to know what they are thinking. So, if they are thinking, "I need more time to think," they should say so. Ms. Nolan has worked diligently to make sure students know that they can always ask for more time to think before speaking in front of the whole class. In fact, she often starts a whole-class discussion with this reminder, "Remember, if I call on you and you're not ready, you can always say, 'You know what? I need another minute' or 'Can you come back to me.' But keep in mind, I *will* come back to you because I want to know what you are thinking." In fact, after calling on Sterling, Ms. Nolan does call again on Latteisha, who offers a very articulate and accurate response.

Leo's final comment in this dialogue is what Ms. Nolan refers to as a pivotal moment in the lesson. He is explicitly connecting the number of minutes to the total cost, which is a necessary step in writing a generalized equation of the relationship between the two variables. In the past, Mrs. Nolan might have repeated Leo's comment herself. Over time, however, she has worked hard to leave the focus on the original speaker and require students to listen to their peers, not just her. Also, because these pivotal moments are so important, she wants to do more than just ask one or two students to repeat the statement. In Line 77, she used partner talk because she wants to give everyone a chance to think about the reasoning of the statement. Then she continued on with the lesson.

78. Ms. N: OK, thanks everybody. What does Leo's group mean that "the rule is times eight"? Victoria?

79. Victoria: He means that to get an answer of one twenty-five, you do twenty-five times eight. To get three dollars and sixty cents, you do forty-five times eight. So, it's times eight when you go across.

80. Ms. N: Jenna, do you agree?

81. Jenna: No, I don't. I did twenty-five times eight and that's two hundred not two-point-zero-zero. I think the rule is times zero-point-zero-eight (0.08) because the cost is dollars, so we have to write the eight cents as point-zero-eight.

82. Ms. N: [Writes *Number of minutes times 0.08 is cost of the phone call* on the board.] This is the same issue we had earlier. Are we representing the eight cents using dollar notation, which is this [points to $0.08] or with cents notation which is this [writes 8¢]? Leo, what does your group think about that?

83. Leo: Oh yeah. We agree. If we did times eight it would be two hundred, which is like pennies. But it's two dollars, so that would be times point-zero-eight.

84. Ms. N: And what's another way to say point-zero-eight?

85. Leo: Eight hundredths.

86. Ms. N: Pete, your hand was up a few moments ago. What did you want to say?

87. Pete: Same thing that Jenna said.

88. Ms. N: Go ahead, say it; it's important.

89. Pete: Every time you do whatever number is in the first column times point-zero-eight to get the number in the second column. So, the rule is, the number of minutes times point-zero-eight, or eight cents, is the cost of the phone call.

90. Ms. N: [Writes *Number of minutes times eight cents is cost of the phone call* on the board.] Leo, does that support your group's reasoning? [Leo nods.] Leo, you said that the chart helped you answer Part A. How? I don't see the cost per minute here.

91. Leo: Um . . . [ten seconds wait time]

92. Ms. N: Well, Leo, you've really helped your group a lot by sharing their ideas. Take a moment and check in with them about this. In fact, let's all talk with the people around us. Where in the chart or in this sentence that Pete gave us is the cost per minute?

After giving all of the students time to think about the statement that "the rule is times eight," Ms. Nolan wanted to check in to see what they talked about. Were they confused, for example, about how Leo and his group members reached that conclusion? Were they able to find a relationship looking across the chart? Could they reconcile the two conflicting statements about the relationship expressed in cents versus dollars? After calling on Victoria, Ms. Nolan called on Pete. At first he was reluctant to share since, he said, his contribution was the same as Jenna's. Ms. Nolan has noticed that her students are often unwilling to say something that has already been said. But, she knows that doing just that will give the students time to process the most important ideas of the lesson. Ms. Nolan was careful to check back in with Leo to make sure that his reasoning was interpreted correctly. She has also noticed that when students comment on each other's ideas, those ideas evolve into new ideas that are not related to the original comment. This can make the original speaker uncomfortable, and it can shift and diminish the focus of the discussion. So, she is careful to revisit with the original speaker to make sure his or her reasoning is being upheld.

When Leo was unable to explain how he used his chart to find the cost per minute, Ms. Nolan used that situation for two purposes. First, she gave Leo a chance to check in with his group members. After all, he is a representative of his group and should have the opportunity to call on them for help. Second, Ms. Nolan used the moment for everyone to "check in" with their group. Students need to be able to identify the unit rate in order to write an algebraic rule generalizing the relationship between time and cost. Using small-group talk at this moment in the lesson increased students' readiness to reach the next objective of the lesson.

After the small-group talk, the lesson continued. On the blackboard were the following two sentences and the accompanying number sentences:

Number of minutes times eight cents is the cost of the phone call in cents. $8 \times 25 = 200$

Number of minutes times 0.08 is the cost of the phone call in dollars. $0.08 \times 25 = 2.00$

93. Ms. N: Go ahead, Clare. [Clare is in Leo's group.]

94. Clare: It's the eight cents. That really means eight cents per minute. [Ms. Nolan writes *per minute* under the *eight cents* in the sentence *Number of minutes times eight cents is cost of the phone call in cents* and under the *0.08* in the sentence, *Number of minutes times 0.08 is cost of the phone call in dollars.*]

95. Ms. N: Nick, what does the eight mean?

96. Nick: Eight cents per minute.

97. Ms. N: Mathematicians use sentences written in words all the time to express relationships. But they also use equations using symbols.

98. Clare: Yeah, we have an equation. It's—.

99. Ms. N: Hold on, Clare, let's all take a moment and check in with our group. We'll try to predict your equation and then you'll tell us if we are right.

After two minutes of small-group talk, the lesson continued as follows:

100. Ms. N: OK, Lia, your hand is up.

101. Lia: We think it is m times eight equals c.

102. Ms. N: [Writes $m \times 8 = c$ on the board] And what do m and c stand for?

103. Lia: The m is the number of minutes and the c is the total cost of the call. [Ms. Nolan adds this information to the board.]

104. Ms. N: Why are there letters here? Why can't we just use numbers?

105. Lia: Because the number of minutes and cost change.

106. Ms. N: Andy, can you repeat that?

107. Andy: They're letters because they can change.

108. Ms. N: Mathematicians call m and c or the number of minutes and the cost of the call *variables*. And the reason is exactly what you said Lia—because they *change*, or *vary*. Clare, what was your group's rule?

109. Clare: Well, it was sort of the same. But we used 0.08. So we had m times zero-point-zero-eight equals c. [Ms. Nolan writes $m \times 0.08 = c$ on the board.]

110. Ms. N: So, we have two equations. I'm wondering if they are both correct. Both equations begin with the number of minutes and end with the cost of the call. And both have multiplication. But I *know* that eight is not the same as eight hundredths. How can both of these equations be correct? [Ten seconds of wait time] I only see a few hands. Turn and talk with your group about this.

While the students were talking, Ms. Nolan listened in. She specifically listened for a group that recognized that the two equations express the quantities in terms of different units. Namely, one rule is defining cost in terms of dollars and the other in terms of cents. As soon as Ms. Nolan heard a group discussing this, she helped that group articulate their thinking and then asked them to share it with the whole class.

111. Ms. N:	OK, thanks everybody. Let me call your attention back to the front. Carlos, go ahead.
112. Carlos:	In the first rule, the eight is eight cents per minute. In the second rule, it's still eight cents but it's like . . . like dollars.
113. Ms. N:	What do you mean by "it's like dollars"?
114. Carlos:	Like in the first one, OK, like if you do twenty-five times eight you get two hundred, but that's two hundred *cents*. In the second one, when you do twenty-five times *point*-zero-eight, you get two-point-zero-zero, which means two dollars.
115. Ms. N:	So, let's look at our two equations again. We can read them in two ways. We can say "*m* times eight equals *c*" ($m \times 8 = c$). What's another way? What does the *m* stand for?
116. Students in unison:	Number of minutes.
117. Ms. N:	What does the eight tell us?
118. Students in unison:	Eight cents per minute.
119. Ms. N:	Eight what?
120. Students in unison:	Eight cents. [Ms. Nolan doesn't respond.] Per minute. Eight cents per minute.
121. Ms. N:	Good. Since we are generalizing, we need to be as specific as possible. What does the *c* stand for?
122. Students in unison:	Cost of the call.
123. Ms. N:	Be more specific.
124. Carlos:	In cents. Cost in cents.
125. Ms. N:	[She writes the following on the board.]

$$m \qquad \times \qquad 8 \qquad = \qquad c$$

m	*8*	*c*
↓	↓	↓
number of minutes	*eight cents per minute*	*cost of call in cents*

126. Ms. N:	So, let's put it all together. How do we interpret this equation? Latteisha?
127. Latteisha:	It means the number of minutes times eight cents a minute and that's—if you do that, you get the cost of the call . . . in cents.
128. Ms. N:	Thanks, Latteisha. Dounte, what does m times eight equals c really mean?
129. Dounte:	It means the number of minutes times eight equals the cost of the call.
130. Ms. N:	Why times eight?
131. Dounte:	Because that's the cost per minute.
132. Ms. N:	OK, so tell us that as you read the equation. Start again.
133. Dounte:	OK, so, m times eight equals c means the number of minutes times eight *cents per minute* equals the cost of the call.
134. Ms. N:	In cents. Good. This is important. Good mathematicians work hard to *understand* an equation. So, talk with your group. How do we interpret this equation? [Writes $m \times 0.08 = c$.]

Ms. Nolan wants to develop her students' understanding of an algebraic equation as a relationship between two quantities. Prior to fifth grade, students have most often encountered alphabet letters in mathematics as labels. For example, $8m$ often means *8 meters* in the primary grades. Ms. Nolan recognized the need to discuss how letters are being used in these equations—as symbols that represent related varying quantities. Ms. Nolan knows that her students must recognize that the 8 in the rule $m \times 8 = c$ is a rate that relates the number of minutes and the cost. She wants her students to understand that the 8 describes how the cost changes in relation to the time. By insisting that students interpret $m \times 8 = c$, Ms. Nolan is focusing on the big ideas of variable and rate of change, and she is preparing her students to generalize and represent more complicated relationships in their future work with algebra.

Summarizing and Solidifying

At this point in the lesson, Ms. Nolan noticed that she had about ten minutes of class time left. She decided to spend this time telling students about the convention of putting the number before the variable in an algebraic expression.

As you will see, this decision gave Ms. Nolan an opportunity to build on her students' understanding of how equations can be used to model the relationship between number of minutes and cost of call.

135. Ms. N:	Thanks, everyone. So, what about *m* times zero-point-zero-eight equals *c*? How do we interpret this equation? Kathleen?
136. Kathleen:	It means number of minutes times eight cents per minute equals the cost of the call *in dollars*.
137. Ms. N:	Good. Now, if you were to see this equation in a math book, you probably would not see it written exactly like this [points to m $\times$ *0.08* = c]. You would see it like this [writes *0.08*m = c]. So, let's try to make sense of this. Mathematicians made an agreement that they would write number values before variables. And, they also made an agreement that if a number was written directly next to a variable, then that meant multiplication. So, what do you think? Is this [points to *0.08*m = c] the same as what we wrote? Talk to the people around you about that for a moment. [Thirty seconds of small-group talk.]
138. Ms. N:	Let me pull everyone back together. Is this [points to *0.08*m = c] the same as this [points to m $\times$ *0.08* = c]? Meena?
139. Meena:	It is. Well, you said that when they are next to each other, it means times.
140. Ms. N:	When they are next to each other, it means times? What do you mean?
141. Meena:	The point-zero-eight and the *m* really means point-zero-eight *times m*.
142. Ms. N:	And how do you know that if we switch the order of the number and the variable, that wouldn't change the product? Nick?
143. Nick:	'Cause order doesn't matter when we multiply. Like, three times eight is twenty-four and eight times three is twenty-four.
144. Ms. N:	OK, everyone, we have seen three equations for the relationship between number of minutes and

	cost of call. And, I think, we all agree that all three are accurate ways of describing the relationship between number of minutes and cost of call. Here is one more for you. What do you think about this? [Writes *0.08*c = m on the board.]
145. Students in unison:	No! That's wrong!
146. Ms. N:	Talk to the people in your groups. I want a convincing argument why the equation I wrote is not accurate for the relationship between cost and number of minutes. [One minute of small-group discussion.]
147. Ms. N:	Let me bring you back together. OK, so this looks like it might make sense to me. After all, the phone plan rate *is* eight cents per minute. [She circles *0.08*c as she says this to challenge the misconception that 0.08*c* means 8 cents.] Convince me I'm wrong. Lia?
148. Lia:	But point-zero-eight-*c* does not mean—can I come up?
149. Ms. N:	Sure.
150. Lia:	This [points to *0.08*c] does not mean eight cents a minute. This [points to *0.08*] means eight cents per minute. Then, the *c* means *cost of call*. So, this [points to *0.08*c] means multiply them and that's totally wrong.
151. Ms. N:	Why? Nick?
152. Nick:	Because that would mean that you would do eight cents per minute times the cost of the call to get the number of minutes. That doesn't make sense.
153. Ms. N:	Rose, do you agree?
154. Rose:	Yeah, you don't do eight cents times the cost to get the number of minutes. You do eight cents times the number of minutes to get the cost of the call. So, its point-zero-eight times *m* equals *c*, like we had earlier.
155. Rachel:	Take an example from our chart. Is point-zero-eight times two equal to twenty-five? No! It's eight cents times twenty-five or, like, twenty-five cents eight times. That's two dollars.

156. Ms. N:	Andy, can you explain how Rachel is using the chart to show that this equation is not accurate?
157. Andy:	I didn't really get what she said. [Another member of Andy's table starts to explain Rachel's example.]
158. Mrs. N:	You know what: This is important. Everyone, talk to the people around you about Rachel's idea of using the chart to show that the equation I wrote is flawed.

After one minute of small-group discussion, Ms. Nolan calls on Andy again. He gives another example from the chart to show that multiplying the cost of the call by eight-hundredths does not result in the number of minutes. Ms. Nolan concludes the lesson as follows:

159. Ms. N:	OK, you convinced me. Let me just make one point. I can see why someone could look at this [points to $0.08c$] and think that it meant eight cents *if* they did not think carefully about numbers and variables. So, that is why it is so important to do two things when we write an equation. First, we must be sure to define our variables—to tell what the letters in our equations stand for. Second, we must be sure about the meaning of the numbers in our equation. Since we are working with money, it gets confusing because there are two ways to represent money—using cent notations and using dollar notations. The number zero-point-zero-eight [points to $0.08m = c$] represents eight cents in dollar notation. But it is eight cents per what?
160. Students in unison:	Eight cents per minute.
161. Ms. N:	Eight cents per minute. Right. When we really make sure we are clear about what the variables and numbers in our equations stand for, we can identify equations that make sense as well as equations that don't.

As her lesson plan shows, Ms. Nolan predicted that some students would reverse the variables representing number of minutes and cost of call when they wrote their equations. Even though she didn't see any students do this during the small-group or whole-class discussion, she chose to bring up the misconception herself. Why? First, it is possible that some students did write this equation while they worked in small groups and Ms. Nolan just didn't see it. Her past experience has led her to believe that it is a common error. Second, Ms. Nolan brought up the misconception to test the strength of students' understanding. If they "took the bait" and agreed that $0.08c = m$ was valid representation, that would indicate that their ability to use equations to model relationships was quite tenuous. This information would, in turn, help inform her future instructional choices.

Ms. Nolan also knows that new understandings do not always replace misconceptions. In this lesson, just because students agree that $0.08m = c$ represents the relationship between number of minutes and cost of call in dollars does not mean that they see the discrepancy with $0.08c = m$. Rather, as they try to make sense of algebraic models, learners need to discuss, evaluate, and compare many forms of equations, including erroneous ones. Furthermore, raising the misconception gave Ms. Nolan a chance to revisit the big ideas of a lesson. Namely, students had one more opportunity to consider the importance of stating and identifying the meaning of variables and number values in an algebraic equation. They were also able to clarify how the equation changed based on whether the number of cents was expressed using dollar notation or cent notation.

For the next lesson, Ms. Nolan plans to have the students make a coordinate graph of the relationship between number of minutes and cost of call. She will ask questions that encourage students to connect the table, graph, and equation. Students will also use these representations to find the length of a call given its cost, and vice versa. Students will discuss the merits of using each representation to answer these questions.

DISCUSSION AND REFLECTION

1. At the end of the class, Ms. Nolan herself raised one of the points listed under the section titled "Anticipating Confusion" in her lesson plan. Which of the other points listed under "Anticipating Confusion" came out in the lesson? How were they dealt with? Were there other confusions that arose that Ms. Nolan hadn't planned for?

2. The students used a question mark symbol in the sentence $? \times 25 = 2.00$ instead of a more formal symbol, such as x. Ms. Nolan did not encourage them to use a more formal symbol. What do you think about this decision? What other decisions might Ms. Nolan have made here?

3. Look back at the questions Ms. Nolan listed in her lesson plan under "Asking Questions." Did she ask each of these questions in the discussion? After seeing what occurred in the lesson, what other questions should she write here?

4. Find at least one line in the dialogue when Ms. Nolan asked a student to repeat a classmate's statement. Why do you think she chose to use this talk move at this point?

5. Find at least one line in the dialogue where Ms. Nolan used revoicing. Why do you think she chose to use this talk move at this point?

3

Grade 6: Fair or Unfair

NCTM Standards:
Data Analysis
    and Probability,
Connections

Grade 6

We will now examine a lesson on probability that Mr. Donnell planned for his second-period class of twenty-eight sixth-grade students. Mr. Donnell is a fictional character, but his words and actions are similar to those of sixth-grade teachers we worked with in Project Challenge. Likewise, this lesson is very similar to a lesson that was taught in Project Challenge classrooms every year.

Mr. Donnell teaches in an urban area, in a city right outside a major city. Many of his students speak a language other than English at home. He was motivated to try using talk in his mathematics instruction as a way to help his students improve their English and he believes that his students' mathematical vocabularies have improved because of his emphasis on productive classroom talk. He knows that even when his students are not terribly articulate, the fact that they are forming their ideas into words is serving multiple purposes. He continually sees progress in mathematical knowledge and fluency with English. Mr. Donnell is an example of a teacher who was convinced of the benefits of talk after he used it for a while, which motivated him to work harder at facilitating discussions. At this point in his teaching career, he can't imagine not using talk to help students explore ideas and learn concepts and facts!

Planning and Projecting

Mr. Donnell's students are coming to the end of a unit on probability. In this unit, they have explored the experimental and theoretical probabilities of simple, independent events involving coins, blocks in a bag, scratch-card contests, and dice. Students have collected data, interpreted the results, and calculated the experimental probabilities as decimals, fractions, and percents. They have discussed the terms *possible*, *impossible*, *probable*, *likely*, and *certain* as they applied to their experiments and other events such as weather, the lottery, and accidents. Students have also analyzed all possible outcomes of these simple, independent events and discussed why the experimental probability of an event was not always the same as its theoretical probability. They have learned about the Law of Large Numbers. This last issue has been particularly difficult for them to talk about and comprehend.

In this lesson, students are learning about the meaning of the word *fair*. (This lesson is adapted from Lappan et al. 2002.) Students play a coin-tossing game. In the game, each pair of students tosses a group of three coins twenty times. One player receives a point every time the coins match (i.e., head-head-head or tail-tail-tail) and the other player receives a point every time the coins do not match (e.g., head-head-tail). After twenty tosses, the player with the most points wins.

Mr. Donnell's Lesson Plan

IDENTIFYING THE MATHEMATICAL GOALS

- Students will understand that the game they are playing is not fair, since a no-match outcome is more likely than a match outcome.
- Students will realize that in a fair game, each player has the same chance of winning; the chances of winning and losing are equally likely.
- Students will understand the difference between experimental and theoretical probability.
- Vocabulary: *theoretical probability, equally likely, experimental probability*

ANTICIPATING CONFUSION

- Students may think a game is unfair simply because they lose.
- Students may not understand why the experimental probably is not the same as the theoretical probability.
- Students may not understand why the coins matched so much less frequently than they did not match.

ASKING QUESTIONS

- What do you think it means to say that a game is fair?
- Do you think the game is fair? Why or why not?

- Why did so many more no-matches than matches occur? Was this just a coincidence?
- How many outcomes are possible in this game? Are they equally likely? Why or why not?
- Are our experimental probabilities the same as the theoretical probabilities? Why or why not?

LESSON OUTLINE

1. Introduce the problem.
2. Make predictions about the game.
3. Student pairs play the game and record their results in the class chart.
4. Whole-class discussion about whether or not the game is fair.

Improvising and Responding: In the Midst of the Lesson

While much of what Mr. Donnell planned actually occurred in the lesson, there were also elements in the lesson that were unexpected. As you read through the lesson, think about the following questions: How, if at all, did Mr. Donnell's talk-based lesson plan help the lesson progress? How does Mr. Donnell use talk to develop students' mathematical understanding?

1. Mr. D: Raise your hand if you have ever heard the term *fair* to describe a game before. What does the term *fair game* mean?

2. Rydell: It means that there are no tricks to it. Like those amusement park games. You never win those 'cause there are hidden tricks to them that you can't see.

3. Deanne: I heard that it was illegal for amusement parks to do that. There are people who check for that kind of cheating. So the games have to be fair.

4. Mr. D: So what do you think *fair* means, Deanne?

5. Deanne: A fair game is when there is no trick to it. You know all the rules and there are no secrets to it.

6. Mr. D: Liam, can you put Deanne's explanation of a fair game in your own words please?

7. Liam: She thinks a game is fair if there are no tricks or secrets to it.

8. Mr. D: Is that what you think, Deanne?

9. Deanne: Yes.

10. Mr. D: Who else would like to explain what the term *fair* means? [No hands after ten seconds of wait time.] Is tossing a coin a fair way to decide who bats first in a baseball game? Why or why not?

11. Barb: Yes, that's fair, because we learned that there's one way to get a head and one way to get a tail. Each outcome is equally likely, so each team has the same chance of getting to bat.

12. Mr. D: So what do you think the term *fair game* means?

13. Barb: I agree with Deanne. I think it means that there are no tricks. Like in the coin toss, there are no tricks to that. It's not like a trick coin or something that really has two heads. Both teams know for sure that there's one head and one tail.

14. Mr. D: Jose, can you repeat what Barb just said?

15. Jose: She thinks that the coin toss is fair since the players know there's one head and one tail and they each have a fifty-fifty chance of coming up.

16. Mr. D: Barb, is that what you said?

17. Barb: Yes, and also that there are no tricks to it.

18. Mr. D: Who else would like to explain the term *fair game*?

When Mr. Donnell did not see any raised hands, he asked the students to talk with their partners about the term *fair*. When he called the students back together, he got more explanations that were based upon trickery rather than likelihood of outcomes. He decided that trying to elicit other ideas about fairness would take up too much class time. While he was reluctant to move on with only one significant explanation of the term, he knew that the next activity would likely bring forth a more mathematical definition of the term *fair*. He finished this phase of the lesson by saying to his students, "Well, we've heard from several people about what a fair game is. Write down what you think the term *fair game* means. It may be the same as what other students have said or it may be different. Also, based on your definition, write a prediction for whether this game will be fair." After students wrote, he added, "As you play the game today, keep in mind two questions: Is the game fair? And what does it mean for a game to be fair? After you play, we will share our results and discuss these two questions as a whole class."

The students' ideas about fairness focused early on the issue of trickery. Mr. Donnell did not anticipate this as a misconception. In addition, when it arose, he was unsure whether or not it really was a misconception. Isn't it in fact true that a game with hidden tricks is not fair? Because Mr. Donnell did not plan to pursue a lengthy discussion of the correct definition of *fairness* at the beginning of the lesson, the students' unanticipated view of fairness did not affect the flow of the lesson. Mr. Donnell knew, however, that the issue of trickery would likely emerge at the end of the class when he did want his students to discuss the mathematical definition. Mr. Donnell used the game time to think about what he would say or do when the issue arose later in the lesson. He also made note to add this idea to his lesson plan for next year.

Mr. Donnell relied heavily on the repeating talk move during this discussion. He did so without making any commentary that may have influenced students' thinking. He wanted to make sure that each student had considered some ideas about fairness before they played the game. He hoped that this would lead to cognitive conflict during the lesson, a state of thinking where students' beliefs or expectations do not match what is actually occurring. In turn, this conflict could lead to a very rich whole-class discussion at the end of the lesson.

When Mr. Donnell asked a student to repeat another's statement, he referred back to the original speaker to make sure that the student who did the repeating did not misconstrue the original comment. Doing this guaranteed that a student's comment was repeated accurately and fairly. Mr. Donnell believes that this is a good way to make sure that his class has a respectful, supportive environment. He knows from past experience that students get very upset when their ideas are misinterpreted, inaccurately reworded, or outright changed. They feel that their reasoning was not given a fair chance, and thus they can be reluctant to participate in the future. Mr. Donnell uses the technique of asking, "Is this what you said?" whenever he revoices to avoid such discomfort in his students. In his classroom, all efforts to revoice or repeat must accurately reflect the mathematical reasoning of the original speaker. If they don't, the original speaker gets to restate his or her idea to provide any necessary clarification before the discussion continues.

After this discussion, Mr. Donnell's students played the game. Mr. Donnell circulated among them, discussing fairness and talking about experimental probabilities—probabilities based on the outcomes from experiments. He then recorded the class outcomes on the following chart:

Group	# Matches	# No-Matches	# of Trials
1	2	18	20
2	5	15	20
3	1	19	20
4	3	17	20
5	2	18	20
6	12	8	20
7	4	16	20
8	6	14	20
9	4	16	20
10	3	17	20
11	2	18	20
12	6	14	20
Totals	50	190	240
P(match) = 50/240 or ≈ 21%		P(no-match) = 190/240 or ≈ 79%	

As a class they determined the experimental probabilities of tossing a match and a no-match.

19. Mr. D:		Before you played the game, we discussed the term *fair game*. We did not, however, settle on a definition. Now that you've had a chance to play the game, I'd like to see if we can define the term *fair game*. What do you think it means? Based on your definition, do you think this game is fair?
20. Vivian:		This game is definitely not fair. It's not even close. Look at our chart—seventy-nine percent of the tosses were no-matches. I was the match person. I lost big time.
21. Mr. D:		So, do you think the game is not fair because you did not win? Is that what makes a game unfair?
22. Vivian:		No, it's just that I didn't even come close to winning.
23. Mr. D:		What do you think the term *fair game* means?
24. Vivian:		It means that each person has to have a pretty good chance of winning.
25. Mr. D:		Tran, do you agree or disagree with Vivian's definition?
26. Tran:		I sort of agree.
27. Mr. D:		Why?
28. Tran:		I think that this game is not fair because we kept getting no-matches. That means that the person who gets a point for a no-match is going to get a lot more points than their opponent. That's not fair.
29. Mr. D:		Vivian defines *fair game* as a game where each player has a pretty good chance of winning. Do you agree with this definition?
30. Tran:		Sort of.
31. Mr. D:		What do you mean, sort of?
32. Tran:		Because it's not like you have to have a pretty good chance. You just have to be as likely to win as your opponent. It's not fair if the game is set up to give one person more points.
33. Mr. D:		Deanne, do you agree with what Tran just said?
34. Deanne:		I couldn't hear.
35. Mr. D:		Well, what should you say?
36. Deanne:		Tran, I couldn't hear you. Could you repeat it please?

37. Tran:	*Fair* means you have the same chance as your opponent. Like as you play, you are just as likely to get what you want as the other person.	
38. Deanne:	I agree. I think a game is fair if each person gets as many points as the other.	
39. Mr. D:	Tran, is that what you said?	
40. Tran:	No. I said that you have to have the *same chance* to get as many points.	
41. Mr. D:	Deanne, do you agree with Tran's definition of fairness? Why or why not?	
42. Deanne:	I agree because in this game, like, looking at the data, the match person got almost nothing.	
43. Mr. D:	Earlier you thought that a game was fair if there were no tricks. Do you still think that that's true?	
44. Deanne:	Yes, but I also think that *fair* means that each person has to have the same chance to win as the opponent.	
45. Mr. D:	Liam, do you agree or disagree with what Deanne just said?	
46. Liam:	I agree.	
47. Mr. D:	Why?	
48. Liam:	[Silence for about ten seconds.] Actually, Deanne, could you repeat it?	
49. Deanne:	A fair game happens when each person has the same chance of winning.	
50. Liam:	Oh. I disagree. I think that *fair* means that each person gets the same number of turns.	
51. Mr. D:	So do you think this game is fair?	
52. Liam:	Yes, because we each got ten turns.	
53. Mr. D:	Which player were you, the player who got a point for a match or the player who got a point for a no-match?	
54. Liam:	I was the match person. I lost.	
55. Mr. D:	And you still think it's fair even though you lost?	
56. Liam:	Yes. Because at the end I was getting a lot of matches. I almost made a comeback.	
57. Mr. D:	So, Liam thinks the game is fair since each player tossed the coins ten times. What do some other people think about this?	

58. Tran:	I disagree with what Liam said. Look at the data. It wasn't even close.
59. Mr. D:	What do you mean?
60. Tran:	There were about four times more no-matches than matches. There is no way that could be fair.
61. Mr. D:	What do some other people think?
62. Lenora:	Well, we don't know if we kept playing if the data would have been different. Maybe it was just this one time that the matches didn't happen.
63. Mr. D:	Lenora, what do you mean it was maybe just this one time that the matches didn't happen?
64. Lenora:	If we played the game again right now, maybe the match people would win.
65. Tory:	I really don't think it was just a coincidence. Look at the data! There's no way this game is fair.
66. Mr. D:	Why not, Tory?
67. Tory:	Because the match person never really had a chance to win. They got crushed.
68. Mr. D:	OK, let's pause for a minute. The two questions we are discussing are: Is this game fair? What does the term *fair game* mean? We have heard several different answers to each of these questions. I've written them on the board as people have said them. Let's hear from some other people. Which of these do you agree with? Or, do you disagree with all of them and have a new idea of your own?
69. Barb:	This game is not fair. Like I said at the beginning of class, *fair* means that each person has the same chance of winning. The probability to match was twenty-one percent and the probability to not match was seventy-nine percent. That doesn't seem fair.
70. Mr. D:	Tracey, your hand was just raised.
71. Tracey:	Oh, Barb took my answer.
72. Mr. D:	If you think similarly to Barb, that's OK. You should put it in your own words. The more we hear from people, the more we will understand each other's reasoning.
73. Tracey:	Well, like Barb said, to be fair, the probabilities should have been the same.

74. Mr. D: And what about the number of turns?

75. Tracey: I don't think that matters. It didn't really matter who was tossing the coins anyway.

Mr. Donnell continued the discussion on fairness for another few moments. At this point, the class had not yet reached a consensus on the definition of *fairness* or whether the game was fair. They had, however, begun to think about fairness in terms of probabilities of outcomes. Mr. Donnell decided to move on to another objective of the lesson, because he knew that fairness would arise in the lesson again.

Throughout the previous discussion, Mr. Donnell used the agree-or-disagree question to increase the productivity of the discussion. At the beginning of the class, Mr. Donnell gave students plenty of opportunity to share their opinions about fairness either orally or in writing. As the lesson progressed, however, he wanted to be more direct. He no longer wanted opinions based on previous experiences. Rather, he wanted students to use specific evidence from the probability lessons to form a mathematically accurate definition of fairness. Vivian did so in Line 20, "This game is definitely not fair. It's not even close. Look at our chart—seventy-nine percent of the tosses were no-matches. I was the match person. I lost big time." Mr. Donnell hoped to focus the discussion of the term *fair* on mathematical evidence.

Every time Mr. Donnell asked students to agree or disagree, he required them to state *why*. Mr. Donnell knows that without the "why" part, many students bluff, usually agreeing with an idea because it seems like the thing to do. Let's recall the exchanges with Liam beginning in line 45.

45. Mr. D: Liam, do you agree or disagree with what Deanne just said?

46. Liam: I agree.

47. Mr. D: Why?

48. Liam: [Silence for about ten seconds.] Actually, Deanne, could you repeat it?

49. Deanne: A fair game happens when each person has the same chance of winning.

50. Liam: Oh. I disagree. I think that *fair* means that each person gets the same number of turns.

Liam was quick to say he agreed with Deanne, but then revealed that he did not really hear what Deanne said. Since it is impossible to agree with something you did not hear, it is likely that Liam was saying he agreed to make it appear that he was listening. Then, Liam further convinced us he was not listening when he went on to explain why he disagreed with Deanne's idea. Mr. Donnell's insistence that Liam explain why he agreed forced Liam to reengage with the lesson. Liam had to ask Deanne to repeat her comment in order to respond to Mr. Donnell's question. Then, Liam's response to Mr. Donnell's question made him an active contributor to the discussion. Mr. Donnell's decision to have Liam explain his position also helped to bring another misconception about fairness to the surface—whether the number of turns makes a game fair or not.

Recall that at the beginning of the class, many students defined fairness in terms of trickery. Mr. Donnell had not anticipated this and was therefore nervous about addressing it in the whole-class discussion. The misconception, however, was not much of an issue in this discussion after all. In fact, when Mr. Donnell reminded Deanne of her initial definition, in Line 43, she quickly brushed it aside and instead defined fairness in terms of the chances of winning. Mr. Donnell was not sure why this has happened. Had the discussion and the game led Deanne toward the mathematical understanding of fairness? Or did she still believe in her original definition, but sensed that the tide was moving in the other direction and became reluctant to stand by it? Mr. Donnell knows that knowledge often does not replace misconceptions by default. Rather, if misconceptions are not dismantled, knowledge will be built upon them. Yet he still wonders whether the idea of trickery is really a misconception. Fairness does depend upon an absence of trickery. Mr. Donnell decides to raise the issue of trickery in future discussions to see whether it still obscures the importance of the mathematical basis of fairness, or whether the two ideas happily coexist. After all, fairness is an important and complex concept—as long as students understand the mathematical aspects of fairness in games of chance, he will have achieved his goal.

Another interesting observation about this discussion comes in Barb's last comment in Line 69. She said, "This game is not fair. Like I said at the beginning of class, *fair* means that each person has the same chance of winning. The probability to match was twenty-one percent and the probability to not match was seventy-nine percent. That doesn't seem fair." But in Line 13 of the discussion earlier in the class, Barb had said, "I agree with Deanne. I think it means that there are no tricks. Like in the coin toss, there are not tricks to that. It's not like a trick coin or something that really has two heads. Both teams know for sure that there's one head and one tail." Barb's comment in Line 13 shows the complexity of this topic: Coin tosses do foreground the idea of probability in judgments of fairness, and the comment suggests that Barb knows that the equal probability of getting heads or tails makes it fair. However, trickery can certainly infiltrate games that use coins. Overlapping ideas of fundamentally different sorts make the term *fair* inherently complex. So, why is Barb now able to give the more mathematically correct definition? Perhaps playing the game, and participating in a discussion before and after, provided her with the additional context she needed in order to expand and generalize this aspect of her understanding of fairness.

The last exchange in this discussion, beginning at Line 71, highlights another technique Mr. Donnell uses. When Tracey said that Barb "took [her] answer," Mr. Donnell asked her to say the same idea in her own words. Mr. Donnell did this because he knew that students needed to hear Barb's idea many times in order to process it. Further, he knows that in real-life conversations and debates, adults rarely say to each other that someone else "took their answers." Rather, adults will state their agreement with a previous point and put that idea in their own words. This is how people create common ground for understanding. Mr. Donnell wants his class discussions to closely mirror those of the outside world. As a result, in his class, he emphasizes revoicing and repeating ideas to lend support and further one another's learning.

After a few more comments about fair games, the class continued. Mr. Donnell worked with the class to systematically list all possible outcomes for the coin-toss game.

Coin 1	Coin 2	Coin 3	
H	H	H	Match
H	H	T	No match
H	T	H	No match
T	H	H	No match
T	T	T	Match
T	T	H	No match
T	H	T	No match
H	T	T	No match

The students agreed that the theoretical probability of tossing a match was $\frac{2}{8}$ or 25 percent and of tossing a no-match was $\frac{6}{8}$ or 75 percent. Following a discussion about the theoretical probability, Mr. Donnell decided to revisit the idea of fairness.

76. Mr. D: By now we agree that the chance of getting a no-match is greater than getting a match. Our theoretical probability shows this and our experimental probabilities support it. First, I want to ask you this question. Does it concern or surprise you that the experimental probabilities and theoretical probabilities aren't the same? Talk to the person next to you about this. [The class engages in partner talk for two minutes. Then Mr. Donnell calls on Reya.]

77. Reya: No, we have talked about this before. It's probability; you never know for sure what's going to happen.

78. Mr. D: Matt, do you agree or disagree, and tell us why.

79. Matt: I agree. Even if it's not the same, it's close. That's good enough.

80. Mr. D: What do you mean "good enough"?

81. Matt: Well, if we had conducted even more trials it would have been closer.

82. Mr. D: Sara, what do you think Matt means that it would have been the closer with more trials? [Sara is Matt's partner.]

83. Sara: It is what the Law of Large Numbers tells us. The greater the number of trials the closer the experimental probability will be to the theoretical probability.

84. Mr. D: Now I want to ask you once again whether or not the game is fair.

85. Barb: I stick with what I've said all along. It's not fair because the no-match person has a better chance of winning.

86. Mr. D: But the match person could still win, right?

87. Barb: Yeah, but that would be really, really strange. And the game would still be unfair based on the probabilities.

88. Mr. D: Who thinks they can explain what Barb just said about the game being unfair based on the probabilities?

89. Liam: She means that the probability of one player winning is bigger than the probability of the other one.

90. Mr. D: Barb, is that what you think? [Barb nods her head yes.] So Liam, what do you think it means for a game to be fair?

91. Liam: It means that each person has to be as likely to win as the other.

92. Mr. D: And what about the number of turns?

93. Liam: Well, I think that matters too but the probability is what makes it fair.

94. Mr. D: I'd like everyone to turn and talk to their partners again about the question we have been discussing. Is this game fair? Why or why not? [He gives the students two minutes of partner talk and then reopens the whole-class discussion.]

95. Yajahira: My partner and I think that this game is not fair. The chance of getting a no-match was three-fourths and the chance of getting a match was one-fourth. That means that one person was three times as likely to win as the other. That's not fair.

96. Mr. D: Frank, can you repeat what Yajahira just said?

97. Frank: She said that the game is not fair since the chance to get a no-match was three times more likely than getting a match.

98. Mr. D: And do you and your partner agree or disagree with this? Tell us why you think so.

99. Frank: We agree. Fair would have had to have been fifty percent for one player and fifty percent for the other to win. In this game, one person has a better chance to win.

100. Mr. D: Let's think back to some of our other lessons. We played a game where two players took turns picking blocks out of a bag. In the bag were three blue blocks and three red blocks. If the block pulled out was red, Player A got a point. If the block pulled out was blue, Player B got a point. Think about what happened when we played this game. Was this game fair? Talk to the person next to you about this for a minute. [After two minutes of partner talk, the whole-class discussion continues.]

101. Vivian: Yes, this game was fair because the red person has a fifty percent chance to win and the blue person does too.

104. Mr. D: How do you know the red person has a fifty percent chance to win?

105. Vivian: Three out of six blocks are red. That's the same as half or fifty percent.

106. Mr. D: Tran, do you agree or disagree with what Vivian said?

107. Tran: I agree because my partner and I said that each person had the same chance of winning.

108. Mr. D: Can you think of another game that we played that was fair? Or, can you think of a game that was unfair? Be ready to convince us why they were fair or unfair. Talk to the person next to you about this. Also, look back in your notes. [Again, he provides two minutes for students to organize their answers in partner talk.] Reya, do you have a game we played?

109. Reya: The one with the spinner? That was unfair.

110. Mr. D: Reya, could you be a little more specific?

111. Reya: There was this spinner. Two sections were marked A and three were marked B. A player got a point for landing on their letter.

112. Mr. D: And why do you think that game was unfair?

113. Reya: Because the chance of landing on B was more than A.

114. Mr. D: Could everyone try to find their notes about this experiment in their notebooks? When we pooled our data, what was the experimental probability of landing on A?

115. Students: There was thirty-six percent for A and sixty-four percent for B.

116. Mr. D: And what about the theoretical probabilities?

117. Students: Two-fifths for A and three-fifths for B.

118. Mr. D: So, does this support what Reya said about the game being fair or unfair?

119. Tracey: Yes, it does. The B person has more of a chance to win. That's not fair.

120. Mr. D: Did we play a spinner game that was fair?

121. Yajahira: Yes, that spinner cut in fourths and two were red and two were blue. That's a fifty percent chance for each player, and that's fair.

This discussion began with Mr. Donnell asking the class to review the theoretical probabilities of the coin game and comparing theoretical and experimental probabilities. Once he had accomplished this objective, he used the same discussion to revisit the idea of fairness. Students' comments suggest that they are making strides in understanding this term. Then, Mr. Donnell sought to strengthen their understanding of the term *fair* by asking them to recall other games that were either fair or unfair. Again, he required students to explain their reasoning. As students began to generalize their knowledge of a mathematical term across contexts, their learning became more solid.

In this lesson, Mr. Donnell repeatedly asked students to agree or disagree with each other's ideas. The purpose of this question was to narrow in on the mathematical meaning of fairness so that the class could continue to move toward a more mathematical understanding of the term. The students' comments revealed that this was indeed happening. While there was no guarantee that every student "had it" yet, they did seem to be headed in the right direction. Note that this forward movement occurred because of the discussion, not what Mr. Donnell said or did not say. In fact, he said very little in any of these discussions, acting instead as a facilitator. At no point did he forcefully tell the students the correct definition or give praise to any of the students who clearly articulated what it meant to be fair. He did not have to. The students appraised the value of each comment based upon what had been said so far, their experiences with the game, and their past knowledge about probability.

Summarizing and Solidifying

Mr. Donnell knows that since his students now have a mathematically sound definition of fairness, they are ready to expand their understanding by adjusting the relationship between likelihood and payout. Mr. Donnell will start tomorrow's lesson by reviewing what students learned and what they are still confused about from this lesson. Then he will proceed to the next lesson where students must make an unfair game fair by adapting rules and/or payout points.

Mr. Donnell was pleased with the way this lesson went. He was particularly impressed by his students' abilities to explain why they agreed with each other in a reasonable and respectful manner. Unlike Mrs. Robert's class in the first case study, his students could respond to this question without the need to revoice the statement first or have the speaker say the comment again. We attribute this to the students' experiences with classroom talk—Mr. Donnell's students had more experience than Mrs. Robert's and Ms. Nolan's students. As a result, they could agree and disagree without much need for prompting. Mr. Donnell was also pleased with the progress his students made in their understanding of the term *fair*. They sought to define *fair* in terms of the mathematics of the lesson. They listened to each other's comments and agreed or disagreed with them on the basis of their reasoning, not personal opinion or bias.

We are confident in saying that you will have fewer classes like Mrs. Robert's and more like Mr. Donnell's or Ms. Nolan's as you and your students gain more experience with classroom talk. However, even when you feel like you and your students have hit your stride with talk, there will certainly be days reminiscent of the early ones. When this happens, we encourage you to be reflective, like Mrs. Robert was. If possible, talk with a colleague, and think specifically about how to move forward with the discussion in the next lesson. Finally, we offer some advice that stems from the three case studies. First, as we have written earlier in this book, make sure to set up classroom rules that honor respectful discourse and equitable participation. This is necessary for both you and your students. Second, commit to the implementation of classroom talk. Don't expect overnight miracles, but don't give up, either. Students will only get better with long-term, consistent implementation. Third, look forward to the days when you will be amazed at what your students say—days when their reasoning and insights will persuade you that your persistent focus on productive talk has resulted in deeper and more robust mathematics learning for all of your students.

DISCUSSION AND REFLECTION

1. The agree-or-disagree talk move is prominent in this case study. Look back through the dialogues for one example of the agree-or-disagree talk move. Why do you think Mr. Donnell chose to use this talk move at this point in the lesson?

2. We certainly don't want to ask our students whether they agree or disagree with every comment. What criteria can help you decide when to use this talk move?

3. In Line 50, Liam explains that he disagrees with Deanne's idea of fairness. However, Deanne's idea of fairness is correct. Describe how Mr. Donnell handles this situation. What else might he have done to help Liam and his classmates understand?

4. Responding to a student who disagrees with a correct notion or agrees with a flawed or incorrect idea can be tricky. Think back to a time when either of these situations occurred during one of your whole-class discussions. How did you respond? What worked? What didn't work?

Questions for Discussion and Reflection

Chapter 1: An Overview

1. One of the key skills you will develop in using this book is the ability to work with students whose contributions are initially unclear, helping them move toward clarity. This kind of work is not easy at first. To prepare for this, try to recall a time when you could not explain your thinking to others because the ideas you were dealing with were new and complex. What would have helped you at that time?

2. This book will also help you develop the ability to tell when talk in your classroom is academically productive. Can you recall a time when you held a discussion in your class that was not academically productive? What happened? What was it like? Can you recall a time when you held a discussion that was academically productive? What were the qualities of that discussion? Do you remember anything you did to make it productive, or did it just seem to happen spontaneously?

3. Think back in your own education. Can you recall a teacher who made you feel that he or she really wanted to understand what you had to say? Try to picture a conversation with that teacher. What was it like?

Chapter 2: The Tools of Classroom Talk

1. For many teachers, the thought of using partner talk as many times as Mr. Harris does in Case 4 may seem disruptive. Go back over the case and consider other ways the discussion might have been conducted. In your own use of partner talk, have you found positive results? Have there been drawbacks? If so, how could you address the drawbacks?

2. One of the main goals of using classroom talk moves like those described in this chapter is to manage the unavoidable complexity

and lack of clarity that occurs when students are learning something new and complicated. Consider each of the five talk moves. Could each be useful when you are faced with a student contribution that is completely unclear? Or are some better than others? Construct a situation in your classroom in which you are faced with an uninterpretable response and describe what you will do.

3. In the cases in this chapter, and throughout the book, you will see instances of students making assertions or observations that are mathematically incorrect. In many cases, because the emphasis is on sustaining student discussion and developing deeper understanding, the teacher chooses not to correct or call attention to these mistakes. What are some of the consequences of such choices? Have you had this experience? How did you deal with it? How might you deal with it in the future?

Chapter 3: Mathematical Concepts

1. This chapter examined the complexities of talking about mathematical concepts. What is a math concept? How are concepts different from skills? For each of the teacher/student vignettes, make a list of the concepts that were discussed.

2. One of the benefits of talking about concepts is that students' misconceptions or confusions often are revealed. Describe some examples from your own teaching experiences in which you learned about a student's misconceptions. For one example, give suggestions on how talk might be used to help students address the misconception.

3. Pictures and models can help students build relationships as long as the salient features of the picture or model are clearly understood by students. How did Ms. Sanchez use classroom discussions to help students understand the pictures of the parallelograms and the relationships between the dimensions and area?

Chapter 4: Computational Procedures

1. Reread the section on Mrs. DeFreitas's fifth-grade class discussion about the three possible answers to the multiplication problem. She chooses to post the three possible answers using letters. It is also possible to set up a discussion using the student names associated with

claims or predictions. Can you think of occasions when one approach might have clear advantages? When might that approach have disadvantages? How do you decide which one to use?

2. After the vignette about Ms. Webster's third-grade discussion of regrouping in subtraction, we make the following claim: "Talking about computational procedures can do more than clarify students' understanding of the ins and outs of those procedures. It may actually promote a more profound understanding of the numbers and mathematical operations at the center of those procedures. In other words, at the same time that talk is building facility with procedures, it may deepen conceptual knowledge as well." Consider Ms. Webster's discussion, or others in this chapter. Do you see evidence for our claim?

3. Sometimes teachers do not want students to discuss errors or misconceptions. What types of errors or misconceptions would you want students to discuss? Why? What type of errors or misconceptions would you rather not discuss? Why?

Chapter 5: Solution Methods and Problem-Solving Strategies

1. Make a list of the problem-solving strategies you think are most important for students at your grade level to be able to use. Write or find a mathematics problem that uses the math you are currently teaching and can be solved using two of these strategies. Design a talk lesson around this problem. See Chapter 9 for planning suggestions.

2. We stated in this chapter that representations can be powerful tools for mathematical thinking. Give an example from your own teaching or this chapter in which a representation (e.g., a picture, manipulative material, graph, equation, or word problem) clearly helped a learner understand a relationship or mathematical idea. How can talk be used to extend an individual student's insights to other members of the class?

3. Sometimes a student whose confidence is quite fragile will present a solution method that is deeply flawed. What might teachers do to help the class see that discussing different solution methods, right or wrong, helps move everyone toward understanding the mathematical truth of the situation? How do we do this and be sensitive to the individual needs of students?

Chapter 6: Mathematical Reasoning

1. National organizations and reports have highlighted the importance of algebra and algebraic reasoning. In the vignette, what did Mrs. Malloy do to focus the discussion on important algebraic concepts and skills?
2. Why talk about reasoning? Can students in grades K–2 reason about mathematical ideas? Explain.
3. Mrs. Wolfe spent a lot of discussion time analyzing the matrix. What are the benefits of spending time discussing representations?
4. Students often have difficulty understanding negations. Find another matrix logic problem in which some clues involve negations (e.g., the use of the words *none, no, not,* etc.). Describe the problem as if you were running a class discussion with students. What should you tell students? What should they figure out on their own?

Chapter 7: Mathematical Terminology, Symbols, and Definitions

1. Can you recall examples from your own teaching where the everyday meaning of a word seemed to cause difficulties with students acquiring the mathematical meaning of the word?
2. Can you recall examples where student knowledge of the everyday meaning of a word helped them understand the mathematical meaning of a word?
3. Consider the meaning of the equal sign in mathematics. How might you define *equal* for students at your grade level? What will your students say the symbol means? Are there particular problem contexts in which we use the term *equal* but perhaps shouldn't? If there are potential confusions at your grade level, how could you plan a discussion that might clarify these?
4. Reread the vignette about Mr. Radulfo's class discussing two-dimensional and three-dimensional shape names. Imagine that they continued talking about cylinders and a student asked how many faces a cylinder has. Mr. Radulfo suddenly realizes that he does not know how many faces a cylinder has! Is it the two ends only, or does the surface of the curved part count as a face? Math discussions sometimes lead to territory where the teacher is not sure of the correct answer. What could he do in this case? What would you do?

Chapter 8: Getting Started

1. Ensuring equitable participation is not always easy. Discuss some of the major obstacles that you face in getting everyone to participate in your classroom, within your school. What kinds of practices or routines could help mitigate your particular set of obstacles?

2. If you are reading this book, chances are that you have tried to use discussion in your classroom before. Can you recall students who had trouble participating in the past? Discuss personal, cultural, social, psychological, or medical issues that might lead to some students not talking at all, or talking too much. Discuss your attitudes and feelings about these things. Identify one or two of the most difficult situations and think about ways to deal with them if they should arise.

3. We have stressed in this chapter that students must feel safe from ridicule or they will not participate. What if you begin to use classroom talk in the ways described in this chapter and some students do not cooperate? Do you and your school have a behavioral system in place that will support you in instituting a zero-tolerance policy for disrespectful behavior? What are the procedures? Is it clear how you would use them in your classroom?

4. It is sometimes more difficult to implement a change in your pedagogical practice if you do not have support from your fellow teachers. If more than one teacher at your school is working on using classroom talk to support math learning, how can you work together to support one another, given your time constraints and resources? What aspects of the five principles covered in this chapter could you help one another implement? Can you involve your principal or department head in your efforts? How?

Chapter 9: Planning Lessons

1. Some teachers find that the Asking Questions part of planning is the most challenging became they aren't sure what questions to ask. Describe what is meant by high-level questions. What resources are available to teachers to help them determine the mathematical goals and related high-level questions when planning?

2. If you have tried using discussion in your classroom, describe what you found was most helpful in planning the use of talk. If you have not yet tried to use talk with students, write a talk lesson plan using the components described in this chapter.

3. In the discussion about the degrees in a circle, Mrs. Carlson did not tell A. J. the "right" answer. She was not the authority on the correctness of the answer. Instead the mathematical logic presented by Arjun and Andrew was used to explain *infinity* and *justify conclusions*. It can be unsettling for a teacher to not be the person who tells students they are right or wrong. What are the benefits of using students' reasoning to justify the correctness of a solution?

4. Write a talk lesson plan that could be used to continue the lesson in this chapter on deriving the area of a circle from the area of a parallelogram.

Chapter 10: Troubleshooting

1. Which of the challenges described in the first part of this chapter have you experienced? Which of the authors' suggestions helped you overcome these challenges? What other strategies have worked?

2. Calling on students is a particularly emotional and complex issue. What do you think about calling on students who have not raised their hands to speak? Do you think calling on them is an effective instructional strategy? Why or why not?

3. The authors describe what happened when they asked their students to react to the use of productive talk in math class. Ask your students what they think about talking in math class. Specifically, ask them to describe how they think talk has or has not helped them learn math.

Case Study 1: Grade 3: Looking at the Shape of the Data

1. This case study highlighted the importance of setting up a respectful, supportive environment for mathematical discourse. What has helped you and your students create and maintain such an environment?

2. What strategies have helped your students get better at listening to each other during a whole-class discussion? What hasn't worked?

3. How have you reacted when a student (such as Martin) makes a disrespectful comment during a discussion? What has worked? What hasn't worked?

4. After teaching her lesson, Mrs. Robert wrote notes to prepare for the next day's class. If you were Mrs. Robert, what would you write in your notes? What strategies might she use to increase the productivity of the next day's discussion?

Case Study 2: Grade 5: Algebra

1. At the end of the class, Ms. Nolan herself raised one of the points listed under the section titled "Anticipating Confusion" in her lesson plan. Which of the other points listed under "Anticipating Confusion" came out in the lesson? How were they dealt with? Were there other confusions that arose that Ms. Nolan hadn't planned for?

2. The students used a question mark symbol in the sentence ? $\times$ 25 = 2.00 instead of a more formal symbol, such as x. Ms. Nolan did not encourage them to use a more formal symbol. What do you think about this decision? What other decisions might Ms. Nolan have made here?

3. Look back at the questions Ms. Nolan listed in her lesson plan under "Asking Questions." Did she ask each of these questions in the discussion? After seeing what occurred in the lesson, what other questions should she write here?

4. Find at least one line in the dialogue when Ms. Nolan asked a student to repeat a classmate's statement. Why do you think she chose to use this talk move at this point?

5. Find at least one line in the dialogue when Ms. Nolan used revoicing. Why do you think she chose to use this talk move at this point?

Case Study 3: Grade 6: Fair or Unfair

1. The agree-or-disagree talk move is prominent in this case study. Look back through the dialogues for one example of the agree-or-disagree talk move. Why do you think Mr. Donnell chose to use this talk move at this point in the lesson?

2. We certainly don't want to ask our students whether they agree or disagree with every comment. What criteria can help you decide when to use this talk move?

3. In Line 50, Liam explains that he disagrees with Deanne's idea of fairness. However, Deanne's idea of fairness is correct. Describe how Mr. Donnell handles this situation. What else might he have done to help Liam and his classmates understand?

4. Responding to a student who disagrees with a correct notion or agrees with a flawed or incorrect idea can be tricky. Think back to a time when either of these situations occurred during one of your whole-class discussions. How did you respond? What worked? What didn't work?

References

Bickmore-Brand, J., ed. 1993. *Language in Mathematics.* Portsmouth, NH: Heinemann.

Bransford, J., A. Brown, and R. Cocking, eds. 2000. *How People Learn: Brain, Mind, Experience, and School.* Washington, DC: National Academy Press.

Cai, J., and J. Moyer. 2008. "Developing Algebraic Thinking in Earlier Grades: Some Insights from International Comparative Studies." In *Algebra and Algebraic Thinking in School Mathematics,* edited by C. E. Greenes and R. Rubenstein (pp. 169–82). Reston, VA: National Council of Teachers of Mathematics.

Chapin, S., and A. Johnson. 2006. *Math Matters: Understanding the Math You Teach, Grades K–8.* 2d ed. Sausalito, CA: Math Solutions.

Chapin, S., and C. O'Connor. 2007. "Academically Productive Talk: Supporting Students' Learning in Mathematics." In *The Learning of Mathematics,* edited by W. G. Martin, M. Strutchens, and P. Elliott (pp. 113–28). Reston, VA: National Council of Teachers of Mathematics.

Cobb, P., T. Wood, and E. Yackel. 1993. "Discourse, Mathematical Thinking, and Classroom Practice." In *Contexts for Learning: Sociocultural Dynamics in Children's Development,* edited by E. A. Forman, N. Minick, and C. A. Stone (pp. 91–119). New York: Oxford University Press.

Cohen, E. G. 1994. "Restructuring the Classroom: Conditions for Productive Small Groups." *Review of Educational Research* 64 (1): 1–35.

Cohen, E. G., and R. A. Lotan. 1995. "Producing Equal Status Interaction in the Heterogeneous Classroom." *American Educational Research Journal* 32 (1): 99–120.

Delpit, L. 1995. *Other People's Children: Cultural Conflict in the Classroom.* New York: New Press.

Delpit, L., and J. K. Dowdy, eds. 2002. *The Skin That We Speak: Thoughts on Language and Culture in the Classroom.* New York: New Press.

Donovan, M. S., and J. Bransford, eds. 2005. *How Students Learn: Mathematics in the Classroom.* Washington, DC: National Academy Press.

Economopoulos, K., J. Mokros, R. Corwin, and S. Russell. 1995. *From Paces to Feet: Measuring and Data.* Palo Alto, CA: Dale Seymour.

Edwards, A. D., and D. P. G. Westgate. 1994. *Investigating Classroom Talk.* 2d ed. Bristol, PA: Falmer Press.

Edwards, D., and N. Mercer. 1987. *Common Knowledge: The Development of Understanding in the Classroom.* 2d ed. London and New York: Methuen.

Elliott, P., and C. Garnett, eds. 2008. *Getting into the Mathematics Conversation: Valuing Communication in Mathematics Classrooms.* Reston, VA: National Council of Teachers of Mathematics.

Gallas, K. 1995. *Talking Their Ways into Science: Hearing Children's Questions and Theories, Responding with Curricula.* New York: Teachers College Press.

Gavelek, J. R., and T. E. Raphael. 1996. "Changing Talk About Text: New Roles for Teachers and Students." *Language Arts* 73: 182–92.

Godfrey, L., and M. C. O'Connor. 1995. "The Vertical Hand Span: Nonstandard Units, Expressions, and Symbols in the Classroom." *Journal of Mathematical Behavior* 14: 327–45.

Goldenberg, C. 1999. "Instructional Conversations: Promoting Comprehension Through Discussion." *The Reading Teacher* 46: 316–26.

Hatano, G., and K. Inagaki. 1991. "Sharing Cognition Through Collective Comprehension Activity." In *Perspectives on Socially Shared Cognition,* edited by L. Resnick, R. Levine, and S. Teasley. Washington, DC: APA.

Heath, S. B. 1983. *Ways with Words: Language, Life, and Work in Communities and Classrooms.* Cambridge, U.K., and New York: Cambridge University Press.

Hicks, D. 1995. "Discourse, Learning, and Teaching." *Review of Research in Education* 21: 49–95.

Hiebert, J., and T. P. Carpenter. 1992. "Learning and Teaching with Understanding." In *Handbook of Research on Mathematics Teaching and Learning,* edited by D. A. Grouws (pp. 65–97). New York: Macmillan.

Inagaki, K., E. Morita, and G. Hatano, 1999. "Teaching Learning of Evaluative Criteria for Mathematical Arguments Through Classroom Discourse: A Cross National Study." *Mathematical Thinking and Learning* 1 (2): 93–111.

Jensen, R., ed. 1993. *Research Ideas for the Classroom: Early Childhood Mathematics.* New York: Macmillan.

Keefer, M. W., C. M. Zeitz, and L. B. Resnick. 2000. "Judging the Quality of Peer Led Student Dialogues." *Cognition and Instruction* 18 (1): 53–81.

Khisty, L. L. 1995. "Making Inequality: Issues of Language and Meanings in Mathematics Teaching with Hispanic Students." In *New Directions for Equity in Mathematics Education,* edited by W. Secada, E. Fennema, and L. B. Adajian (pp. 279–97). Cambridge, U.K., and New York: Cambridge University Press.

Kieran, C., and L. Chalouh. 1993. "Prealgebra: The Transition from Arithmetic to Algebra." In *Research Ideas for the Classroom: Middle Grades Mathematics,* edited by D. Owens (pp. 179–98). New York: Macmillan.

Kilpatrick, J., J. Swafford, and B. Findell, eds. 2001. *Adding It Up: Helping Children Learn Mathematics.* Washington, DC: National Academy Press.

Lampert, M. 1990. "Connecting Inventions with Conventions." In *Transforming Children's Mathematics Education: International Perspectives*, edited by L. P. Steffe and T. Wood (pp. 253–64). Hillsdale, NJ: Lawrence Erlbaum.

———. 2001. *Teaching Problems: A Study of Classroom Practice.* New Haven, CT: Yale University Press.

Lampert, M., and M. L. Blunk, eds. 1998. *Talking Mathematics in School: Studies of Teaching and Learning.* Cambridge, U.K., and New York: Cambridge University Press.

Lampert, M., P. Rittenhouse, and C. Crumbaugh. 1996. "Agreeing to Disagree: Developing Sociable Mathematical Discourse in School." In *Handbook of Psychology and Education: New Models of Learning, Teaching, and School*, edited by D. R. Olson and N. Torrance (pp. 731–64). Oxford, U.K.: Basil Blackwell.

Lappan, G., J. Fey, W. Fitzgerald, S. Friel, and E. Phillips. 2002. *How Likely Is It?* Upper Saddle River, NJ: Prentice Hall.

Lemke, J. 1990. *Talking Science: Language, Learning, and Values.* Norwood, NJ: Ablex.

McKeown, M. G., I. L. Beck, R. L. Hamilton, and L. Kucan. 1999. *"Questioning the Author" Accessibles: Easy-Access Resources for Classroom Challenges.* Bothell, WA: The Wright Group.

Mehan, H. 1979. *Learning Lessons: Social Organization in the Classroom.* Cambridge, MA: Harvard University Press.

Moschovich, J. 1999. "Supporting the Participation of English Language Learners in Mathematical Discussions." *For the Learning of Mathematics* 19 (1): 11–19.

———. 2000. "Learning Mathematics in Two Languages: Moving from Obstacles to Resources." In *Changing the Faces of Mathematics: Multiculturalism and Gender Equity*, edited by W. Secada (pp. 85–93). Reston, VA: National Council of Teachers of Mathematics.

Moses, R. P., M. Kamii, S. Swap, and J. Howard. 1989. "The Algebra Project: Organizing in the Spirit of Ella." *Harvard Educational Review* 59 (4): 423–43.

Murray, M. 2004. *Teaching Mathematics Vocabulary in Context.* Portsmouth, NH: Heinemann.

National Council of Teachers of Mathematics. 2000. *Principles and Standards for School Mathematics.* Reston, VA: National Council of Teachers of Mathematics.

National Research Council. 2000. *How People Learn.* Washington, DC: National Academy Press.

Nystrand, M. 1997. *Opening Dialogue: Understanding the Dynamics of Language and Learning in the English Classroom.* New York: Teachers College Press.

O'Connor, M. C. 1998. "Language Socialization in the Mathematics Classroom: Discourse Practices and Mathematical Thinking." In *Talking Mathematics in School: Studies of Teaching and Learning*, edited by M. Lampert and M. L. Blunk (pp. 17 55). Cambridge, U.K., and New York: Cambridge University Press.

———. 2001. "'Can Any Fraction Be Turned into a Decimal?' A Case Study of a Mathematical Group Discussion." *Educational Studies in Mathematics* 46: 143–85.

O'Connor, M. C., and S. Michaels. 1996. "Shifting Participant Frameworks: Orchestrating Thinking Practices in Group Discussion." In *Child Discourse and Social Learning*, edited by D. Hicks (pp. 63–102). Cambridge, U.K., and New York: Cambridge University Press.

Orsolini, M., and C. Pontecorvo. 1992. "Children's Talk in Classroom Discussions." *Cognition and Instruction* 9: 113–36.

Owens, D., ed. 1993. *Research Ideas for the Classroom: Middle Grades Mathematics*. New York: Macmillan.

Paratore, J. R., and R. L. McCormack, eds. 1997. *Peer Talk in the Classroom: Learning from Research*. Newark, DE: International Reading Association.

Pimm, D. 1987. *Speaking Mathematically: Communication in Mathematics Classrooms*. London: Routledge & Kegan Paul.

Polya, G. 1945. *How to Solve It*. Princeton, NJ: Princeton University Press.

Rectanus, C. 2006. *So You Have to Teach Math? Sound Advice for Grades 6–8 Teachers*. Sausalito, CA: Math Solutions.

Rowe, M. B. 1986. "Wait Times: Slowing Down May Be a Way of Speeding Up." *Journal of Teacher Education* 37 (1): 43–50.

Russell, S. J. 1999. "Mathematical Reasoning in the Elementary Grades." In *Developing Mathematical Reasoning in Grades K–12*, edited by L. V. Stiff and F. R. Curcio (pp. 1–12). Reston, VA: National Council of Teachers of Mathematics.

Russell, S. J., and R. B. Corwin. 1993. "Talking Mathematics: 'Going Slow' and 'Letting Go'." *Phi Delta Kappan* (March): 555–58.

Schuster, L., and N. C. Anderson. 2005. *Good Questions for Math Teaching: Why Ask Them and What to Ask, Grades 5–8*. Sausalito, CA: Math Solutions.

Secada, W., E. Fennema, and L. B. Adajian, eds. 1995. *New Directions for Equity in Mathematics Education*. Cambridge, U.K., and New York: Cambridge University Press.

Sfard, A. 2001. "There Is More to Discourse than Meets the Ears: Looking at Thinking as Communicating to Learn More About Mathematical Learning." In *Learning Discourse*, edited by C. Kieran, E. Forman, and A. Sfard (pp. 13–57). Dordrecht: Kluwer Academic Publishers.

Sheffield, L., and D. Cruikshank. 2001. *Teaching and Learning Elementary and Middle School Mathematics.* 4th ed. New York: John Wiley & Sons.

Stacey, K., and M. MacGregor. February 1997. "Ideas About Symbolism That Students Bring to Algebra." *Mathematics Teacher* 90 (2): 110–13.

Stein, M. K., M. S. Smith, M. A. Henningsen, and E. A. Silver. 2000. *Implementing Standards-Based Mathematics Instruction: A Casebook for Professional Development.* New York: Teachers College Press.

Van Zee, E. H., and J. Minstrell. 1997. "Using Questioning to Guide Student Thinking." *Journal of the Learning Sciences* 6 (2): 227–69.

Van Zee, E. H., M. Iwasyk, A. Kurose, D. Simpson, and J. Wild. 2001. "Student and Teacher Questioning During Conversations About Science." *Journal of Research in Science Teaching* 38 (2): 159–90.

Wagner, S., and S. Parker. 1993. "Advancing Algebra." In *Research Ideas for the Classroom: High School Mathematics*, edited by P. Wilson (pp. 119–39). New York: Macmillan.

Wells, G. 1985. *Language at Home and School.* Cambridge, U.K., and New York: Cambridge University Press.

———. 1999. *Dialogic Inquiry: Toward a Sociocultural Practice and Theory of Education.* Cambridge, U.K., and New York: Cambridge University Press.

Whitin, P., and D. Whitin. 2000. *Math Is Language Too: Talking and Writing in the Mathematics Classroom.* Urbana, IL: National Council of Teachers of English.

Willes, M. 1983. *Children into Pupils: A Study of Language in Early Schooling.* London: Routledge & Kegan Paul.

Wood, T., and E. Yackel. 1990. "The Development of Collaborative Dialogue in Small Group Interactions." In *Transforming Early Childhood Mathematics Education: An International Perspective*, edited by L. P. Steffe and T. Wood (pp. 244–52). Hillsdale, NJ: Lawrence Erlbaum.

Yackel, E., P. Cobb, and T. Wood. 1991. "Small Group Interactions as a Source of Learning Opportunities in Second Grade Mathematics." *Journal for Research in Mathematics Education* 22: 390–408.

Index